D1225260

With Christ in Prison

With Christ in Prison

JESUITS IN JAIL
FROM ST. IGNATIUS TO THE PRESENT

George M. Anderson, S.J.

Fordham University Press
New York
2000

Copyright © 2000 by Fordham University Press

All rights reserved. No part of this publication may be reproduced, stored in a retrieval system, or transmitted in any form or by any means—electronic, mechanical, photocopy, recording, or any other—except for brief quotations in printed reviews, without the prior permission of the publisher.

Library of Congress Cataloging-in-Publication Data

Anderson, George M., S.J.
    With Christ in prison : Jesuits in jail from St. Ignatius to the present / George M. Anderson.
      p. cm.
    Includes bibliographical references and index.
    ISBN 0-8232-2064-8—ISBN 0-8232-2065-6 (pbk.)
    1. Jesuits—History   2. Prisoners—History.   3. Persecution—History.
    I. Title.

BX3706.2 .A53   2000
272—dc21   00-055122

Printed in the United States of America
00 01 02 03 04 5 4 3 2 1
First Edition

CONTENTS

CHART OF IMPRISONED JESUITS BY COUNTRY OF INCARCERATION

This chart lists only the Jesuits discussed in this book. See the glossary for a short account of each one's life. Many other Jesuits have been imprisoned in the countries listed below (and in other countries), but I have not found personal or eyewitness accounts of their prison experiences.

Albania
Dajani, Daniel. 1906–1946
Fausti, Gjon. 1889–1946
Gardin, Giacomo. b. 1905
Karma, Gjon. 1896–1975
Luli, Anton. b. 1910
Pantalija, Gjon. 1887–1947

Argentina
Jalics, Franz. b. 1927
Moyano Walker, Juan Luís. b. 1946

Chile
Cariola, Patricio. b. 1928

China
Beaucé, Eugène. 1878–1962
Chu, Francis Xavier. 1913–1983
Clifford, John W. 1917–1984
Esteban, Tomás. 1879–1933
Fahy, Eugene E. 1911–1997
Fekete, Michael. 1907–1973
Havas, John A. 1908–1994
Houle, John A. 1914–1997
Phillips, Thomas. 1904–1968

Shen, Louis. b. 1936
Tang, Dominic. 1908–1995
Thornton, James Enda. 1910–1993
Ts'ai, Francis Xavier. 1907–1997
Wong Jen-Shen, Aloysius. b. ca. 1910
Wong, George B. b. 1918

Czechoslovakia

Korec, Ján. b. 1924

England

Briant, Alexander. 1553–1581
Campion, Edmund. 1540–1581
Colombière, de la, Claude. 1641–1682
Corby, Ralph. 1598–1644
Emerson, Ralph. d. 1604
Garnet, Henry. 1555–1606
Garnet, Thomas. 1575–1608
Gerard, John. 1564–1637
Holtby, Richard. 1552–1646
Lillie, John. b. ca. 1560
Lusher, Edward. 1587–1665
Middleton, Robert. 1570–1601
More, Henry. 1586–1661
Morse, Henry. 1595–1645
Owen, Nicholas. d. 1606
Pounde, Thomas. 1539–1615
Prescott, Cuthbert. 1592–1647
Robinson, John. 1598–1675
Sherwin, Ralph. b. ca. 1560
Southwell, Robert. 1561–1595
Turner, Anthony. 1628–1679
Walpole, Henry. 1558–1595
Weston, William. 1550–1615
White, Andrew. 1579–1656

Ethiopia

Paez, Pedro. 1564–1622

France

Bengy, Anatole de. 1824–1871
Caubert, Jean. 1811–1871

Clerc, Alexis. 1819–1871
Clorivière, Pierre Joseph de. 1735–1820
Cordier, Jean-Nicolas. 1710–1794
Ducoudray, Léon. 1827–1871
Imbert, Joseph. 1720–1794
Olivaint, Pierre. 1816–1871
Salès, Jacques. 1556–1593
Saultemouche, Guillaume. 1557–1593

Germany

Beschet, Paul. b. 1921
Cavanaugh, Paul W. 1901–1975
Coninck, Léo de. 1889–1956
Delp, Alfred. 1907–1945
Frater, Robert. 1915–1987
Gestel, Peter van. 1897–1972
Grimm, Alois. 1886–1944
Jabrun, Louis de. 1883–1943
Koláček, Aloysius. 1887–1970
Lenz, John. b. 1902
Mayer, Rupert. 1876–1945
Menzel, Josef. b. 1916
Moussé, Jean. b. 1921
Müldner, Josef. 1911–1984
Pies, Otto. 1901–1960
Rösch, Augustin. 1893–1961
Rueter, Wilhelm. 1911–1987
Sommet, Jacques. b. 1912

Honduras

Carney, James Guadalupe. 1924–1983

India

Bouchet, Venantius. 1655–1732
Brito, John de. 1647–1693
Laynez, Francis. 1656–1715
Maya, Sebastian de. 1598–1638
Nobili, Roberto de. 1577–1656

Italy (Papal States)
Ricci, Lorenzo. 1703–1775

Ireland
Collins, Dominic. 1567–1607

Japan
Fernandes, Ambrose. 1551–1620
Kisai, James. 1533–1597
Miki, Paul. 1564–1597
Nagascima, Michael. 1582–1628
Pacheco, Francis. 1565–1626
Sampo, Peter. 1582–1620
Soan de Goto, John. 1578–1597
Spinola, Carlo. 1564–1622

Lithuania
Matulionis, Jonas Kastytis. b. 1931
Šeškevičius, Antanas. b. 1914
Tamkevičius, Sigitas. b. 1938

Mexico
Hernández López, Jerónimo. b. 1955
Pro, Miguel. 1891–1927
Rosas Morales, Gonzálo. b. 1955

Peru
Wicht, Juan Julio. b. 1932

Philippines
Hausmann, Carl W. 1898–1945
Kavanagh, Joseph J. 1915–1999
Martin, Clarence A. b. 1918
McSorley, Richard T. b. 1914

Portugal
Eckhart, Anselm. 1721–1809
Malagrida, Gabriel. 1689–1761

Russia
Ciszek, Walter. 1904–1984
Dunda, Gerardas. 1914–1996

Scotland
Ogilvie, John. 1579–1615

Spain
Ignatius of Loyola. 1491–1556
Arrupe, Pedro. 1907–1991 (incarcerated in Japan)
Arbona, Bartolomeo. 1862–1936
Battles, Constantine March. 1877–1936

Sudan
Evans, Michael A. b. 1954

United States
Berrigan, Daniel. b. 1921
Bichsel, William J. b. 1928
Dear, John S. b. 1959
Hagerty, Francis O. 1916–1997
Kelly, Stephen M. b. 1949
Mulligan, Joseph E. b. 1943
Murphy, Edward J. b. 1937

(North American martyrs)
Brébeuf, Jean de. 1593–1649
Goupil, René. 1607–1642
Jogues, Isaac. 1607–1646
Lalemant, Gabriel. 1610–1649

Uruguay
Pérez Aguirre, Luís. b. 1941

Vietnam
Doan, Joseph Nguyen-Công. b. 1941

PREFACE

While studying theology at Woodstock College in New York City in the early 1970s, I began doing volunteer work at Rikers Island, the immense jail and prison complex near LaGuardia Airport. After ordination in 1973, I continued at Rikers as a full-time chaplain until l978. Upon reassignment to St. Aloysius, an inner-city parish in Washington, D.C., I engaged in part-time prison ministry as a volunteer at the D.C. jail for six years during the 1980s. After returning to New York City in 1994, I occasionally went back to Rikers Island to celebrate Mass when one of the regular chaplains was absent.

What has struck me throughout my entire prison ministry experience is the degrading treatment to which prisoners are subjected: the crowding, when two are often forced to share a cell designed for one; the solitary confinement for those accused of "infractions"; the constant noise; the substandard quality of the food and medical care; the shabby treatment of visiting family members. It came as no surprise to me that such conditions could lead to periodic outbursts of rage and brutal behavior on the part of inmates and guards alike. Above all, however, I came to the realization that prisoners are, for the most part, now as in the past, here as in other nations, from backgrounds marked by poverty.

What comes to mind, therefore, are the words of the American Eugene V. Debs—several times the Socialist candidate for president in the early part of the twentieth century—who wrote in his autobiography *Walls and Bars:* "From the hour of my first imprisonment in a filthy county jail, I recognized that prison was essentially an institution for the punishment of the poor."[1] Not just here, but in nations around the world, those who fill the jails and prisons tend to be from the lowest income and educational strata of their populations.

---

[1] Eugene V. Debs, *Walls and Bars* (Chicago: Charles H. Kerr and Co., 1973), 224. The autobiography was originally published in 1927. Besides spending several months in the Cook County jail in Chicago, Debs (1855–1927) also served three years in a federal penitentiary on politically related charges.

Though not impoverished in the traditional sense, imprisoned Jesuits have implicitly been in solidarity with the poor and the disenfranchised. Most have embraced this solidarity willingly, even gladly, as a way of being linked more closely to the poor and humiliated Christ who was arrested, beaten, and executed. By and large, they have been subjected to the same treatment as other prisoners. Many have been forced to exist in conditions so inhuman—like Jean-Nicolas Cordier and Joseph Imbert in France in the late 1700s—that they died from the effects of their confinement. And yet some saw in their experiences a relationship to what the apostles endured, as described in the Acts of the Apostles: experiences sustained by the joy of realizing they were walking in the steps of Christ (Acts 5:41). In this scriptural context, one thinks, too, of what Paul says of himself in his Letter to the Ephesians: "I Paul, a prisoner for Christ Jesus" (3:1). Carlo Spinola, one of the prisoners who appears in this book, imitated this very phrase in signing the letters he wrote from his seventeenth-century prison in Japan: "I Carlo, a prisoner of Christ." Like Paul, he was eventually put to death.

Ignatius's *Spiritual Exercises* have always been a primary source of support for Jesuits in prison. From the time of Ignatius to the present, every Jesuit makes the *Exercises*, first as a novice and then again after ordination as a prerequisite for taking final vows. The *Exercises* are divided into four weeks. Early in the first week, there is a specific reference to prisoners in a spiritual sense; Ignatius asks the retreatant to see the soul "as a prisoner in this corruptible body," in exile here on earth (#47). This imprisonment in a physical body and its implied transitoriness in terms of the brevity of life here on earth would have had a freeing effect on the perception of those Jesuits held in stone-and-iron prisons for varying lengths of time.

Similarly, in the second week's meditation on the three kinds of humility, incarcerated Jesuits would have resonated with what Ignatius says of this most advanced state of humility: To imitate Christ ever more closely, he invites the retreatant to desire "insults with Christ loaded with them [and to be] accounted worthless and a fool for Christ" (#167). No matter where in the world Jesuits found themselves to be behind bars, they knew firsthand what these insults could be and what it was like to be accounted a fool. They accepted the world's evaluation of them because in their eyes, such a derogatory view brought them closer to Christ on the cross. The meditations of the third week, on Jesus' passion and death, were a source of great strength to those subjected to particularly harsh conditions. Their intimate knowledge of the various meditations gave them the will to endure their sufferings, and many referred to that fact in their writings.

A number of the incarcerated Jesuits not only survived but also wrote extensively about their ordeals, either while still in prison or after their release. The superiors of the Elizabethan Jesuit John Gerard actually ordered him to provide (for the edification of novices) an autobiographical account of what he had undergone in England.[2] And edified they must have been to read such a testimony of a faith that never faltered even under torture. Others have also put down on paper descriptions of their long years of incarceration. First-person narratives such as these, along with interviews and letters to the author, form the backbone of this book.

The incarceration experience also had a darker side, however: Jesuits who were crushed in both body and spirit. This darker side is the theme of *Silence*, the 1980 novel by the Japanese novelist Shusaku Endo. The novel is the story of two Jesuit missionaries in Japan during a time of intense persecution of Christians. Arrested and incarcerated, they are subjected to various pressures by their captors; as a result, first one and then the other apostatizes. While the story is fictitious, it realistically underscores the fact that the outcome of the imprisonment of Jesuits is not always to be seen in terms of triumph over adversity. Often, the outcome may point to an at-oneness with the brokenness and frailty of humanity.

Among the more striking features of the Jesuit incarceration experience is the diversity of those who have been imprisoned. They have included brothers and priests, novices and scholastics; the old, like Cordier and Imbert, as well as the young and the middle-aged; the learned and those who had less education. It is noteworthy that provincial superiors, too, have been incarcerated. During World War II, the Gestapo arrested and held Augustin Rösch, the Bavarian provincial who was superior for Rupert Mayer and Alfred Delp. Another who endured incarceration was Pedro Arrupe; in the late 1960s he would become the superior general of the entire Society of Jesus. He

---

[2] John Gerard, *The Autobiography of a Hunted Priest*, trans. Philip Caraman (New York: Pelligrini and Cudahy, 1952), xviii.

was arrested on December 7, 1941, in Yamaguchi, Japan, where he was serving as a parish priest. Because he was a foreigner, he was suspected of espionage and was held for five weeks.[3] And during the suppression of the Society, its then superior general, Lorenzo Ricci, not only was imprisoned but ended his life in a papal dungeon in eighteenth-century Rome.

Others have been beatified and later canonized as well, like Claude de la Colombière. After a year and a half at Paray-le-Monial, where he was spiritual advisor for Margaret Mary Alacoque, he was sent to England in 1676 as chaplain and preacher to the Catholic Duchess of York. As a foreign priest, he was permitted by English law to function in this capacity, in contrast to English-born priests who were forbidden to exercise their sacramental ministry on English soil.

Nevertheless, in the aftermath of the so-called Popish plot fabricated by Titus Oates in 1678, de la Colombière was falsely accused of treasonous speech by a lapsed convert whom he had assisted. His imprisonment lasted only three weeks, but confinement in the damp, cold dungeon in the King's Bench prison undermined his already fragile health. After Louis XIV negotiated his release, he was able to return to France, where he died two years later of tuberculosis at the age of only forty-one.

In my approach to this book, I have tried to be as broad as possible with regard to time and place, making use of resources illustrating situations in both the East and the West over a 400-year span. The availability of the source material has varied, however. Initially, it was difficult to locate much material on Latin America. As one Jesuit working in El Salvador—Dean Brackley—put it, Jesuits in Central and South America have tended to be murdered outright rather than being imprisoned. Such was the case with Rutilio Grande in 1977, as well as the Bolivian, Luís Espinal, who was tortured and riddled with bullets in 1980, only two days before the murder of Archbishop Oscar Romero. His "crime"? Criticizing the military regime through his weekly review of opinion, *Aquí*.

Nevertheless, several Jesuits in that part of the world have written of their incarceration. Arrested in Santiago in 1975 in the aftermath of the Pinochet coup, Patricio Cariola describes his time in the Capu-

---

[3] Miguel Pedro Lamet, *Arrupe: Una Explosión en la Iglesia* (Madrid: Ediciones Temas de Hoy, 1989), 148–67.

chinos jail in "Dos Meses" (Two Months). The arrest stemmed from his efforts to obtain medical assistance for Nelson Gutierrez, a member of the leftist party MIR, who had been wounded in a confrontation with Chilean security forces. His six-page reflection appeared in *Noticias Jesuitas Chile* for July–August 1976. Other accounts have also come to my attention. Juan Luís Moyano Walker and Franz Jalics were both imprisoned in Argentina in the 1970s, as was Luís Pérez Aguirre in Uruguay in the 1980s. The reflections of all three are included in this book.

In contrast, we know little of the experiences of others who were imprisoned in Latin America. James Guadalupe Carney, an American ministering in Central America, described his first detention by the Honduran military police in his posthumously published autobiography, *To Be a Revolutionary*. Held in custody for a day, he was expelled from the country in 1979. Carney returned to Central America a year later, working for three years in Nicaragua before crossing over into Honduras as chaplain to a group of revolutionaries in July of 1983.

Captured with them that same summer, he was imprisoned for two weeks at the Aguacate military base. Carney was never heard from again. According to family members who spent eight years investigating his disappearance, he was tortured at Aguacate and later killed by being pushed from a helicopter over the jungle. In the later stages of its investigation, the family came into contact with a member of the Honduran death squad who had defected to Canada. The defector, Florenzio Caballero, had been at Aguacate at the time of Carney's capture and corroborated the fact that Carney had been tortured and the manner of his execution.[4]

Ironically, whereas through his work with the campesinos of Honduras, Carney came to believe it was essential to be a revolutionary—his statement "To be a revolutionary is to be a Christian" is the title of the last chapter of his autobiography—Miguel Pro, a Mexican Je-

---

[4] Carney was a member of the Missouri Province of the Society of Jesus for thirty-five years. In June, 1983, realizing that his conscience-based decision to return to Honduras was incompatible with his remaining a Jesuit, he left the Society. Soon after crossing the border from Nicaragua into Honduras, he disappeared. In a telephone interview on June 27, 1994, Virginia Smith, his sister, said, "In his heart, Jim was always a Jesuit. He loved the Jesuits." For this reason he was included in this book. His autobiography, *To Be a Revolutionary* (San Francisco: Harper and Row, 1985), was published posthumously by his family.

suit living earlier in the century, fiercely opposed the revolutionary government of his country. During the Mexican government's open persecution of the church in the 1920s, Pro was arrested and confined to the Mexico City jail for ten days prior to his execution before a firing squad on November 23, 1927. With his brother Humberto, he was accused of being implicated in an attempt on the life of General Álvaro Obregon. There was no trial. As will be seen later, lack of due process followed by summary execution is a frequent component of the stories of incarcerated Jesuits.

If they were to speak to us today, Carney and Pro would probably be poles apart in their views of the relationship between politics and religion. And yet both were Jesuits who died while imprisoned. Again, one realizes that those who have undergone the incarceration experience were diverse in both background and outlook.

The stories of Jesuits imprisoned in the East, in nations such as China and Vietnam, also appear in the pages of this book. As in the case of several Latin American Jesuits, some were still living at the time of this writing. Several granted me interviews, responded through letters to my requests for their stories, or directed me to the appropriate material. From his residence in Taiwan, for example, the late Eugene E. Fahy referred me to a first-person account he had written soon after his release from a Chinese prison and which had appeared, in abbreviated form, in *Life* magazine in the early 1950s.

The fact that Fahy's story was published more than forty years ago in such a widely circulated magazine as *Life* serves to remind us that much valuable material of this kind falls into the category of what might be called fugitive pieces—articles in popular magazines and small local publications that could easily have remained scattered, such as the Cariola reflection, which appeared in a publication of his province. Equally valuable first-person accounts have appeared in periodicals as diverse as *The New Yorker*, *The Catholic Mind*, and the *Woodstock Letters*. One purpose of this expanded version of the original "Jesuits in Jail" essay, therefore, has been to gather these fugitive pieces and place them in a unified setting that helps to complete the overall picture of how Jesuits dealt with their various forms of incarceration.

At the end of the book is a glossary of names, along with thumbnail sketches of most of the Jesuits mentioned. Many Jesuits have helped both with the initial essay and with this expanded version. To try to mention each would risk omitting some names, and so I must thank them as a group as my brothers in the Society of Jesus. However, one Jesuit friend deserves special thanks—Charles M. Whelan, S.J., an associate editor at *America* and a professor at the Fordham University School of Law. Fr. Whelan was a main supporter of this project from the beginning, and it was he who guided me through the complexities of computers to bring it to completion. His patience in the latter regard was infinite.

INTRODUCTION

After my essay "Jesuits in Jail: Ignatius to the Present" was published in September, 1995, as one of the *Studies in the Spirituality of the Jesuits,* John W. Padberg, S.J., the editor of *Studies,* suggested that it be expanded into a book. This book, which incorporates a great deal of new material, is the result of that suggestion. Much of the new information is in the form of first-person accounts of Jesuits whose prison experiences are of mid-to-late twentieth-century origin. In most cases, the choice of which Jesuits to include depended on how much information was available about their time behind bars.

Jesuits who have been imprisoned were largely confined to cells; however, incarceration is not limited to cells alone. It can apply to any area or place of confinement, even on the water. For example, in seventeenth-century Maryland, Andrew White was arrested and transported in chains to Newgate prison in London by ship, charged with the treasonable offense of serving as a Catholic priest on what was considered to be English soil.

Other Jesuits were condemned to spend long periods in floating prisons during the French Revolution. In his 1994 book, *Les Prêtres Déportés sur les Pontons de Rochefort,* Yves Blomme describes the grim and frequently fatal conditions to which more than 800 priests were subjected for refusing to swear their allegiance to the Constituent Assembly's civil constitution of the clergy, a move denounced by Pius VI in 1791. These non-jurors, as they were called, were for the most part confined to the holds of two ships—the *Washington* and the *Deux Associés*—anchored off l'île d'Aix and l'île Madame near Rochefort during the reign of terror between 1793 and 1795. Two-thirds of them died from typhus epidemics, malnutrition, and overall ill treatment.[5]

At least two of the priests had been Jesuits before Louis XV dis-

---

[5] Yves Blomme, *Les Prêtres Déportés sur les Pontons de Rochefort* (Saint Jean d'Angély: Editions Bourdessoules, 1994), 33, 75.

solved the Society of Jesus in 1764. One was the 84-year-old Jean-Nicolas Cordier from Lorraine. As he was painfully making his way up the gangplank of the *Washington,* the captain snatched his cane and flung it into the sea. According to the brief account of Cordier's life in Abbé Aimé Guillon's *Les Martyrs de la Foi pendant la Révolution Française,* the captain shouted: "Old wretch! If I had let you keep your cane, you might have been capable of using it to stir up a counter-revolution aboard my ship." Then pushing him toward the other prisoners going aboard, he struck him across the shoulders with the flat side of his saber, shouting imprecations at him all the while. It is difficult to imagine the elderly Cordier fomenting rebellion, but there is probably enough truth in the physical details of the story—the blow across the shoulders with the sword and the imprecations—for it to serve as an example of what Ignatius of Loyola (1491–1556), founder of the Society of Jesus, calls the third degree of humility in his *Spiritual Exercises.* There, he speaks of the way in which the follower of Jesus is encouraged to imitate Christ even to the point of desiring poverty and insults in order to achieve perfect humility. Cordier later died of typhoid in one of the makeshift prison hospital tents set up by the government on the l'île Madame, not far from where the two ships were anchored.[6]

Another elderly Jesuit, Joseph Imbert, was a prisoner on the companion ship, the *Deux Associés.* Referring to him, Guillon says that his age—he was seventy-five—did not allow him to resist for long the crowded and unwholesome below-deck atmosphere. He died in the ship's hold on June 9, 1794. Both Jesuits, along with sixty-two other French priests who perished around the same time, were beatified by John Paul II on October 1, 1995.[7]

An incident described by Guillon suggests just how inhuman the shipboard conditions actually were. So fetid was the air because of crowding and the lack of provision for sanitary needs that a doctor who came aboard the *Deux Associés* felt at the point of fainting at the entrance to the hold, saying: "If someone put 400 dogs there just for one night, the next day they would be either dead or maddened."[8]

---

[6] Abbé Aimé Guillon, *Les Martyrs de la Foi pendant la Révolution Française* (Paris: Chez Germain Mathiot, 1821), (2):460.

[7] Ibid., (1):333–34.

[8] Ibid., (1):361. Guillon notes that the original intent of the government was actually to deport the prisoners to Guinea in West Africa, but the plan was abandoned and the ships with their prisoners remained anchored off the French coast.

A decade and a half earlier, at the time of the suppression of the Society of Jesus in Portugal, a group of 198 Portuguese Jesuits, expelled from their missions in Brazil, were similarly jammed into the holds of two small ships and were not permitted to go on deck during the long voyage back to Europe. Their worst torment was thirst. Their daily ration of water was so small that some were driven to drink their own urine.[9]

If one considers incarceration as primarily the deprivation of freedom, it does not matter whether one is imprisoned in quarters on sea or on land. Isaac Jogues, for instance, was held in an Iroquois village. Writing to his provincial in France, he says of himself and René Goupil: "They left us in a kind of free slavery."[10] In that state of free slavery, however, Jogues was at least able to minister to other prisoners.

To some degree, the same could be said of the American Jesuit Walter Ciszek. Within the confines of his Siberian labor camp, he had considerable mobility and used it to baptize, hear confessions, and celebrate the Eucharist, albeit at great risk. A similar situation prevailed for the Jesuits in Dachau. As will be seen later, the determination to continue ministering despite often life-threatening obstacles has been one of the most remarkable aspects of the lives of imprisoned Jesuits.

The causes of incarceration varied, but it is also worth remembering that some are of relatively recent origin. When Henry David Thoreau refused to pay his poll tax in nineteenth-century Massachusetts because the state condoned the buying and selling of slaves, he committed an act of civil disobedience that led to his arrest and brief confinement. In the United States, at least, he set the stage for what would occur on a large scale more than a hundred years later when—following in the footsteps not only of Thoreau but also of Gandhi and Martin Luther King—a number of American Jesuits deliberately courted imprisonment to protest government actions that they perceived to be immoral. In so doing, they accepted what might be called voluntary incarceration. A name like Daniel Berri-

---

[9] Auguste Carayon, *Documents Inédits sur la Compagnie de Jésus* (Poitiers: Henri Oudin, 1865), (9):92.

[10] Reuben Gold Thwaites, ed., *Jesuit Relations and Allied Documents* (Cleveland: Burrows Brothers Co., 1898), 39:199.

gan's immediately comes to mind in this regard because of his protests against the Vietnam War; however, others have continued to follow his example by performing acts of civil disobedience aimed primarily at the United States' manufacture and use of weapons of destruction.

With Christ in Prison

ONE

Voluntary Incarceration

OPPOSITION TO THE VIETNAM WAR manifested itself in acts of civil disobedience that resulted in the incarceration of a number of Jesuits, both scholastics and priests. The daytime burning of draft records in the parking lot outside the Selective Service office in Catonsville, Maryland, in 1968 led to the swift arrest of Daniel Berrigan. In an attempt to heighten public awareness regarding the destructive effects of the Vietnam War, his supporters videotaped the incident, as well as the arrival of the police to arrest the members of the group that came to be known as the Catonsville Nine. Later that same day, hundreds of thousands of Americans in living rooms around the country witnessed the event on television. Berrigan's arrest could therefore be regarded as the most public arrest of a Jesuit in the history of the Society. This instance contrasts sharply with the secrecy that surrounded the arrests of Jesuits by police agents in Communist-ruled governments in countries like Albania around the same time. Berrigan's action also set the stage for what other Jesuits would do: engage in forms of civil disobedience that resulted in imprisonment.

Thus, in 1970, then-scholastic Joseph E. Mulligan spent two years at Sandstone, the medium-security federal facility in Minnesota. His act of civil disobedience was similar to Berrigan's: As one of the Chicago Fifteen, he took part in the burning of draft records outside the Selective Service office in Chicago. Like Berrigan, he was convicted of the charge of destruction of government property.

More than two decades later, in 1993, John Dear, a young Maryland Province priest, together with three lay persons who described themselves as the Pax Christi-Spirit of Life Plowshares, entered the grounds of the Seymour Johnson Air Force Base in Goldsboro, North Carolina, and repeatedly struck an F-15E fighter plane with a hammer. The act, which was deliberately scheduled to coincide with the anniversary of the December 7th bombing of Pearl Harbor, was meant to symbolize the Isaian image of beating swords into plowshares. Dear spent seven and a half months in two North Carolina jails and another four and a half months under house arrest in Washington, D.C., in the small, inner-city Jesuit community in which he had been living prior to his arrest.

During the same year that Dear was arrested, Francis O. "Skip" Hagerty, a Jesuit in his seventies, also went to jail, although for a different reason. Hagerty was arrested for blocking the entrance to an abortion clinic in Brookline, Massachusetts—an act of civil disobedience for which he served more than four months in a local detention facility. As he described the scene in a telephone interview, Hagerty, dressed in clerical attire, along with two lay people, drove to the clinic at 1297 Beacon Street and pulled their van up to the front door at 7 A.M.

"The air was let out of the tires, and the floor of the van removed, so that though still inside the vehicle, we were actually sitting on the sidewalk," he said. "The police arrived, and since they couldn't get us out, they called the fire department. The firemen cut open the roof of the van and pulled us out through the top."[1]

It could be argued that although their motivations were different, both Dear and Hagerty were driven to their acts of civil disobedience by a deep sense of the sanctity of life, as were Mulligan and Berrigan. All four, moreover, were implicitly witnessing to their belief that a life of active fidelity to the gospel could place Jesuits in conflict with the generally held notion of what it means to be a law-abiding citizen.

Another who witnessed through civil disobedience was Edward J. "Ned" Murphy, a New York Province Jesuit who, albeit briefly, was jailed approximately ten times for protests of various kinds during the Vietnam era, starting in the late 1960s. In an interview at Fordham University's Murray-Weigel Hall on November 27, 1994, Murphy spoke of how his personal faith served as the basis for what he had done.

"What we're here for," he said, "is the building of the kingdom of God, and building the kingdom usually means very normal activities, like feeding the hungry and taking care of one another and comforting the people. But the kingdom," he continued, "also demands at times bolder action: I did most of what I did with fear and trembling, but I was convinced that this was, at that moment, what the kingdom of God demanded."[2]

---

[1] Telephone interview with Francis O. Hagerty, S.J., January 17, 1994. (Father Hagerty died on April 24, 1997.)

[2] Interview with Edward J. Murphy, S.J., November 27, 1994.

In a similar vein, William J. Bichsel of the Oregon Province was incarcerated on a number of occasions in the early 1980s for illegally entering the grounds of the Trident submarine base on Hood Canal, just off Puget Sound. During a telephone conversation on January 24, 1995, he explained why he undertook these acts of civil disobedience: "We're called upon to share the wealth and resources of the world. But those in power, instead of seeing to it that they're shared with the poor, use them to create weapons of mass destruction like the Trident submarine." Bichsel added that another reason for entering the grounds of the naval base was to "reclaim the land for peace." He explained that part of the land had once been the site of a settlement of Native American Indians.

Although his periods of incarceration were generally brief and spent in the county jail in Seattle, he also served four months at the Lompoc federal prison in California.[3] In 1997, he was arrested again and sentenced to eighteen months for civil disobedience protests calling for closure of the U.S. Army's School of the Americas at Fort Benning, Georgia.

Another antiwar act of civil disobedience resulting in imprisonment occurred in California on August 7, 1995. Stephen Kelly, along with Susan Crane, a schoolteacher, broke into the Lockheed Martin Missiles and Space complex in Sunnyvale, where they hammered on parts of two nuclear missile components—again, the image of beating swords into plowshares—and splashed their own blood on two Trident casings used by the navy to fire nuclear weapons from submarines. The date of their act of civil disobedience, which they called the Jubilee Plowshares Action, was chosen to coincide with the fiftieth anniversary of the bombing of Hiroshima and Nagasaki in August, 1945.

In a statement released afterward, Kelly said, "Jesus calls us to be brother and sister to each other. How can we say we have love in our hearts when we are planning to kill each other?" But his act of civil disobedience was also meant—as was John Dear's—as a protest against the massive sums of money spent on armaments rather than on programs to help the poor.

Kelly and his codefendant spent seven months in jail before being sentenced on March 13, 1996. Both were given ten more months to

---

[3] Telephone interview with William J. Bichsel, S.J., January 24, 1995.

serve. In contrast to the anger shown by some of the judges who have sentenced Jesuits convicted of other acts of civil disobedience, the magistrate in this case referred to the defendants'commitment to peace and their willingness to accept responsibility for their act.[4] Like William Bichsel, Kelly was subsequently involved in other acts of civil disobedience that led to additional time behind bars.

---

[4] *National Jesuit News*, October 1995; *San Jose Mercury News*, March 14, 1996. The following year, Kelly and five other peace activists, including Philip Berrigan, were tried in Bath, Maine, May 5–7 1997, and found guilty of conspiracy and damaging government property after an action the preceding Ash Wednesday. The group, calling themselves the Prince of Peace Plowshares, boarded the guided missile destroyer U.S.S. *The Sullivans,* hammered on the missile's hatch covers, poured their own blood on them from baby bottles, and displayed a banner with the words: "They shall beat their swords into plowshares and their spears into pruning hooks." *National Jesuit News*, June, 1997, 4.

TWO

Ignatius's Own Experience and Ecclesiastical Prisons

THE FIRST INCARCERATION of Ignatius of Loyola occurred in 1527 as a result of the Inquisition. His pilgrim style of dress and speaking in public on religious themes aroused the suspicion of religious authorities in Alcalá, Spain, in the early years of his conversion and long before the founding of the Society of Jesus. Following a preliminary interrogation by an inquisitor, Ignatius was led off to jail by an officer of the law. For eighteen days, he was given no reason for his confinement—again, a common occurrence in the lives of incarcerated Jesuits. Having undergone further examination, Ignatius was finally released after spending a total of forty-two days in custody.

His second incarceration took place in Salamanca the same year. His Dominican confessor invited him to dinner, although he was warned that the prior would probably question him and his companion, Calixto, about their preaching. After the meal, the two were confined to the Dominican monastery for three days. They were then transferred to the Salamanca jail, where they were kept chained to a post in the middle of the building.[1]

During this period, four ecclesiastical judges examined Ignatius's copy of the *Spiritual Exercises* and interrogated him on a variety of theological issues. The only fault they could find in these sessions

---

[1] Ignatius's experience of being chained to a post suggests the similar but much longer ordeal of the Jesuit astronomer, Adam Schall (1590–1666), who worked as a missionary in Peking in the seventeenth century. He held the prestigious position of head of the bureau of astronomy and mathematics and was a friend of the emperor. As a result of anti-Christian sentiment and professional jealousy on the part of Chinese astronomers, he was arrested with three other Jesuits in 1664 and chained to a post for six months. See George H. Dunne, S.J., *Generation of Giants: The Story of the Jesuits in China in the Last Decades of the Ming Dynasty* (South Bend, Ind.: University of Notre Dame Press, 1962), 361–62.

concerned what they considered his ill-preparedness in describing the difference between venial and mortal sin. Warning him to speak no further on such matters until he had studied theology for four more years, the judges ordered his release from the jail after twenty-two days.[2]

The fact that Ignatius spent the first few days of his Salamanca confinement in a Dominican monastery rather than the city jail is significant. By the fourteenth century, virtually all religious orders had made provision for incarceration of one kind or another. Most monasteries and convents had actual cells with bars, where religious could be confined for offenses ranging from lying and stealing to pride. In serious cases, confinement could be life-long and might include obligatory fasting, chains, and beatings. St. Teresa of Ávila herself accepted the practice and introduced it into her constitutions. Her friend, John of the Cross, spent nine months locked in a barred cell in the Carmelite monastery in Toledo.[3]

The *Constitutions* of Ignatius, therefore, were a notable exception to those of other religious orders in that they did not include such provisions. According to one anecdote, when Ignatius sought approval for the *Formula of the Institute*, which was his first sketch of what would eventually become the *Constitutions of the Society of Jesus*, he was asked why it included no arrangements for confinement. Ignatius, it is said, replied that none were necessary because there was always the door, that is, expulsion.[4]

In a somewhat related context, in the early days of the suppression of the Society in 1773, civil authorities arrested three English Jesuits at the English College in Bruges—Charles Plowden, William Aston, and Thomas Angier—and sent them to the college of the Augustinian friars in Ghent. The Jesuits remained there in close custody for nine months. Similarly, civil authorities turned religious houses into prisons during the French Revolution, and later in France at the time of the Commune in the 1870s. The same seizure of monasteries and

---

[2] *St. Ignatius' Own Story*, trans. William J. Young, S.J. (Chicago: Loyola University Press, 1956, reprinted in 1980), 46–50.

[3] E. Pacheco, "Carcere e Vita Religiosa." In *Dizionario degli Istituti di Perfezione*, vol. II, ed. Guerino Pellicia and Giancarlo Rocca (Rome: Edizioni Paoline, 1975), 2:272–76.

[4] Anecdote told to the author by John W. Padberg, S.J., director of the Institute of Jesuit Sources in St. Louis, Mo.

convents occurred during the Spanish Revolution. More recently, after his release from a German prison during World War II, Rupert Mayer was kept under house arrest at the Ettal Monastery until March 1944. Although the Benedictine monks treated him kindly, they were obligated by the Gestapo to impose severe restrictions on his movements. The first of the Gestapo's orders read: "Father Mayer is not to have contact with the outside world in any way, shape, or fashion. You are therefore to see to it that he does not leave the monastery."[5] Buildings that were constructed by religious orders but that are no longer under their control have continued to be used as prisons into our own time. The Italian-born Jesuit, Giacomo Gardin, who was arrested in Albania after years of work there, writes in his prison diary in November, 1950: "Two of the new prisons incorporated into the [Albanian] prison system were formerly residences for Franciscans and Jesuits."[6] Attempting to escape from the former, the Albanian Jesuit, Brother Gjon Pantalija, suffered injuries in a fall that hastened his death.

Perhaps the most famous ecclesiastical prison to be used by the Roman Catholic Church itself was the Castel Sant'Angelo in Rome. It was there that the Congregation of Cardinals, under political pressure from the Bourbons and other enemies of the Society such as the Portuguese Sebastião José de Carvalho—better known as the Marquis [Marquês] de Pombal—ordered the incarceration of the superior general, Lorenzo Ricci. The order came after Clement XIV promulgated *Dominus ac Redemptor*, the papal decree that dissolved the entire Jesuit order.

Accordingly, on the evening of September 23, 1773, Ricci was transferred from the English College in Rome—where he had been subjected to interrogations but was relatively well treated—to the Castel Sant'Angelo. Imprisoned with him were his secretary, Gabriele Comolli, five Jesuit assistants, and several others. Their treatment immediately grew harsh to the point of cruelty. To prevent communication with the outside world, the windows of their cells were boarded up, a move that also eliminated all natural light. The pope was persuaded to order the governor of the castle to reduce the

---

[5] Anton Koerbling, S.J., *Father Rupert Mayer* (Cork: Mercier Press, 1950), 177.

[6] Gjon Sinishta, *The Fulfilled Promise: A Documentary Account of Religious Persecution in Albania* (Santa Clara, Calif.: H and F Composing Service, 1976), 145.

funds spent on food for the Jesuits by half. When cold weather arrived, Ricci and his companions were not allowed to have even a small fire with which to warm themselves. Most seriously, however, they were denied the right to celebrate Mass, which was a source of suffering to them as well as to many other imprisoned Jesuits over the years.

Ricci's frequent interrogations were based largely on allegations that he had hidden or sent large sums of money out of the country. He vigorously denied the charge: "The rumor that we are in possession of millions, which we have hidden or invested, is just a lie . . . which our enemies, no doubt, have bruited abroad with great delight." He was also charged on suspicion of wishing to restore the Society.

When the interrogations found no actions that would merit his continued incarceration, Ricci petitioned the Congregation of Cardinals to end it, pointing out that he was seventy-two years old and in failing health. The petition went unanswered. Eleven months after the death of Clement XIV in September, 1774, Ricci appealed again. The new pope, Pius VI, was sympathetic, but the Spanish ambassador to Rome, José Monino, opposed the release of the Jesuits, although they were granted freedom to move about the castle. By then, however, Ricci's health had so greatly deteriorated that this concession was of no help. He died on November 24, 1775. His secretary, the seventy-year-old Comolli, had died the preceding January.[7]

Fifteen years before the promulgation of *Dominus ac Redemptor,* Jesuits were already feeling the effects of the coming suppression in Portugal, where Pombal's influence reigned supreme. In fact, more Jesuits were incarcerated in that one country in the eighteenth century than in any other part of the world, or, one might add, at any other period in the Society's history. Not even in Elizabethan England or in Germany under the Third Reich did its members undergo such massive persecution. As one of the most inveterate enemies of the Society, Pombal wielded such power that he succeeded in persuading King Joseph I to expel all Jesuits from Portugal in 1759. The expulsion order came after Pombal convinced the king that a

---

[7] Ludwig Freiherr von Pastor, *History of the Popes,* trans. E. F. Peeler (St. Louis: B. Herder Book Co., 1952), vol. 38, 320–25.

group of Jesuits had been involved in an attempt on his life the year before.[8]

One of the ten Jesuits accused of being implicated in the plot was Gabriel Malagrida, who had already incurred Pombal's animosity with his pamphlet, "The Real Cause of the Earthquake That Ruined Lisbon on November 1, 1775." In it, Malagrida contended that the earthquake was God's vengeance on Lisbon's inhabitants for their sinfulness. The allegation was especially offensive to Pombal who, as a man of the Enlightenment, scorned what he regarded as religious superstition.[9]

Imprisoned first in Lisbon's Belem Tower and then in the Junquiera fort, Malagrida became mentally unbalanced during his two and a half years of confinement in underground dungeons. He claimed to hold conversations with saints such as Ignatius, Philip Neri, and Teresa of Avila. The civil authorities thus turned him over to the inquisitors, who locked him in a dungeon of their own prison on Lisbon's principal square, the Rossio. Relentlessly questioning the enfeebled and confused old man, they condemned him to death for heresy. Malagrida was taken to a large scaffold on the square where he was first strangled and then burned at the stake.[10] His imprisonment and execution vividly illustrate the way in which secular and religious authorities worked together, leading to devastating results for those accused of crimes considered to be within the purview of both groups.

Before the century ended, many other Jesuits suffered in Portugal's dungeons, including the hundreds brought back from the missions in prison ships that often became floating death chambers. Of the 127 Jesuits who were forced to embark from Goa in February, 1761, for example, 23 had already died by the time their ship reached Lisbon three months later. Eighteen others arrived so near death that when they were taken to the Junquiera fort, they were simply placed on the ground in front of the prison and were anointed in preparation

---

[8] William V. Bangert, S.J., *A History of the Society of Jesus* (St. Louis: Institute of Jesuit Sources, 1972), 366–69.

[9] Sir Marcus Cheke, *Dictator of Portugal: A Life of the Marquis of Pombal, 1699–1782* (London: Sidgwick and Jackson, 1938), 96.

[10] António Lopes, S.J., *Roteiro Historico dos Jesuítas em Lisboa* (Braga: Livraria A.I., 1985), 80.

for their imminent demise. Only 10 of the original group of 127 remained well enough during the voyage to assist their ill companions.[11]

In *Les Prisons de Marquis de Pombal,* a nineteenth-century account of what actually transpired within the Portuguese prisons, Auguste Carayon provides a list of 222 names of those who were confined in them, along with brief biographical information about each one. In age, they ranged from young scholastics to Jesuits over ninety years old. Their origins were equally diverse—Italian, Irish, French, German, Hungarian. Among them were two provincials, Francisco de Costa, provincial of the Japanese province, and António de Torres, a former provincial of Portugal itself. When de Costa returned to Portugal from Macau, he was held in the St. Julien prison from October, 1764, until his death in August, 1766. De Torres was imprisoned first at the Almeida prison and then at St. Julien, where he died in October, 1762, at the age of seventy-two.

Carayon notes that the list is "far from giving the number of all the religious of the Society of Jesus who suffered during Pombal's persecution." He observes that "it would be necessary to add to it the names of over 1500 Jesuits violently torn away from Portugal, Brazil, the Indies, and Macao, and most of those exiled on pontifical territory."[12]

[11] Ibid., 76.
[12] Auguste Carayon, *Les Prisons de Marquis du Pombal* (Paris: L'Ecureux Librairie, 1865), 233–59.

THREE
Arrest and Trial

THE SUMMARY JUDGMENTS imposed on Malagrida and his Jesuit brothers imprisoned in Portugal bear little resemblance to what we would call jurisprudence today. And yet a similar absence of equitable justice can be found in the arrest and trial of Jesuits of the twentieth century. In this respect, Malagrida's experience is not unlike that of Alfred Delp, who was tried and condemned by a Nazi tribunal for alleged complicity in a plot on Hitler's life.

In a "Letter to the Brethren" at the end of his *Prison Meditations*, Delp used words that call to mind Pombal's detestation of the Society: "The actual reason for my condemnation was that I happened to be, and chose to remain, a Jesuit," he said. Continuing, he notes: "There was nothing to show that I had any connection with the attempt on Hitler's life. . . . There was one underlying theme—a Jesuit is a priori an enemy and betrayer of the Third Reich."[1] In *The Jesuits and the Third Reich,* Vincent Lapomarda points out that the Nazis loathed Jesuits almost as much as they hated the Jewish people, whom they tried to destroy. They feared them for their outspoken criticism of national socialism in their preaching in churches and their teaching in schools and universities.[2]

Because of the Society's close ties with the Vatican, being branded an enemy and betrayer of the state has long been a major cause of the incarceration of Jesuits. The representative of the state could be Hitler or Pombal or Elizabeth I of England. It could also be the revolutionary forces of the 1871 French Commune or the Spanish Civil War or the Communist regimes in China, Albania, Czechoslovakia, and the Soviet Union.

Often viewed as subverting the state's control, Jesuits have been hunted, imprisoned, and frequently put to death because their pri-

---

[1] Alfred Delp, *The Prison Meditations of Alfred Delp* (New York: Herder and Herder, 1963), 193.

[2] Vincent A. Lapomarda, *The Jesuits and the Third Reich* (Lewiston, N.Y.: Edwin Mellen Press, 1989), 11–24.

mary commitment was to the gospel's authority rather than to the authority of the state. "Why should I not obey Christ rather than the King?" asked the martyr John Ogilvie at his trial in seventeenth-century Scotland.[3] His question helps us to understand the willingness of Jesuits to stand firm against temporal powers that demand total allegiance. Virtually none of them, however, believed their activities to be primarily motivated by political considerations. To them, it was the need to oppose the actions of governments that, in their eyes, were attempting to crush the gospel values of their faith. Rupert Mayer, who was imprisoned three times under the Nazis for speaking out against Hitler's party, said during one of his trials: "Never did I give a political speech! Never! With respect to politics I am completely ignorant. What got me started was religion."[4]

But in the view of some governments, the very fact that they were Catholic priests made them suspect because it meant that they had vowed obedience to an authority other than their own—namely, that of the pope. Given sixteenth- and seventeenth-century England's not unjustified fear of invasion by Catholic forces, divided allegiance was a particular issue in pseudo-trials like those of Delp, Ogilvie, and many other Jesuits.

During Robert Southwell's trial, the prosecuting attorney claimed that the pope had sent "Jesuits and seminary priests, instruments of the King of Spain, to stir up sedition in all countries, whereby he might subdue them."[5] As late as 1644, even as the mood of the government had temporarily grown more tolerant of Catholics, the sheriff said to Ralph Corby as he stood on the gallows waiting to be hanged: "Having been made priest in foreign parts . . . you have returned to England and seduced the King's subjects."[6]

---

[3] John Ogilvie, *An Authenic Account of the Imprisonment and Martyrdom in the High Street at Glasgow, in the year 1675, of Father John Ogilvie, of the Society of Jesus*, trans. Charles J. Karslake S.J. (London: Burns and Oates, 1877), 45.

[4] Koerbling, *Father Rupert Mayer*, 141–42.

[5] Henry Foley, S.J., *Records of the English Province of the Society of Jesus* (London: Burns and Oates, 1877), I:368. The English Mission was begun in 1580, but during the worst years of the persecution, few Jesuits were in England—by 1598, there were only eighteen, according to Thomas M. McCoog, S.J., ed., "English and Welsh Jesuits: Catalogues 1555–1640," in vol. 1 of *Monumenta Angliae*, in *Monumenta Historica Societatis Jesu*, vol. 142 (Rome: Institutum Historicum Societatis Jesu, 1992), xxxvi. A century later, in 1680, ninety-two were assigned to the English Mission (Francis Edwards, S.J., *The Jesuits in England: From 1580 to the Present Day* [London: Burns and Oates, 1985], 90).

[6] Foley, *Records of the English Province*, 3:84.

Even in our own time, particularly in Communist countries, governments continue to be suspicious of religious because of their ties with the Vatican. In Soviet-ruled Lithuania, Gerardas Dunda, a pastor in Juodeikei in the Joniskis region, was arrested late in the afternoon of October 28, 1948. "Men with automatic rifles and machine guns surrounded the rectory," he wrote in a ten-page account years later. His captors at least allowed him to fill a pillowcase with food—a loaf of bread and a side of bacon—and even advised him to take some warm clothes, because winter was not far off. Then, along with a number of his parishioners who were also being arrested, he was transported by truck to the KGB's headquarters in Zagare. A fortnight of intense interrogations followed, after which he began to serve seven years of imprisonment in labor camps in Russia. There was no trial; he was simply sentenced in absentia.[7]

Ten years later, in 1958, four Jesuits engaged in pastoral work in East Germany—Robert Frater, Josef Menzel, Wilhelm Rueter, and Josef Müldner—were arrested and charged with espionage. Menzel, the only one of the four still living in 1997, wrote of his arrest, trial, and imprisonment in his recollections. He states that the very fact that he studied in Rome was, in the eyes of the STASI [state security police], an incriminating circumstance. To the STASI, it meant that he "was purposely educated and schooled in Rome, the center of resistance against world peace and socialism."[8]

The same fear of foreign influence from the Vatican brought about the arrest of Walter Ciszek in the early 1940s and Archbishop Dominic Tang in Canton in 1958. Both men served many years in prisons and labor camps in China and Russia. Although subjected to repeated

---

[7] Gerardas Dunda, untitled memoir, n.d., p. 1. It was sent to the author by Antanas Saulaitis, acting provincial of the Lithuanian Province, in August, 1997, and had been translated into English by Ms. Ramune Lukas, secretary at the Lithuanian Jesuit community in Chicago, Illinois.

[8] "Personal Recollections of Fr. Josef Menzel, S.J.," n. d., p. 1. Fr. Menzel sent the author a copy of his recollections in October, 1997—about a dozen pages. Soon afterwards, following a request to Bernd Gunther, S.J., for additional information about the four Jesuits who had been incarcerated in East Germany in the late 1950s, I was put in touch with Josef Ullrich, S.J., at the provincialate of Northern Germany. Fr. Ullrich sent me a report of the experience of all four arrested Jesuits, which was assembled from material in the Society's archives. Both the recollections and the report were translated into English for the author by Thomas Schwarz, S.J., a German scholastic teaching at Santa Clara University in California, and James Torrens, S.J.

interrogations, neither received a formal trial. Nor did Miguel Pro, imprisoned in Mexico in the earlier part of this century.

The night before Pro's execution on November 23, 1927, General Roberto Cruz, uneasy over the lack of due process in his condemnation to death, suggested to the Mexican president, Plutarco Elias Calles, that it might have been wiser to follow normal legal forms after his arrest. Calles is alleged to have replied: "I don't want legal forms, but deeds!"[9] Pro's execution before a firing squad in the courtyard of the Mexico City jail went ahead as scheduled.

Defense procedures in such situations were either nonexistent or conducted under circumstances that made it impossible for the defense attorney to be an effective advocate for his client—assuming that the lawyer was even committed to representing the interests of the accused Jesuit. In his *Prison Meditations,* for instance, Alfred Delp observes that his lawyer told him "while the proceedings were still in progress, that as a matter of fact he was against Jesuits too." To make matters worse, Delp's trial took place before a judge known to be "anti-Catholic and a priest-hater."[10] Fifteen years later, the four Jesuits arrested in East Germany on espionage charges at least had attorneys who were not prejudiced against them because they were Jesuits; however, the two lawyers assigned to their defense "needed to be very careful because of their own situation" in East Germany. "The authorities did not allow a Western attorney, who alone could have answered the accusations freely and objectively."[11] All four were found guilty and served prison terms of between one and two years. Much of Menzel's time was spent in solitary confinement.

The arrests of priests in England under Elizabeth I and her successors were all the more frequent not only because the government viewed priests as traitors, but also because there was the lure of monetary gain. A statute enacted in 1606 offered rewards to anyone who provided information leading to the arrest of priests who celebrated Mass or engaged in other sacramental work, such as baptizing and hearing confessions.[12]

[9] Antonio Dragon, S.J., *Blessed Miguel Pro,* trans. Sr. Mary Agnes Chevalier F.M.I. (Anand, India: Gujarat Sahitya Prakash, 1959), 136.

[10] Delp, *Prison Meditations,* 12, 162.

[11] Josef Ullrich S.J., ed., "Regarding the Trial of Four Jesuits in the Year 1958 in the Former GDR [German Democratic Republic]" (Archives, North German Province of the Society of Jesus, n.d.) pt. 2, p. 1.

[12] Philip Caraman, *Henry Morse: Priest of the Plague* (New York: Farrar, Straus, and Cudahy, 1957), 115.

Jesuits on the English Mission tried to avoid arrest by adopting aliases and disguises. Aliases were needed in part because agents of the crown had secret access to lists of Englishmen studying abroad for the priesthood. Edmund Campion's superior, Robert Persons, who sometimes used the name John Howlett,[13] arrived in England in the guise of a Flemish captain, "in a dress of buff layd [sic] with gold lace, and hatt [sic] and feather suited to the same." Seeing Persons attired in this manner, Campion wrote with amusement to the superior general in Rome, Everard Mercurian, that "a man must needs have very sharp eyes to catch a glimpse of any holiness or modesty shrouded beneath such a garb, such a look, such a strut!"[14] The strutting and the bold look added to the actual disguise, made all the more necessary by the watchful eyes of pursuivants at English ports.

By and large, English Jesuits chose the garb of gentlemen as their disguise so that they could easily move about among the homes of the English gentry who, at great risk to themselves, provided them with shelter and the opportunity to celebrate Mass for their families and trusted Catholic friends in the neighborhood. In his *Autobiography of a Hunted Priest,* John Gerard explains that he selected this style of dress because he could "stay longer and more securely in any house or noble home where my host might bring me as his friend."[15]

The use of exterior disguises was complemented by changes in outward behavior that would otherwise have been uncharacteristic. While staying at the country home of Lady Agnes Wenman near Oxford, Gerard was seemingly engaged in a game of cards with the ladies of the household when a Protestant doctor of divinity paid an unexpected visit. But as he explains, "actually we had put the cards away to attend to better things as soon as the servants had gone downstairs, and we resumed our game when this gentleman came in."[16]

In other times and places, too, Jesuits have resorted to disguises and aliases to carry on their ministry undetected. Ciszek entered Russia as a laborer with the assumed name of Wladimir Lypinski. Centuries earlier, when Pedro Paez set sail at Diu on a Turkish ship

---

[13] E. E. Reynolds, *Campion and Persons: The Jesuit Missions of 1580–81* (London: Sheed and Ward, 1980), 88.

[14] Gerard, *The Autobiography of a Hunted Priest,* 18.

[15] Ibid., 18.

[16] Ibid., 170.

for Massawa, the gateway to Ethiopia, he and his fellow Jesuit, Antonio Monserrate, were dressed as Armenian merchants.[17]

So too, before his arrest, did Miguel Pro adopt a disguise in order to exercise his priestly ministry after the government had closed Mexico City's churches and suppressed public worship. His ministry included secretly distributing communion both in public places like parks and in private homes. His resourcefulness in eluding the police in such situations is evident from his own description of one particularly narrow escape.

As Pro was giving out communion in one of these home "eucharistic stations," a servant entered the room crying, "The police!" According to Pro, the people "turned white with fright." Urging them to remain calm, he told them to spread out into the other rooms and urged the women to remove and hide their veils. He himself was wearing a cap and a gray overcoat, "which had become quite dirty." He hid the Blessed Sacrament over his heart. Finally, with planned sang-froid, he took out a long cigarette holder and, fitting a cigarette into it, awaited the police.

As they entered the room, the officers announced accusingly, "There is public veneration going on here." "Come along now, sirs, you are mocking me," Pro replied. The officers responded, "We have seen a priest enter." "What humbug! I bet you half a glass of whiskey that there is no priest here," Pro said. Undeterred, the police answered, "We have orders to search this house. Follow us!"

Pro obligingly accompanied them, indicating "what was to be found beyond each door, but," he adds with humor, "as it was my first visit to the house I was nearly always mistaken. I announced a bedroom when it was a study; then as a sewing room what proved to be a lavatory." After the police allowed him to leave, he went on to distribute communion at other homes. "When I returned from my round of Holy Communions, I found them still at the door," he observes, "but the famous priest had not yet turned up!"[18]

In Latin America, government action against religious frequently resulted in arrest and incarceration—and death—during the 1970s and 1980s. Arrests were more common when basic constitutional

---

[17] Philip Caraman, *The Lost Empire. The Story of the Jesuits in Ethiopia 1555–1634*. (London: Sidgwick and Jackson, 1985), 17.

[18] Dragon, *Blessed Miguel Pro*, 94–95.

rights were rescinded on the pretext of maintaining public order, such as in Argentina in the mid-1970s. Juan Luís Moyano Walker, a scholastic at the time, was living in the barrio of San Martín in the Province of Mendoza, where he coordinated an adult literacy program. He was also active in the Movement of Priests for the Third World—a movement that, in his words, was regarded by both the military and right-wing groups as "very suspicious."[19]

A few days after civil rights were suspended in Argentina in November 1974, Moyano Walker and others were arrested at the close of a meeting of the literacy program's coordinators. Most were quickly released, but he and another person were held in jail, charged with illegal assembly and the possession of weapons. Within a week the attorney engaged by the Society proved his innocence and his release was ordered.

Caught up in a totalitarian regime intent on sequestering political prisoners by any means necessary, Moyano Walker describes how he—like Franz Jalics, another Jesuit working in Latin America, whom we will meet later—became one of the "disappeared": "It was at this moment [when his freedom seemed assured] that the problems began in earnest," he notes, "through a methodology that was systematically applied throughout the country after the 1976 military coup that resulted in the death of more than 30,000 people." He continues: "Although I was officially at liberty, with my release papers signed, the federal police removed me through a back door. For three days I was in the category of 'disappeared.' " During this three-day period, he was subjected to interrogations, accompanied by torture, concerning his work in the barrio and with the Movement of Priests of the Third World.[20]

Under pressure from the church to disclose his whereabouts, the military authorities finally acknowledged that even though nothing had been found to incriminate him, they were indeed holding Moy-

---

[19] Letter from Juan Luís Moyano Walker to the author, April 18, 1995.

[20] By causing an arrested person to be "disappeared," the authorities prevent the family and friends from pressing specific charges of harming the prisoner. As the authors of *The Book of Christian Martyrs* (New York: Crossroads, 1990, 16–17)—Bruno Chenu, Claude Prud'homme, France Quere, and Jean-Claude Thomas—point out, "the victim is carried off and disappears. Who should be accused?" If the prosecutor were to allow a trial, "he would cause general indignation and would be giving the accused the opportunity of bringing the iniquity of his politics into broad daylight."

ano Walker "at the disposition of the national executive power." He remained in the Mendoza prison for four months and was then transferred to a prison for political prisoners in the city of Resistencia in the northern part of Argentina. There he remained for another three months—deprived of all books, the Mass, and the ability to write letters. Finally, the authorities permitted him to go into exile in Germany, where he finished his theology studies prior to ordination.

In traditionally Catholic Latin American countries, the arrest and imprisonment of Jesuits like Moyano Walker often occurred because military dictatorships viewed them as part of groups they perceived as left-wing communist threats. However, actual Communist governments have treated religious prisoners with particular harshness because they feared Vatican influence as exercised through the religious engaged in apostolic work within their borders.

Thus, when George Wong refused to cooperate with Chinese authorities in condemning Ignatius Pei Kung, then-bishop of Shanghai, as an imperialist "running dog," he himself was arrested on September 26, 1955, two weeks after Bishop Kung's arrest. Wong's interrogations over the next six months focused on his relationships with foreigners. Including time spent in a labor camp as well as in various prisons, he was incarcerated for a total of twenty-six years.

The arrest of Francis Xavier Ts'ai two years earlier led to an even longer period of incarceration. Serving as pastor of St. Ignatius Church in Shanghai at the time, Ts'ai was taken into custody along with six other Chinese Jesuits and was held for thirty-five years, from 1953 until 1988. Neither man had even the pretense of a trial until several years after the actual arrest; the charge against both of them was the usual one—antirevolutionary activities.

Francis Xavier Chu, one of the other Chinese Jesuits arrested around the same time as Ts'ai, was, like him, named after the sixteenth-century Jesuit missionary, Francis Xavier. Also like Ts'ai, he was incarcerated for three decades, both in actual prisons and in labor camps. His witness to his faith is all the more remarkable in that several of his blood brothers were imprisoned as well, although for shorter periods. Whereas Francis Xavier Ts'ai was eventually released, Chu was still a prisoner when he died at the age of seventy-one.

In Vietnam in 1981, the same charge was leveled against Joseph Nguyen-Công Doan, the regional superior for Vietnamese Jesuits.

According to Doan's account in an interview, the authorities "saw me as dangerous, both because I was [the] superior of the Jesuits and because I worked with the [Vietnamese] bishops . . . and they knew that the bishops trusted me. They even suspected that I was secretly a bishop!"

After another Jesuit in Hanoi was arrested for mimeographing and distributing commentaries on the Sunday gospels—it was forbidden to print anything without permission—it was Doan's turn. On January 8, 1981, "Government agents came to the Jesuit residence and invited me to go to the police station. . . . 'Invite' is the word they use when you're being arrested. The chief of the investigators questioned me, and at noon they locked me up in the central jail for political prisoners there at the station. The 'invitation' to the police station led to nine years spent in prisons and labor camps."[21]

Arrests could sometimes be combined with demands for ransom. Such was the case with Tomás Esteban, a Spanish Jesuit who arrived in China in 1917 to work as a missionary at the Wuhu mission. Communist soldiers arrested him in 1931. His religious superiors tried to meet the demands of his captors, but each time they offered a sum, his captors demanded a larger amount. During his two years of confinement, Esteban developed tuberculosis and died, still imprisoned, in 1933.[22]

Nor have Jesuits been arrested only individually or in small groups. Entire communities have been placed under arrest at virtually the same moment, particularly during the suppression, as noted earlier. For example, before the Jesuits were actually expelled from Paraguay, there was a loud knock on the door of one of the Jesuit colleges in the predawn hours of July 17, 1767. When a brother came to inquire who was there, a voice outside said that a priest was needed to assist a dying person. But it was a ruse. As soon as the brother opened the door, a captain—followed by a contingent of soldiers—rushed in, aimed his pistol at the brother's chest, and demanded to be taken to the rector. In the latter's presence, he ordered the notary accompanying him to read aloud the decree of expulsion signed by Charles III of Spain. The entire community was then herded into the refectory

[21] Joseph Nguyen-Công Doan, interview with author, April 11, 1995. The interview later appeared in *America* magazine, September 16, 1995.

[22] Pablo Gil, S.J., *Misionero y Mártir. Vida del Padre Tomás Esteban, S.J.* (Pamplona: Ediciones los Misioneros, 1956), 132.

where the decree was read aloud again. One novice, Dominico Perez, was told that he was free to go because he had not taken vows. However, in a gesture of fidelity to the Society, he told the captain to add his name to the list of those who were to be expelled and deported.[23]

The same abruptness characterized the arrest and deportation of the Jesuits in Mexico City in 1767, starting on June 25—the vigil of the feast of the Sacred Heart. Arriving at the house of the professed fathers (la Casa Profesa) at 4 a.m., soldiers pounded on the door. Two of them then seized the brother porter who answered the door, while others took up positions as guards there and at all other doors. The officer in charge, José Antonio Areche, summoned the superior, José Otrera, and ordered him to call together the members of the community to the chapel. He then read aloud the royal decree whereby Jesuits were banished from Mexico.

As the stunned members of the community stood in the chapel listening to the proclamation, one observed aloud that the Blessed Sacrament was reserved there. Areche apologized and said that it should be removed to another part of the building. "No," replied the Jesuit who had made the observation. "It would be more fitting that we ourselves consume the Sacrament and [thereby] fortify ourselves with this celestial food." "What? Now?" asked the surprised officer. "Yes," the Jesuits responded in unison. "It is the viaticum of pilgrims and the afflicted," one Jesuit movingly observed. The minister of the community, Juan Francisco Iragorri, then distributed the consecrated hosts to all the Jesuits, including a Jesuit who was so ill with erysipelas that he had to be carried to the chapel. At noon, they were sent to their rooms, while the soldiers removed the chalices and other liturgical vessels and ornaments and converted the chapel into their barracks. The next day no one was allowed to say Mass or receive communion even though it was the feast of the Sacred Heart.

On the same day that the soldiers occupied the Casa Profesa, soldiers also arrived before dawn at the houses of other Jesuit communities: San Andres, the Colegio Mazimo, San Ildefonso, and San Gregorio. Similar expulsion procedures were carried out there, as well as in California, where there were missions at Sinoloa and Sonora. Over the next few months, the members of the now-dissolved communities began their long voyage back to Europe. Of the 678

---

[23] Carayon, *Documents Inédits*, 16:183–84.

Jesuits who had lived in Mexico, 101 died either on their way to the port of Veracruz or aboard the ships onto which they had been herded. For some, the voyage included a stop of several months in a prison in Havana, which meant that they spent two years as prisoners in transit before they even arrived in Spain. In an effort to maintain a sense of community life, each ship had a superior who oversaw the sharing of the limited provisions, and who—the semidarkness of the ships' holds notwithstanding—read aloud from their breviaries as a means of both personal and communal support.[24]

More recently, Jesuits have simply been arrested as prisoners of war. Carl Hausmann, for example, was serving as a chaplain with the U.S. Army in a hospital in Mindanao in the Philippines during World War II. He spent three years in a penal colony at Davao before dying aboard a prison ship in circumstances that will be described later. A number of scholastics were also interned in the Philippines at the same time.

In Europe, another army chaplain, Paul W. Cavanaugh, was captured by the Germans on December 19, 1944. During his five months of captivity, he and hundreds of other prisoners participated in a forced march through Bavaria for thirty-five days, narrowly escaping death from allied bombings along the way: "April 5. Were bombed by Americans at Nurnburg [sic]—24 killed outright, about 40 others seriously wounded. A 500-pounder landed 15 yards from me." Never one to forget his sacramental duties even in these dangerous circumstances, he "anointed all the dead and seriously wounded."[25] For many incarcerated Jesuits, arrest and detention were no barriers to the exercise of their ministry—a theme that will be addressed in chapter 12.

---

[24] Gerard Decorme, S.J., *La Obra de los Jesuitas Mexicanos durante la Epoca Colonial 1572–1767* (Mexico City: Antigua Libreria Robredo de José Porrua y Hijos, 1941) I, 445–78.

[25] Paul W. Cavanaugh, circular letter to other Missouri Province military chaplains, dated July 23, 1945 (Missouri Province archives, Colombiere Center, Clarkston, Michigan).

FOUR

Spectators

THE ARREST OF JESUITS has frequently been marked by a certain public quality. As previously noted, perhaps the most public arrest of all was that of Daniel Berrigan in Catonsville, Maryland, in 1968, which was viewed by hundreds of thousands of Americans on the evening news. But even in earlier times, crowds were often present as Jesuit prisoners were taken from place to place, and the mood of those gathered could be hostile. When the seventeenth-century inhabitants of the Arabian town of Tarim learned that the missionaries Pedro Paez and Antonio Monserrate did not believe in Mohammed, they "spat on our faces and punched us with their fists. There was nothing the guards could do."[1] Similar maltreatment greeted the scholastic Paul Miki and his companions in 1597 as they were led from one village to another on their weeks-long journey from the prison in Miyako to their place of execution in Nagasaki.[2]

A century later in India, John de Brito was arrested for disobeying the rajah of Marava's order not to preach the gospel in his territory. Soldiers apprehended him on January 8, 1693, and forced him to walk through a series of villages to the prison in Ramandabouram. At one village, he was placed in chains in the type of cart used by Brahmin priests to carry their idols. In a letter to the other Jesuits of the mission, Francis Laynez, the superior of the Madurai Mission, describes how de Brito was left in the cart for a whole day "exposed to the laughter of the public."[3]

A few decades after de Brito's death, another Jesuit assigned to the Madurai Mission, Venantius Bouchet, was also arrested and forced to undergo public humiliation on the way to the fortress in which he

[1] Caraman, *Lost Empire*, 30.

[2] Joseph N. Tylenda, S.J., *Jesuit Saints and Martyrs* (Chicago: Loyola University Press, 1983), 41.

[3] *Lettres Edifiantes et Curieuses Ecrites des Missions Etrangères par quelques missionaires de le Compagnie de Jésus*, ed. Charles le Gobien, S.J. (Paris: Nicholas le Clerc, 1707), 2:22.

was to be imprisoned for a month. "All the streets were filled as I went by," he writes. "Some seemed compassionate, others—the greater number—hurled insults at me, and said I deserved all kinds of punishment for having despised their gods."[4]

A far harsher experience lay in store for Isaac Jogues after his capture by the Iroquois in 1642. He was forced to travel through their villages, together with René Goupil and the Hurons who had been taken captive with him. All were subjected to torture along the way. Jogues writes in his letter to his superior in France, "Now for seven days they had been leading us from village to village, from stage to stage [wooden platforms erected specifically for the torture of captives]—being made a spectacle to God and to the angels, and the contempt and sport of the barbarians."[5]

The animosity of the captors and onlookers of Bouchet, de Brito, Miki, Monserrate, and Paez was anti-Christian in nature; however, that of the spectators in Elizabethan England was specifically anti-Catholic and could lead to harsh treatment of the Jesuits, who were seen as being in league with Catholic powers like Spain intent on occupying the kingdom. After being dragged through the streets of London to the Marshalsea prison, Thomas Pounde—whose story is told later—wrote from his cell to his fellow Jesuits, "Bareheaded, I went with a heavy iron [chain], while the mob shouted 'Crucify!' "[6]

William Weston's arrest in 1586 coincided with the discovery of the so-called Babington plot to assassinate Queen Elizabeth and place Mary Queen of Scots on the English throne. Though not implicated himself, Weston writes in his autobiography of the crowd's reaction upon learning of the plot. From the house in which he was confined, he could hear angry shouting nearby. He observes, "Great crowds gathered in the street . . . talking wildly all the time against the Pope, the King of Spain, and the Queen of Scots." Significantly, Weston adds, "and not least, as you can guess, against the Jesuits."[7]

---

[4] Ibid.

[5] Thwaites, *Jesuit Relations*, 39:197.

[6] *The Elizabethan Jesuits: Historia Missionis Anglicanae Societatis Jesu (1660) of Henry More*, trans. Francis Edwards, S.J. (London: Phillimore, 1981), 37.

[7] William Weston, *An Autobiography from the Jesuit Underground*, trans. Philip Caraman (New York: Farrar, Straus and Cudahy, 1955), xxv. In *Campion and Persons*, E. E. Reynolds notes on p. 112: "Religion no longer plays a determinative part in the lives of the vast majority of people, but from, say, 1550 to 1650, it was part of men's thinking and was inevitably interlocked with politics."

Similarly, Robert Southwell's letter of August 31, 1588, to the superior general of the Society, Claudio Acquaviva, reflects an awareness of the English crowd's anti-Catholic virulence. In his letter, Southwell describes an execution during which the condemned person begged any Catholics in the crowd to pray for him. When a bystander fell on his knees, the crowd turned on him. "Hereupon the people raised a great outcry, and he [the bystander] was hurried off to prison."[8]

The mood was not always hostile, however. As Southwell stood on the gallows awaiting his own execution, he publicly declared that he had never meant any harm to the queen and that he had prayed for her daily. He asked only for God's mercy for himself. His humility and the simplicity with which he spoke were such that "the people were so moved with his charitable ending, that no one of them (contrary to the accustomed wont) did speak any evil words against him."[9]

The fickleness of the crowd's mood is even more evident in the events surrounding the arrest and eventual hanging of John Ogilvie twenty years later in Scotland. After being incarcerated in Glasgow, he was taken to Edinburgh, where he was questioned by council members appointed by James I. As he was being led out of his place of confinement in Glasgow, relatives of other captives being held there, believing that Ogilvie had betrayed their Catholic family members, brutally turned on him. "Whilst I am being led through the crowd of the friends and wives of the condemned," he wrote, "I am greeted with mud, snow and curses. . . . A certain woman cursed 'my ugly face.' "[10] Unperturbed, Ogilvie looked at the woman and said, "The blessing of Christ on your bonnie countenance," an impressive example of following the scriptural injunction to return good for evil.

After his return to Glasgow from Edinburgh where he received his death sentence, Ogilvie was greeted quite differently by some of these same people. In the conclusion of his account, which was written by several others who had shared his imprisonment, we are told

---

[8] Catholic Records Society, *Unpublished Documents Relating to the English Martyrs*, vol. 1, 1584–1603, coll. and ed. John Hungerford Pollen, S.J. (London: J. Whitehead and Son, 1908), 1:327.

[9] Foley, *Records of the English Province*, I:375. Foley says that he takes his information from a mansucript by Henry Garnet S.J., "A brief discourse on the condemnation and execution of Mr. R. Southwell."

[10] *An Authentic Account of the Imprisonment and Martyrdom of Father John Ogilvie*, 20.

that as he was being led to the scaffold, "people of all sexes and conditions came running together to the sight, and amongst them the wives and relatives of his condemned fellow prisoners who, a few days before, had heaped reproaches upon him, and pelted him with snow-balls, regarding him, as they did, as the cause of all their miseries." But instead of cursing him, "they were invoking every blessing on his head, and not without tears." What caused this change in their attitude? It came about because they now knew that "he had not discovered [revealed] a single one of the Catholics."[11] Such refusal to implicate other Catholics, despite being subjected to torture, is an underlying theme in the writings of a number of Jesuit prisoners during this and other periods.

Similarly, so widely known and admired in England was Henry Morse's work among the plague-stricken that when he was publicly executed in 1645, an eyewitness described the onlookers as "an almost infinite crowd that [stood] looking on in silence and deep emotion." By the same token, earlier in the same century Henry Garnet, superior of the English Mission, proclaimed his innocence from the scaffold in regard to the so-called Gunpowder Plot in such a way that it dissipated whatever animosity the crowd may have previously felt.[12] In fact, when the hangman had quartered Garnet's body and held up his heart with the traditional cry of "Behold the heart of a traitor," the crowd refused to utter the corresponding replies of "Aye, aye" and "God save the king."[13]

The reaction of Catholic crowds tended to be entirely sympathetic. With their expulsion from Mexico during the suppression, a group of Jesuits at one college there were stripped of all personal belongings except their breviaries and loaded onto carts. Of those who gathered to watch, "each wanted to say, weeping, a last goodbye to the Fathers [and] many threw their purses into the carts for the needs of the

---

[11] Ibid., 41.

[12] In a faxed communication to the author dated October 30, 1995, the English Jesuit historian, Francis Edwards, stated: "I am convinced that the gunpowder plot and the other plots . . . were put up jobs to discredit the Catholics. Of course, all this is backed up by evidence which is persuasive if not conclusive. Conclusive it could not be in the absence of so much destroyed or lost."

[13] Philip Caraman, *Henry Garnet, 1555–1606 and the Gunpowder Plot* (New York: Farrar Straus and Co., 1964), 439.

voyage, having no other way of offering their affection."[14] Though the
description of the crowd's sorrow at the forced departure of the Jesuits might be exaggerated, it does show that the citizens may not have
agreed with the suppression of the Jesuits and had come to appreciate the value of their apostolic efforts on their behalf.

Even in India, Japan, Ethiopia, and other non-Christian countries
there were converts to Catholicism who eagerly showed support for
Jesuits in custody. Such was the situation with Carlo Spinola in
seventeenth-century Japan. Word of his arrest soon spread throughout the Christian community. Consequently, as soldiers led Spinola,
Ambrose Fernandes—the Jesuit brother arrested with him—and a
catechist to a prison in Omura, "the streets were full of Christians
from Nagasaki and other nearby towns [who] with tears and lamentations, grieved by this loss, moved the hearts of the confessors of
Christ." Following an overnight stop, the three captives continued
on toward Omura. Once in sight of the prison, they began to sing
psalms and hymns. Hearing them, Christians held inside the prison
sang back by way of answer and support. "Then, entering the prison,"
Spinola's first biographer writes, "it would not be easy to explain the
joy of both groups, accompanied by embraces."[15]

Also in Japan, during the period of persecution that culminated
with the execution of Paul Miki in 1597, two catechists who had
worked with him and a group of Franciscans and their lay helpers
were also condemned to death. Large numbers of Christian converts
converged on the Nagasaki site where the crucifixions were to take
place. Michael Cooper, in his biography of the Jesuit João Rodrigues—who, along with fellow Jesuit Francisco Passio, was permitted to be present—describes the scene as follows: "Lines of
[Japanese] soldiers armed with lances and muskets surrounded the
site to keep back the crowds. Only Rodrigues and Passio were allowed to stand within the circle by the side of the crosses and comfort
the martyrs in their agony. As the sympathetic spectators pressed

---

[14] Carayon, *Documents Inédits,* "Notes historiques sur l'expulsion de la Compagnie de J. de la Province de Mexique et de la Californie en 1767" 16:354–55. The
name of the college is not given.
[15] P. Fabio Ambrosio Spinola, *Vita del P. Carlo Spinola* (Bologna: L'Herede del
Benacci, 1628), 124–25. The author of the biography, published only ten years after
Spinola's death, was a relative who had access to Spinola's letters written from
prison.

forward, the guards used their staves and clubs to beat them back."
Cooper adds that in the melee, the two Jesuits were accidentally
struck by the guards' staves. The sheer confusion of the scene, with
the crowds surging forward, suggests the degree of sympathetic support felt by the Japanese Christians intent on witnessing the martyr-
doms.[16]

During the inquisition, however, Catholic spectators were likely
to keep their views to themselves at large public executions such as
that of Gabriel Malagrida in eighteenth-century Portugal. An account
of the execution appears in the journal of Anselm Eckhart, another
Jesuit imprisoned by Pombal. Eckhart, a German who had been assigned to the Portuguese mission in Brazil before being forcibly returned to Portugal at the time of the suppression, heard the account
from a Spanish Dominican who had been present at the execution in
1761 in Lisbon's Rossio Square.

Eckhart writes that an enormous scaffold was erected for the execution of Malagrida and others condemned for heresy. Assembled
around the scaffold were the judges of the inquisition, along with
large numbers of religious from various congregations. Facing the
scaffold was "an immense multitude." The forty condemned prisoners, including Malagrida, were brought forward carrying signs indicating the seriousness of their heretical offenses. Holding lighted
candles, they had to abjure their errors and make a profession of
faith. A priest described as "a minister of God" prayed at great length
about the truths of the faith. The proceedings began in the morning
and continued until night.

Malagrida was distinguished from the others by the garb he was
obliged to wear. On his head was a mitre-like headdress similar to
those placed on the heads of accused heretics in ceremonies of public

---

[16] Michael Cooper, S.J., *Rodrigues the Interpreter* (New York: Weatherhill, 1974),
138. The cause of the 1597 persecution had its origins in the mishap of a Spanish
galleon, the *San Felipe*, that had gone aground the year before on the coast of Japan.
Several Franciscan missionaries were on board. Cooper notes (pp. 132–36) that the
pilot had allegedly told a Japanese official that Spanish missionaries generally prepared the way for conquest. When the news reached Japan's supreme lord, Toyotomi
Hideyoshi, he threatened to execute all missionaries in the country. His anger, however, was mainly directed toward the lately arrived Franciscans, not the Jesuits, with
whom he had been on relatively good terms for a number of years. Miki and the two
catechists "had been caught in the Jesuit residence at Osaka and by error had been
included on the list of condemned Christians."

degradation.[17] His cassock was "embroidered with figures of frightening serpents and monstrous devils in flames." In his mouth was a bridle, "suggesting that he was a blasphemer or to prevent him from trying to proclaim to the assembly his innocence."

Two Benedictine priests accompanied Malagrida to the spot on the platform where he was to be garroted. At the moment of the actual execution, bystanders heard him murmur the words, "Merciful God, receive me in this hour and have mercy on my soul. Lord, into your hands I commend my spirit." Once he had been strangled, his body was thrown onto a nearby pyre, and the ashes were subsequently cast into the sea from the square. The macabre as well as the public quality of the scene is accentuated in Eckhart's description of the ecclesiastical formality of the arrangements, including the presence of many religious, besides the judges themselves, who were the official witnesses.[18]

A different type of crowd response emerges during periods of revolution. At these times, anger often stemmed from the perception that the clergy—including Jesuits—was allied with an oppressive regime that favored the rich over the poor. Such was the situation during the French Revolution. In *The Crowd and the French Revolution,* George F. Rudé notes that in 1789, "the degree of disrespect for the Church . . . had by this time become general in the markets . . . [and] this anti-clerical feeling was on the increase among the 'menu peuple' [sic]."[19]

The mood of popular anger paved the way for the arrest and month-long incarceration of twenty-three French Jesuits early in September 1792. Like the priests aboard the prison ships near Rochefort, they had refused to take the oath of support for the constitution of the clergy, which called for the establishment of a national

---

[17] When Jan Hus was condemned as a heretic at the Council of Constance in 1415, his tonsure was "defaced with scissors . . . [and] they put on his head a paper crown with three demons on it, and the explanation 'This man is a heresiarch.' " Chenu, Prud'homme, Quere, and Thomas, *The Book of Christian Martyrs,* 112.

[18] Anselm Eckhart S.J., *Memórias de um Jesuíta Prisioneiro de Pombal* (Braga: Livraria A.I., 1987). The account also appears in Carayon's *Documents Inédits,* vol. 16, p. 105. Carayon uses Eckhart as his source. The two accounts differ in some details. Eckhart, for example, speaks of a bronze effigy of Malagrida placed near him, which was evidently intended to represent him as a heretic, but the exact meaning of the effigy is unclear.

[19] George F. Rudé, *The Crowd and the French Revolution* (Oxford: Clarendon Press, 1959), 66.

church, independent of the pope. But it is unlikely that the crowd's hatred was stirred by such an intellectual consideration. Rather, its hatred was aimed at them as priests. Thus, when the Jesuits were brought forth with others from their confinement in a Vincentian seminary on September 3, the crowd's cry was "Death! Death!"[20] All twenty-three were killed.

On the same day in Paris, another onslaught occurred against the captives at a city prison called La Force. Of the five priests who were there, three were slain. Among the latter was the Jesuit, Hyacinthe Le Livec. He was chaplain to the convent of the Daughters of Calvary and also spiritual director for the Princesse de Lamballe, who, like her close friend Marie Antoinette, was beheaded. In his book on men and women religious during the French Revolution, *Refractory Men, Fanatical Women,* Edwin Bannon quotes a passage from a Jesuit martyrology that briefly describes Le Livec: "He had accepted with heroic courage the suffering of exile and penury [as a result of the suppression] in order to remain faithful to the Society . . . His virtue, learning and meritorious qualities had caused him to be held in the highest esteem in Germany. As chaplain to the Lamballe family he was regarded as a saint."[21] Bannon does not give a precise description of how Le Livec and the other two priests at La Force met their end, but he does quote extensively from eyewitness accounts of the massacre at the St. Fermin seminary the day before. Once the seminary was invaded, the non-juring priests were thrown from the windows to the mob below, which included women who were waiting to help in the slaughter. Drawing on these accounts, Bannon says: "Armed with kitchen implements they helped to deal successively with the victims thrown down from the windows of the seminary. One of them . . . earned on this occasion the nickname of 'La Tueuse'—the Killer—and she was referred to by that name for the rest of her life."[22] If not precisely in the same way, it is probable that Le Livec and the other Jesuits killed during the September massacres were dispatched with similar ferocity.

---

[20] Tylenda, *Jesuit Saints and Martyrs,* 297.

[21] Edwin Bannon, *Refractory Men, Fanatical Women. Fidelity to Conscience during the French Revolution* (Leominster, Herefordshire HR OQF: 1992; publisher in USA: Morehouse Publishing, P.O. Box 1321, Harrisburg, Pa. 17105), 76. Bannon's source here is E. de Guilhermy, *Menologie de la Compagnie de Jésus: Assistance de France* (Schneider, 1892).

[22] Ibid., 72.

Although the priests held aboard the prison ships at Rochefort were not put to death in such a brutal fashion, the crewmembers of the *Deux Associés* were as vociferous as the Parisian crowd. They cried out "with an infernal joy, 'Long live the nation! Down with the calotins [clerics[23]]! When will death come for the last of these wretches?'" In his *Les Martyrs de la Foi*, Guillon adds that if a priest died in one of the crude hospital tents set up by the government on l'île Madame, "this cry [of joy] uttered around the dying body was taken up by the crew" aboard the nearby prison ship.[24]

By then, the French monarchy had already been dissolved, replaced by the form of government known as the Commune. The same term reappeared in the nineteenth century as the name of the insurrectionary government that briefly took control of Paris in the spring of 1871. During this latter period, five Jesuits were imprisoned for a month and then slain in another outburst of anticlerical violence. Alexis Clerc and Léon Ducoudray were killed by a firing squad on May 25th. The next day, as Pierre Olivaint, Jean Caubert, and Anatole de Bengy were being led, along with other prisoners, through the streets of Paris on the way to their execution, communard women and children followed "with imprecations and a thousand cries of death."[25] Pushed into a courtyard, the entire group was massacred by the mob.

During the Spanish civil war of the 1930s, religious were again perceived to be linked to the oppressors of the working class and the poor. Thus, a number of Jesuits were imprisoned and executed. The authors of one study of the Spanish civil war assert that the Church was largely regarded as "an instrument . . . of the rich, as the defender of property and an iniquitous social order, and as . . . the enemy of the workers."[26] Jesuits were especially singled out for persecution. In 1932, legislation pertaining to the separation of Church and state included a provision that dissolved the Society in Spain—in

---

[23] Edwin Bannon, 32, defines "calotins" as "a term of contempt derived from the use, by many clergy, of the calotte or skull-cap."

[24] Guillon, *Les Martyrs de la Foi*, 1:363–64.

[25] Armand de Ponlevoy, S.J., *Actes de la Captivité et de la Mort des RR. PP. P. Olivaint, L. Ducoudray, J. Caubert, A. Clerc, A. de Bengy*, 5th ed. (Paris: G. Téqui, Librairie Éditeur, 1872), 116. (There are variations between the fifth and sixth editions. The edition cited will be noted in the future.)

[26] Pierre Braie and Emile Temimé, *The Revolution and the Civil War in Spain* (Cambridge: MIT Press, 1970), 371.

effect, a second de facto suppression of the Society almost two hundred years after the first and universal suppression by the pope.

The hostility engendered in some segments of the population is epitomized in the events surrounding the arrest of a group of Jesuits at the St. Joseph Retreat House in Barcelona on July 21, 1936. That morning twenty soldiers arrived to search the house for arms. Although none were found, the four Jesuits in the house were taken into custody anyway. During the drive through the city, young men walking alongside their car hurled insults and urged the soldiers to kill the four because they were religious.[27]

Although three of the four Jesuits in this instance were killed before they could even be incarcerated, a number of other Spanish Jesuits did spend time in jail. Merely having a crucifix on the wall of one's room could result in arrest. Brother Constantine March Battles was in hiding with a relative when searchers came to the apartment. Although Battles was surreptitiously using an identity card stating that he was a businessman from Orihuela, a crucifix on the wall prompted the searchers to ask if he were a priest. He replied that he was not but acknowledged being a Jesuit brother. He was subsequently held for a month in the San Elias prison, a former Poor Clare convent, before being shot with sixteen others.[28]

Jesuits at Dachau also felt the contempt of the crowd, although in this case the crowd was composed largely of lay prisoners who despised their fellow prisoners who were priests. The Belgian, Léo de Coninck, who wrote of his Dachau experiences after the war, speaks of encountering this kind of hostility in the course of carrying out assigned tasks:

> Twice a day we had to go to the kitchen for heavy cauldrons used for our food: they weighed 180 lbs. each. An equal weight of soup (so-called!) was poured in, and two of us, shod in wretched sandals we could scarcely keep on our feet, had to carry them to all the other blocks. This was seldom accomplished without one or other of the carriers stumbling, amid the hostile jeers of spectators who seemed to be consumed with a bestial hatred for Pfaffen [priests].[29]

[27] Tylenda, *Jesuit Saints and Martyrs*, 432.

[28] Ibid. In *The Revolution and the Civil War in Spain* (p. 151), Braie and Temimé note that the ban on public worship included a prohibition against the ownership of religious objects such as crucifixes and holy pictures. Indeed, "the revolutionary rear militias tracked down their owners, carried out searches, and made arrests."

[29] Léo de Coninck, S.J., "The Priests of Dachau," *The Month* CLXXXII (950) (March–April 1946):117.

For de Coninck, such cruel jeers may well have called to mind the meditation on the third degree of humility in the *Exercises*. As one who secretly gave retreats at Dachau to bolster the morale of Jesuits and other religious prisoners, de Coninck would surely have pondered this particular meditation, as, indeed, would other Jesuits over the centuries, exposed as they were to ridicule and hatred during their time as prisoners.

Jeers, insults, and threats were also the lot of three Jesuits in Albania after the Communist persecution of religious began at the end of World War II. On January 1, 1946, the vice provincial for Albanian Jesuits, Gjon Fausti, together with Daniel Dajani, president of St. Xavier College, and a scholastic, Mark Cuni, was arrested for alleged anticommunist activities. Their trial lasted for six days. Each day, along with several others, they were forced to walk chained together from the jail to the courthouse. "Along the way, they were insulted by people yelling, "Death to the traitors.' Father Fausti . . . would walk in front of the seminarians. He was often hit or spat upon while he proceeded in resignation."[30] Taken to a wall outside the Shkodra Catholic cemetery, they were machine-gunned and buried in a mass grave.

Two years after Communists assumed control in China, the police arrested four members of the Aurora Prep community in Yangzhou city: Eugene E. Fahy, who at the time was the apostolic prefect of Yangzhou; James E. Thornton; William D. Ryan; and Eugène Beaucé. The arrests took place on the morning of July 31, 1951—the feast of St. Ignatius. But the police officials were not alone; a hostile crowd accompanied them. As noted in Peter Joseph Fleming's *Chosen For China*, 300 people surrounded the Jesuit residence. When Fahy refused to renounce his authority as apostolic prefect, "the crowd began to shout, 'Down with American Imperialism!' "[31]

In this situation, however, the crowd's negative attitude was not spontaneous but rather was carefully orchestrated by the authorities

---

[30] Giorgi Silvestri, "Fr. Gjon Fausti, S.J., Strength in Serenity: The Account of an Eyewitness of His Mission," in *The Fulfilled Promise: A Documentary Account of Religious Persecution in Albania*, by Gjon Sinishta (Santa Clara, Calif.: H and F Composing Service, 1976), 104–9.

[31] Peter Joseph Fleming, "Chosen For China: The California Province Jesuits in China 1928–1957. A Case Study in Mission and Culture." (Unpublished Ph.D. diss., Graduate Theological Union, Berkeley, Calif.) (Ann Arbor: University of Michigan Dissertation Services, 1994), 452.

and even involved its encircling the building. Fahy makes this clear in his own twenty-six-page account written while he was recuperating in the St. Francis Hospital in Hong Kong after his expulsion from China in 1952. Various Chinese Catholics had been forced to be present in the crowd in the garden. Of these, he says: "When some of the good Christians attempted to hide or push to the rear, they were rounded up and shoved to the front. The whole show," he adds, "was painful for them and they took no more part than what was physically forced on them."[32]

Another instance of prearranged hostility took place a week later at a so-called mass accusation meeting (K'ung Su Hui). Again, Fahy gives a detailed description of what transpired:

> A squad of a dozen, sporting tommy-guns, rifles and side-arms, paraded us through town to the Government Middle School which had the largest auditorium available. We were lined up between guards at the side of the stage. At center stage sat various city officials. . . . One of the "people," a non-Catholic who had been a former secretary in our Middle School, demanded that we stand "in order to see the strength of the Chinese people." We stood and saw the strength of the "people"—the usual crowd of unwilling sheep, vigorously shepherded by Red bellwethers who made sure everyone came in on cue. We were to remain standing for the next three hours.

Six officials addressed the 400 people in the auditorium, leveling various accusations. Between accusations, "a yell leader furnished slogans which the mob obediently sang out." But, Fahy adds, "little energy was put into the cries against us and the accusations were flat and stale." They were, at this point, confined to crimes like "resisting the Independence Movement."[33]

Another instance of public humiliation took place in China eighteen years earlier, before its total takeover by the Communists. While being held for ransom by Communist soldiers in 1931, Tomás Es-

---

[32] Eugene M. Fahy, S.J., Prefect Apostolic of Yangchow, Kaingau, China, "The Red Take-Over of a Mission and My Ten Months in Communist Jails," n.d., 5. Sections of this twenty-six-page account of Fahy's incarceration appeared in much shortened form in the *Life* magazine article, "Buried above Ground," September 8, 1952. The full typed account was never printed. A copy was sent to the writer by Guilbert Guerin, S.J., on October 12, 1996. Fr. Guerin found the account in Msgr. Fahy's room in the Jesuit residence in Taiwan, two months after his death in August, 1996.

[33] Ibid., 6–7.

teban spoke in a letter of having "been exposed to public shame three times." On a later and more painful occasion, he adds, "[T]hey stripped me of my clothes to ridicule me in plays." However, in the same letter, he is able to say that although "insults abound, and three times I thought my end had come, I fear nothing: to live and work for Christ, or to die to reign with him." Two years after his imprisonment began, death did overtake Esteban, brought on by illness stemming from the conditions of his captivity.[34]

In the early 1970s, Edward Murphy was subjected to hate-filled jeers during his first night of incarceration at a local jail in Washington, D.C., where he was being held for an anti-Vietnam War demonstration: "I was in a cell in the isolation unit," he explained, "and all night long there were two guys outside saying that Allah had ordered them to murder the white minister, meaning me. They said the same kinds of things to me the next day," he continued, "and the following night they were still outside my cell, saying they were going to pour kerosene in and set it on fire."

The threat of setting fire to his cell was not carried out, but Murphy had no way of knowing that it would not happen. Observing that the threats and harassment took place on the weekend of Good Friday and Easter Sunday, he said in an interview: "I experienced great fear, and prayed: 'Get me out of this.' Good Friday has never been the same since then, never as real as it was in those two nights. I can still see their faces and hear their voices. Praying then was a talking to Jesus with a sense that there was no distance at all between him and me. The immediacy of the situation made the presence of God very real."[35]

How prayer and the sense of God's presence became sources of strength for those imprisoned will be examined later at some length.

---

[34] Gil, *Misionero y Mártir*, 115.
[35] Interview with Edward J. Murphy, November 27, 1994.

FIVE

Joyful Acceptance of Incarceration for Christ's Sake

ALTHOUGH WHEN JESUITS were arrested, their initial reaction might well include shock and fear, in a number of accounts they also express a note of joy. For example, Rupert Mayer, who was arrested for anti-Nazi preaching and for refusing to give the Gestapo the names of royalist party members, describes his feelings as follows: "When the door [of the cell] snapped shut . . . tears came to my eyes, tears of joy that I was accounted worthy to be imprisoned for the sake of my profession and to await an uncertain future."[1]

John Lenz, who was in a concentration camp in Germany around the same time, had a similar response. In *Christ in Dachau*, he writes that "despite all the hardship and suffering it brought me, Gusen [a branch of the Mauthausen camp, where he was confined before going to Dachau] also brought me joy, the special kind of joy that comes through suffering." He then describes what happened one evening as he walked in the camp with a friend after their meager supper: "I remember . . . suddenly bursting out laughing for sheer joy. I was half-shocked at the time by my own laughter in such a situation, it seemed almost grotesque. And yet," he goes on to explain, "it was my deep inner happiness which had made me laugh, the happiness which, thank God, never forsook me even during the worst days of tribulation and suffering."[2]

Later Lenz relates another incident in which the awareness of God's sustaining presence shone through an otherwise intolerable moment. A priest told him of an SS officer who, during a Mass at

---

[1] Koerbling, *Rupert Mayer*, 164.

[2] John M. Lenz, *Christ in Dachau*, trans. Barbara Waldstein (Modling Bei Wien: Missionsdruckerie St. Gabriel, 1960), 71.

Dachau, had seized the host from the priest's hand and thrown it on the floor. "If that's your God," the officer cried, "then let Him help you if He can." Having heard the story, Lenz comments, "He did help us. He helped us all the time, night and day. . . . Looking back to those years in Dachau, we still cannot thank God sufficiently for His merciful Providence."[3]

By the same token, the Jesuits arrested during the uprising of the Paris Commune in 1871 "went rejoicing that they were accounted worthy to suffer reproach for the name of Jesus." One of them, Léon Ducoudray, describes the scene in a deliberate paraphrase of Acts 5:41, regarding the reaction of the apostles after their arrest and beating: "Then they left the presence of the council, rejoicing that they were counted worthy to suffer dishonor for his name."[4]

It was precisely the memory of the apostles' imprisonment, as described in Acts, that led Patricio Cariola to "explode with joy" on finding himself in a Chilean jail in 1975. During an interview in Washington, D.C. on July 2, 1994, he explained why: "From reading Acts in my cell in the Capuchinos, I suddenly realized that the leaders of the early church had all suffered in prison—it was part of the tradition to be respected for going to jail, and so I felt joy at being part of that same tradition."[5]

Joy mingled with gratitude was also part of the experience of Juan Luís Moyano Walker during his four and a half months in the Mendoza prison in Argentina the same year. In the personal notes he wrote during this period, he addresses God in these words: "Thank you, Lord, for all this—for the insecurity of what may come, for staying close to me, and through me, the pain of many others." He con-

---

[3] Ibid., 87.

[4] Lady (Baroness Mary Elizabeth) Herbert, *A Martyr from the Quarterdeck: Alexis Clerc, S.J.* (London: Burns and Oates, 1890), 209.

[5] Interview with Patricio Cariola, July 2, 1994, in Washington, D.C. An initial rush of joy on being incarcerated for one's religious convictions—whether Catholic or Protestant—is not unusual. During the reign of Queen Mary, many English Protestants were imprisoned in the mid-1550s. In his *Book of Martyrs*, originally published in 1563 as *Acts and Monuments of these latter and perilous Days*, John Foxe mentions a wealthy English Protestant named John Glover who, in a letter to his wife, wrote as follows: "After I came into prison, and had reposed myself awhile, I wept with joy and gladness, musing much on the great mercies of God, and saying to myself, 'O Lord, who am I, on whom thou shouldst bestow this great mercy, to be numbered among the saints that suffer for the Gospel's sake?" (*Book of Martyrs*, ed. Marie Gentert King [Westwood, N.J.: Fleming H. Revell Co., Spire Books, 1968], 207.)

tinues, "After a month and a half you made me see that, just as the weakness of others manifests itself physically or psychologically in a state of depression, in me it was a state of euphoria accompanied by a certain denial. . . of my fears." He adds that within him was "a basic acceptance of whatever may happen, a belief that you, Lord, are guiding this story and each story in the lives of everyone."[6]

Later we shall see that this basic acceptance of incarceration as part of God's will was also part of the thinking of Walter Ciszek and other Jesuits—a trust in God's plan so strong that it could drive away all fear. Joseph Nguyen-Công Doan had just such a reaction. When asked during an interview with the author whether he felt fear at the time of his arrest or at any time during his nine years of imprisonment in South Vietnam after Saigon fell into Communist hands in 1975, he replied: "No. Even at my arrest I felt no fear. I had already been praying a lot over Matthew 10:19–20: 'When they deliver you up, do not be anxious how you are to speak or what you are to say, for what you are to say will be given to you in that hour, for it is not you who speak, but the spirit of your Father speaking through you.' I felt I'd received a grace, then, through the Holy Spirit that took away my fear."

During one of Doan's many interrogations, the North Vietnamese official questioning him mockingly observed that his faith had not saved him from arrest: "You are the third Jesuit to be arrested, so your prayers did not help you to escape our hands." Doan replied, "We did not pray to escape your hands, we prayed to be in the hands of God." He added that his interrogator: "had no answer for that."[7]

This sense of God's care was also evident to Jean Moussé soon after his terror-filled arrival at Buchenwald. Initially, he was certain that he and the other prisoners who tumbled from the airless cattle cars, into which they had been packed for days, would soon be massacred. As they ran through a wooded area in a column five men across, the SS guards beat them with the barrels of their rifles and the stony road cut their bare feet. Moussé records his reaction: "I told myself I was going to die any minute . . . buried in a common grave, and my

---

[6] Carcel de Mendoza, July 1, 1975; personal notes of Juan Moyano Walker photocopied by him and sent to author.

[7] Interview with Joseph Nguyen-Công Doan, April 11, 1995. Fr. Doan had returned to Saigon on April 24, 1974, just days before the city's fall, after several years of study in Rome. His actual arrest did not occur until 1980.

parents would never know where or when I died. I imagined their sorrow and suffered from it in advance."[8]

Not only did Moussé grieve at the thought that his parents might never know how or when he died, he was also stricken with concern that he might not achieve his goal of becoming a Jesuit. While in Paris in 1943, he had spoken to the Jesuit provincial about joining the Society. By then, however, the Germans already occupied France, and it was impossible for him to enter. He was twenty-two at the time. While attempting to cross the border into Spain to join Gaullist supporters there, he and a dozen other young Frenchmen had been arrested and shipped to Buchenwald.[9]

During the forced run along the stony road, however, Moussé realized that his deeper goal was to be even more closely united with God, with or without religious vows. This realization brought with it a sense of peace and ultimately actual joy.

> I wanted to be a Jesuit and would have liked to make my vows before dying. But I understood that if I died right away, it would make no difference to have formally pronounced the vows, since I would be joined to God. Thus, whether or not there were vows no longer had any importance. I was ready to accept death, and from that moment, I was filled with a great joy. Truly, if they had massacred us at that moment, I would have died joyous.[10]

Suddenly, the forced run from the cattle cars to what he knew could be a violent death ceased to be the central reality. Instead he says, "I looked up at the sky and the moon over the trees, and beyond the sound of the blows and the cries of pain, I thought of God's love."[11] It was a love that, coupled with the joy now invading his heart, drove out all fear.

Another young Frenchman, Jacques Sommet, who had entered the Society just before the outbreak of the war, was working with the Resistance at the time of his arrest in Paris. Instead of joy, he felt the sensation of a burden's being lifted—that the pressure of knowing himself to be constantly hunted was over. "I experienced a certain relief," he writes in *L'honneur de la liberté*. "Over were the almost

---

[8] Jean Moussé, letter to author, November 7, 1995.
[9] Ibid. Moussé finally succeeded in entering the Society after the war.
[10] Ibid.
[11] Ibid.

unbearable anxieties pervading daily life that were a part of being in the Resistance. . . . That explains the strange comfort of being taken prisoner. . . . Without knowing how things would end, I could say that I regretted nothing." Once this realization came to him, it "brought me a sufficient degree of consolation."[12]

In his memoirs *How Inscrutable His Ways!*, Dominic Tang speaks of his own positive reaction when taken into custody. It was an acceptance that included happiness at sharing the fate of Catholics who had been faithful to him, their bishop: "While I was being arrested, I was happy; for priests and many Catholics had also been arrested because they had obeyed my orders; they had not joined the CCPA [Chinese Catholic Patriotic Association] nor had they admitted that the Legion of Mary was counter-revolutionary." Then he asks, "How could I not be like them?"[13]

Tang had foreseen that incarceration might be an actual part of his vocation and could, in fact, amount to a vocation itself. In 1951, seven years after his appointment as apostolic administrator of Canton, Tang was told by a nun: "Your vocation to be a bishop is a vocation to be imprisoned." Commenting on her remark, he writes, "I always asked God for the grace to realize this vocation."[14]

For some, the desire for imprisonment was accompanied by a longing for martyrdom. Augustin Rösch, the Jesuit superior for both Mayer and Delp, who was himself incarcerated by the Gestapo, later wrote of a wish to die for Christ that had been with him since childhood: "Since my first communion, I have asked every day for the grace of shedding my blood for the faith."[15] Though he never received this grace, he displayed extraordinary courage in supporting both Delp and Mayer when they came under attack by the Nazi authorities. His unswerving support of them, in his capacity as provincial, brought about his own imprisonment.

---

[12] Jacques Sommet, *L'honneur de la liberté* (Paris: Editions du Centurion, 1987), 64.

[13] Dominic Tang, *How Inscrutable His Ways! Memoirs, 1951–81* (Hong Kong: Aidan Publicities and Printing, 1987), 91. Another Chinese Jesuit who endured many years of incarceration was Francis Xavier Chu (1913–1968), who was either in prison or in labor camps for thirty-two years and who died while still incarcerated. For an account of his life, see *If the Grain of Wheat Dies*, written by a Carmelite Sister in Macao (Sr. Teresa of Jesus) and available through Xavier House, 167 Argyle St., Kowloon, Hong Kong.

[14] Ibid., 118.

[15] Lapomarda, *Jesuits and the Third Reich*, 31.

The Nazis already suspected Rösch because of his membership in the Kreisau Circle. Organized in 1940 by Count Helmuth von Moltke, this was a group made up of Catholic and Protestant intellectuals who opposed the Nazi regime. Like Delp and Mayer, Rösch was subjected to interrogations that lasted for days, and during them, he says, "I was frequently beaten."[16]

If the Elizabethan Jesuit Robert Southwell did not specifically pray for martyrdom, he nonetheless welcomed the prospect of his imminent death. After his condemnation by the Lord Chief Justice, he "went joyfully with them [the guards] through the streets where many of his friends and acquaintances awaited his coming . . . beholding him full of consolation; his countenance nothing dismayed, they never knowing him to look better or more cheerful." The next morning, February 21, 1595, the keeper of Newgate prison informed him that the sentence was to be carried out within a matter of hours. On hearing this, Southwell gave him his nightcap as a remembrance and said: "I thank you most heartily for your good news. If I had any better thing to give, you should have it."[17]

Even when the conditions of confinement were inhuman, some Jesuits were able to maintain a sense of happiness. On their journey to Omura in 1618, Carlo Spinola and his two fellow prisoners—the elderly Brother Ambrose Fernandes and the Japanese catechist, John Kingocu—were forced by their guards to make a lengthy halt at a nearby village before proceeding. In the full heat of July, they were kept for eighteen days in a small straw hut that lacked ventilation and water for bathing. Their accumulated excrement caused an overpowering stench. Not surprisingly, all three fell ill. And yet on entering the cage-like hut, Spinola told the soldiers that he was content to enter "so narrow a prison for love of God."[18] Two years later while at the prison in Omura, he wrote to the superior general, Mutio Vitelleschi, in a letter dated February 18, 1620, about that early period of incarceration in the hut: "We were happy, and more than ever sang

---

[16] Ibid., 61, n. 81.

[17] Foley, *Records of the English Province*, 1:373, note.

[18] Spinola, *Vita del P. Carlo Spinola*, 156. The hut was twenty-four palms long and sixteen wide. According to the Oxford English Dictionary, a palm, as a measure of length, was either the breadth of the palm of the hand, that is, about three or four inches; or the length of the hand from the wrist to the fingertips, that is, seven to nine inches.

psalms, praising God for having made us worthy of suffering for his love."[19]

Another who found illness no impediment to a sense of happiness in prison was Claude de la Colombière. Consumptive and already spitting up blood while imprisoned in London on suspicion of involvement in the Titus Oates plot in 1605, he was eventually banished to France. As he wrote in a letter after his banishment: "It would take me too long to tell you all the mercies God did me. . . . What I can tell you is that I was never so happy as I was in the midst of that storm."[20]

As for Spinola, as horrific as were the conditions of his hut, his long-term place of confinement at Omura was worse. Most of the four years of his incarceration preceding his execution were spent in a kind of cage; instead of three prisoners, however, there were two dozen—four Dominicans, three Franciscans, and fifteen Japanese catechists—resulting in extreme overcrowding. There was no room to lie down and no separate place to relieve themselves. Again, the resultant stench was overwhelming. Their only clothes were what they wore at the time of their arrest, and as these items disintegrated, the prisoners were left in a state of near nakedness. The cage was located on top of a mountain, which meant that the prisoners were exposed not just to the heat of summer but, more dangerously, to the winds of winter. As noted previously, exposure to the extreme cold caused the death of one of the Jesuits, Brother Fernandes, at the age of seventy-nine.

In a rare acknowledgment of just how difficult their life was during the winter, Spinola wrote to the Jesuit provincial of Japan, Matteo de Couros: "I must confess to your reverence that there is not one of us who would not willingly . . . be readier to be burned alive [as they eventually were] than to stay in this prison, because they have not . . . provided us with so much as a straw mat to defend ourselves from the wind, rain, and snow, and the cold is extreme."[21]

Willing acceptance of incarceration and its attendant hardships could go hand in hand with a refusal to make any attempt at escape. Following his arrest, John Gerard makes clear his position on this

---

[19] Ibid., 129–30.

[20] Georges Guitton, *Perfect Friend: The Life of Blessed Claude de la Colombière, S.J.*, trans. William J. Young, S.J.(St. Louis: B. Herder Book Co., 1955), 374.

[21] Spinola, *Vita del P. Carlo Spinola*, 136

subject: "All idea of escape had gone, and in its place I felt a great happiness that I had been allowed to suffer this much for Christ's sake."[22] The embrace of suffering for Christ's sake, even when confronted with his own death sentence, also led another Jesuit, Thomas Garnet, to decline an opportunity to escape: "When certain Catholics amongst the crowds that flocked to Newgate . . . offered him a rope by means of which he might have effected his escape from prison, he said that he had rather be raised up by a rope than leap down to the ground by the same means."[23] The lightheartedness of this reply illustrates the inner serenity that sustained him during his incarceration.

The often-expressed desire to undergo imprisonment for Christ's sake can be seen as a link to the wish to embrace the third degree of humility of the *Exercises*—that is, the desire to choose poverty and insults and to be counted as worthless and a fool because it meant following Christ more closely. Indeed, young men seeking to enter the Society during the reign of Elizabeth I were questioned along these very lines: "Do you consent to put on the livery of humiliation worn by Him, to suffer as He did and for love of Him, contempt, calumnies, and insults?"[24] Edmund Campion and other young candidates of the period were accepted as novices only after they assented to these and similar questions.

It was not just Jesuits on the English Mission but others, too, who, by their acceptance of the degrading treatment to which they were subjected, demonstrated their willingness to put on the livery of humiliation and suffering. Anton Luli, an Albanian Jesuit, quickly came to know the third degree of humility in the treatment he received after his arrest on December 19, 1947, charged with speaking against communism. He had been pastor of a parish in Shkreli for a year and a half when the arrest took place. Here is his description of what happened then: "The guard opened the door to a small room, hurled me against the wall, and then slammed the door. . . . I found myself in a bathroom full of hardened excrement. . . . Never in my life did I

---

[22] Gerard, *Autobiography of a Hunted Priest,* 66.

[23] Foley, *Records of the English Province,* 2:492. Thomas Garnet was the nephew of Henry Garnet, superior of the English Mission. Both were executed, though at different times. Thomas Garnet was canonized in 1970.

[24] Reynolds, *Campion and Persons,* 53.

feel the real and true presence of the Lord as in that instant. Calvary began right away."

Luli then describes how his calvary gained momentum with the appearance of the police chief: "He . . . punched me in the jaw, and then called in two or three guards. They stood in a circle around me. Then they shoved my body first toward one and then toward another like a ball. All the while they yelled and cursed." More pain and humiliation were to follow during his seventeen years of imprisonment and forced labor; nevertheless, this segment of Luli's account suggests both the level of anguish to which he was reduced and his own sense of "the real and true presence of the Lord" in the midst of it as the guards beat and cursed him.[25]

---

[25] Anton Luli, S.J., "Dearest: The Painful Ordeal of an Albanian Jesuit," *National Jesuit News* (December–January 1994):6.

SIX

Physical Suffering and Torture

THE SUFFERING experienced by imprisoned Jesuits could take on very specific forms, sometimes determined by the conditions of their confinement. As a galley slave, for example, Pedro Paez endured not just hunger, thirst, and—as with Carlo Spinola in seventeenth-century Japan—the overpowering stench of accumulated feces, but also the greater torment of lice, a torment well known to prisoners everywhere, down to our own times. Lice prevented the prisoners from getting even a little rest aboard the galley: "Right through the night to dawn we were forced to remain sitting up, trying all the time to rid ourselves of the lice. As they fell from us from above we threw them into the sea; if when we were overcome by fatigue or sleep we lay down and covered our faces, the lice forced us to get up and went on torturing us until morning."[1]

For army chaplain Paul W. Cavanaugh, too, lice proved to be a particular torment after his capture in Belgium during the Battle of the Bulge, especially during a forced march of prisoners that lasted for thirty-five days. "Suffered most from lice," he wrote to his provincial in Detroit. But his spirits were high enough for him to be able to joke: "I am literally a lousy chaplain."[2]

Similarly, the Lithuanian, Gerardas Dunda, had to deal with bedbugs in his barracks in the coal mining labor camp in the Soviet Union. "Everything was infested with bedbugs. They would crawl on the walls in the day and at night. At first we fought them," he writes

---

[1] Caraman, *The Lost Empire*, 38. Lice have been the painful lot of many Jesuit prisoners. In his prison memoirs, *Banishing God in Albania: The Prison Memoirs of Giacomo Gardin, S.J.* (San Francisco: Ignatius Press, 1988), Giacomo Gardin speaks of his prison in Shkodra as being "totally infested with fleas, roaches, and, most of all, ferocious lice" (p. 41).

[2] Letter dated July 23, 1945, Detroit Province archives. The letter was actually a form letter to fellow chaplains of the same province, with a copy sent to the provincial. The provincial was not named.

in his memoir of that period in the late 1940s. In desperation, he and his barracks mates "would sleep in bags, tying ourselves in."

Far more dangerous than lice and bedbugs was the hunger that threatened the lives of many incarcerated Jesuits. Working in the Soviet coal mines all but sapped the starving Dunda's remaining strength. "When we walked home from work," he writes, "we had to hold on to each other so that we would not fall down." But once back at the barracks, he often did fall down on the floor as he tried to remove his shoes. Even climbing up to the wooden platform that served as a bed required the help of another prisoner. Dunda describes the intensity of his hunger in commenting on the sight of one prisoner who had surreptitiously "gotten a loaf of bread [and] was eating it in hiding." Watching him, Dunda "thought how great it would be if a crumb of bread would fall to the ground . . . but the bread disappeared, not a trace was left." [3]

Paez had faced the same situation centuries earlier as he pulled on the oars of the galley on which he was a slave, his daily ration of food just a few handfuls of rice. And Carlo Spinola could write to the Jesuit provincial of Japan: "Our hunger is such that, a few days ago, when our guards gave us a little badly baked bread, already hard, each of us ate it as if it were marzipan [a sweet made of almonds and sugar]." [4]

As Walter Ciszek toiled in a Siberian labor camp in Soviet Russia, "the whole aim of life became the acquisition, somehow, of food. We thought of it constantly." [5] Similarly, Louis Shen, whose weight dropped to eighty-two pounds while confined in a labor camp in China a few decades later, felt that he would not survive and prepared for death. But after praying to God for help, he learned how to catch fish in a lake within the camp precincts and thus regained sufficient strength to hold on to life. [6] Not all found that strength, however. Less fortunate was fellow Chinese Aloysius Wong Jen-Shen, who was arrested by the Communists in 1953. Given a sentence of

[3] Dunda, unpublished memoirs, 5.

[4] Spinola, *Vita del P. Carlo Spinola,* 134. The date of the letter is not given, but it would have been written during his four years of imprisonment at Omura, 1618–22.

[5] Walter Ciszek, S.J., *With God in Russia* (New York: Image Books/Doubleday, 1966), 174.

[6] Louis Shen, S.J., "Growing Up in the Church: China and the USA," *America* (January 23, 1993):11.

twenty years, he was sent to the White Lake labor camp, where he died of hunger seven years later.[7] In the 1940s at Dachau, Jesuits like the Austrian John Lenz also experienced life-threatening hunger. In *Christ in Dachau,* he comments, "Many of our comrades, especially Poles, died of starvation [and] we were driven in desperation to eating mice, earthworms, weeds, grass, anything we could lay our hands on."[8]

Although few died of starvation, Jesuits interned by the Japanese in the Philippines during World War II were also acquainted with hunger. In a series of reflections on their experiences at Los Baños, the huge detention camp near Manila, an unidentified scholastic wrote that "the real torture of a prison camp is hunger." He added that by late 1944, beriberi was common, with internees living on seven ounces of rice mush a day. A decade later in China, James Thornton described what happened to his own body as beriberi took hold: "Every afternoon my calves would begin to swell and glisten, until my ankles had completely disappeared.[It] reduced my pace to a shuffle."[9]

Thornton survived, but an American who did die primarily from hunger was Carl W. Hausmann, an army chaplain who—like Paul Cavanaugh—became a prisoner of war in the 1940s, though for a far longer period. After three years in a Japanese labor camp in the Philippines, he and 500 other American prisoners were locked in the hold of a transport ship as the Japanese began to withdraw. John E. Duffy, a fellow Jesuit chaplain who was also on the ship, described what happened:

> Carl died partly because he gave his food away. We were getting two spoonfuls of rice every third day and he gave it away. And the shame of it was that the men he gave it to weren't worthy of it. He gave it to the whiners. . . . When they complained he'd lean over and dump his ration into their cup, without a word. After his death from hunger and

---

[7] *Jesuits in China, 1949–1990: Ignatian Year* (Hong Kong: China P. Macau Hong Kong P. DCA, 1990), 11. Attending Fr. Wong at the time of his death from starvation was fellow prisoner Francis Xavier Chu. Other Chinese Jesuits who died in prison or in labor camps were Frs. Ng Ying Fun (1979) of Sacred Heart Church and Beda Chang (1955) of St. Ignatius Church.

[8] Lenz, *Christ in Dachau,* 149.

[9] James Enda Thornton, "The New Proletarian Man," unpublished ms. n.d., sent to author by Msgr. Eugene Fahy in August 1994, pp. 15–16.

exposure, the Japanese simply dropped his body, along with those of many others, over the side of the ship into the sea."[10]

Also during World War II, the French Jesuit Jacques Sommet writes in his autobiography of how the effects of hunger were especially deadly for the youths held at Dachau, whose bodies wasted away at a rapid pace: "The progressive effect of hunger is visible, particularly in regard to young men of twenty and twenty-two. In the showers, one realizes that the very structure of their bodies is changing, and one says, 'Look, these young fellows have lost their buttocks, they're on a downward slide. Their muscles have disappeared.' Then," he adds, "one day they collapse."[11] The same situation prevailed at Buchenwald. Jean Moussé speaks of a hunger there that "danced on the horizon," one whose "traits were clearly visible in the skeletal silhouettes of the survivors."[12]

Two centuries earlier in India, Sebastian de Maya, a Portuguese Jesuit, wrote to his provincial in Malabar of the hunger and other deprivations that he and Roberto de Nobili underwent in the Madurai jail during an anti-Christian persecution: "For the last seventeen days we are living in utter destitution; no linen to change, no water to wash; no other food than a handful of rice." De Nobili was sixty-three at the time and nearly blind.[13]

Especially grim were the conditions endured by the many Jesuits thrown into Portuguese prisons at the order of the Marquis de Pombal, after they were forcibly returned from their missions elsewhere following the suppression. Anselm Eckhart, mentioned earlier in connection with the public execution of Gabriel Malagrida, describes in his journal what he and other Jesuits had to contend with in Lisbon's St. Julien prison. In addition to the inevitable lice, fleas, and bedbugs that effectively deprived them of sleep, rats abounded: "Nothing was safe from their voracity—the oil in the lamps and even the wick, all disappeared." During the winter months, the cells were

---

[10] John E. Duffy, "He Kept Silence in Seven Languages: A Short Sketch of Carl W. Hausmann, S.J.," *Woodstock Letters* 75(4) (December 1946):334.

[11] Sommet, *L'honneur de la liberté*, 83. Though not quite as young as these youths whose bodies were visibly wasting away, Sommet himself was a scholastic (seminarian) at the time. He had been arrested in Paris because of his resistance work.

[12] Jean Moussé, "La Planète Buchenwald," *Etudes* (Paris: March 1985), 362/3:338.

[13] S. Rajamanickam, "De Nobili in the Madurai Jail: A Letter of Sebastian de Maya," *Indian Church History Review* XVIII(2) (December 1984):92.

periodically inundated with rainwater that left the floors covered with mud.[14]

Darkness added to their misery. A French prisoner at the St. Julien prison, Père du Gad, who had been serving as a missionary in China until his arrest and expulsion in 1762, wrote of it, saying: "One is entirely in darkness, which obliges us to keep a lamp lighted to read our breviary. . . . The walls are windowless. There is a little skylight, but it is boarded from the outside." Thus, his situation was similar to what Lorenzo Ricci, superior general of the Society, had to endure in his dark cell in the Castel Sant'Angelo in Rome at the time of the suppression.[15]

Many incarcerated Jesuits over the centuries have also experienced the hardship of noise, which could take many different forms. Its omnipresence weighed on Daniel Berrigan, confined in the Danbury prison in Connecticut. "The hardest thing (at times) is the noise. One seems awash in it," he writes in *Lights On In The House Of The Dead*.[16] Loud, repetitive noise could amount to a form of torture. Centuries earlier in Portugal, blacksmiths fashioned armor near the cells in which Anselm Eckhart and others were confined. Not only during the day but throughout the night as well, six of them pounded on their anvils, creating a constant din that Eckhart said almost caused their eardrums to burst. To the noise were added fumes from the burning coals, which were so thick that they made breathing difficult. Were the noise and fumes deliberately intended to create added suffering? It would appear so. Eckhart writes that the Marquis de Pombal's brother, Paulo Carvalho de Mendonça, a cleric, came to the prison and personally exhorted the blacksmiths to "proceed with their deafening task," which continued uninterruptedly for six months.[17]

For those incarcerated, noise brought with it another discomfiting aspect—the pain of hearing the screams of other prisoners. Describing his prison experience in China in the 1950s, John Clifford speaks of being suddenly awakened one night to "a new sound [that] jerked me into a sitting crouch. Somewhere in the cellblock a prisoner was

---

[14] Carayon, *Documents Inédits* 16:89.

[15] Ibid., 16:137.

[16] Daniel Berrigan, *Lights On In The House Of The Dead* (New York: Doubleday, 1974), 200.

[17] Eckhart, *Memórias de um Jesuíta Prisioneiro de Pombal*, 121–22.

screaming in terror. Over and over he shouted in French, 'I refuse! I refuse! I protest in the name of the Catholics of the whole world.' " Next, Clifford heard the scuffling of several pairs of feet, then the sound of blows, a thud, and finally "the heavier sounds of an object being dragged across the rough floor." He identifies the prisoner as a French priest "who had been questioned and did not give the proper answers." Such sounds of abuse were frequent, he adds, and "came regularly to our sharpened ears."[18]

Rupert Mayer, too, had to endure hearing the sounds of prisoners being beaten after he arrived at the Sachsenhausen concentration camp during World War II. Rather than being placed in a barracks, he was housed in a cell. The walls separating him from the other prisoners were very thin, however. As a result, "whatever happens, even in the remotest corners of the prison, is audible throughout the whole prison. Nearly twenty times I heard a prisoner being beaten; what with and how I do not know," he writes, adding, with a note of surprise, that he never heard cries of pain—just the sound of the beating itself. But what was transpiring became evident when he "arrived by chance on the scene as a prisoner was being flogged with a whip right behind the entrance."[19]

On the other side of the globe in the Philippines, Richard McSorley was temporarily confined with other American scholastics at a jail while on their way to the Japanese detention camp at Los Baños. He, too, had to endure the sounds of others' suffering. In his autobiography, *My Path to Peace and Justice*, he describes his horror at having to listen to the sounds of a Filipino prisoner being beaten during an interrogation: "The guard asking the questions held a baseball bat. . . . From our cell I heard the screams and thuds of the baseball bat against flesh and bone. . . . It was bad enough," he continues, "to hear such savagery, so foreign to my experience, but to hear it while I was locked in the bat holder's prison made the horror even more acute. It was as though I felt the blows." A few days later he heard that the Filipino was still alive, "suffering in the cell across the yard from us." For McSorley and for others who had to "hear such savagery," the sounds clearly heightened their own anguish. [20]

---

[18] John W. Clifford, S.J., *In the Presence of My Enemies* (New York: W.W. Norton and Co., 1963), 83.

[19] Koerbling, *Rupert Mayer*, 167.

[20] Richard T. McSorley, S.J., *My Path to Peace and Justice* (Marion, S. Dak.: Fortkamp Publishing/Rose Hill Books, 1996), 11–12.

In the prisons of twentieth-century China, punishment was often inflicted for perceived infractions of prison rules. In the fifth year of his imprisonment that began in 1950, George Wong was punished for teaching the Hail Mary to two other prisoners interested in becoming Catholics. "I tried to explain that the Hail Mary was a prayer, not an organization, and that it did not refer directly to the Legion of Mary, which the authorities had condemned as counter-revolutionary," he said. "But nevertheless, they handcuffed my hands behind my back for fifty days, which shocked the others in my cell."[21]

The reference to others in Wong's cell illustrates yet another dimension of the physical and psychological suffering endured by the prisoners, namely, overcrowding. Though not as extreme as that endured by Carlo Spinola in seventeenth-century Japan, the crowding Wong experienced was burdensome. At the time of his extra punishment, there were twenty-two prisoners in his cell. "We slept on the floor with our heads to the wall," he said, adding dryly: "We couldn't move much." For Joseph Doan in Vietnam, the crowding brought with it an added burden: "The hardest part was never being able to be alone."[22]

In addition to the lack of privacy, prisoners were also tormented psychologically by being promised a release that would be continually deferred. The experience of Franz Jalics in Argentina offers a striking example. Five days after his arrest in 1976—in the wake of the military coup that ousted Isabel Martínez de Perón, widow of the dictator Juan Perón—he was informed that his innocence had been proven and that he and the Jesuit with whom he shared a small house in a poor section of Buenos Aires would be released the following Saturday, the only day of the week when releases occurred. "I was happy, because that was a Friday," he wrote. "But Saturday went by and we were not set free."

His initial response was anger. "I was secretly raging at the injustice, despite our evident innocence, of holding us; it conjured up a horrible nausea." Then, after the day of rage, "a terrible anxiety came over me" at the thought of possible execution—a reasonable anxiety, since the military group that had carried out his abduction was ulti-

---

[21] Interview with George Wong, May 29, 1995.

[22] *America* (September 16, 1995):14. The *America* article by the author deals with various incarcerated Jesuits; the section on Joseph Nguyen-Công Doan was based on the author's interview with him on April 11, 1995.

mately responsible for the deaths of more than 6,000 people. The anxiety lasted a day and a half and then was followed by severe depression: "All is lost," Jalics believed. On the fourth day, he said, "I sank into an indescribable sadness. . . . I cried for hours."

As the second Saturday approached with its promise of release, his mood lightened and he felt more at peace. But the peace was short-lived. "When, this time, we weren't set free, the whole process was triggered again: rage, anxiety, depression, and sobbing. For three or four days I went through all these feelings once more." Then, "hope flared up again on the next Saturday [and] this process went on for three and a half months." The wrenching mood swings brought on by the uncertainty of his situation were no small part of what he endured.[23]

During the same mid-1970s period, Juan Luís Moyano Walker's torturers combined physical and psychological methods. The physical part involved beatings. In the course of the three days when he was among the "disappeared," two men "entered my cell and hit me with their fists and with sticks for more than half an hour—they did it over my whole body." In addition, he said in a letter to the author, "they made me remain in almost unendurable positions and prevented me from moving in spite of their blows. During this time they questioned me about my activities in the barrio, in the university, and with the Movement of Priests for the Third World."

The psychological component then followed: "Soon after the two men left, another official came in and tried to convince me that he was not in agreement with this kind of violence and that they wanted to help me. Later he asked me the same questions." A few hours later the whole process would be repeated, with four or five sessions a day. Moyano Walker notes that this method of what he calls "bad and good" treatment was standard in all the Argentinean detention and torture centers.[24]

Josef Menzel had a similar experience with East German state security officials in 1958. Although his treatment did not involve physical torture, he was interrogated by a method that he calls "hot and cold." He describes them in his recollections: "After an initial, rather

---

[23] Franz Jalics, S.J., *Ejercicios de Contemplación* (Buenos Aires: San Pablo Press, 1995), 161.

[24] Juan Luís Moyano Walker, letter to author, June 6, 1995.

polite game of questions and answers, the tone of the questioner changed. I thought that something was going to happen, and indeed, something did happen: he started to scream at me." The first interrogation took place late at night. Through the open door, Menzel could hear the sound of another interrogation taking place in a neighboring room, and he later came to realize that this was deliberate— "pure acoustic background, for the purpose of intimidation and to throw me off my composure, since I became more and more tired."

Eventually, "the hot-and-cold method escalated to psychological terror." The sense of terror was induced in different ways involving additional players in a carefully constructed scene. Menzel gives an example: "One morning, on the usual route to the interrogation room by way of a set of stairs, there was an officer from the STASI [state security police] on the top step in full officer regalia. . . . His outfit was meant to frighten. . . . During my interrogations, a captain appeared, just as if he belonged there. He did not say anything, he listened, he made frightening faces, and then left. That happened several times."

Menzel adds that one day the captain brought a man with him "whom without remorse I would group into the category of 'slashing brutes.'" The man was not in uniform and said nothing. But he loosened the studs from his sleeves and let them fall noisily to the floor. "If I would have helpfully risen . . . to pick them up, this would have counted as an 'attack on a representative of state power,' and some well-placed blows would have answered this 'attack.'" Fellow prisoners later interpreted the incident for him in this way.[25]

To break down their prisoners' resistance, captors frequently conducted interrogations during the night. After his 1948 arrest in Lithuania, Gerardas Dunda was initially held in a KGB facility in Vilnius. Over the next six months, he was interrogated thirty times, and the sessions "would always take place at night, from 10 P.M. to 4 A.M."— the hours when, for most people, fatigue lessens clarity of thought and instincts of self-preservation. Dunda describes how the interrogations proceeded. Having come for him, the guards "would bend my arm behind my back, and on a quick run would hurry me to the interrogation room, which was located on the fourth floor." Once there, he had to remain seated for the next six hours. "If I moved, a

---

[25] Menzel, "Personal Recollections," 5.

guard with an automatic rifle would hit me on the shoulders or on my back." When the six hours of questioning were over, he was escorted back to his cell, with his arm again bent behind his back. "If, to or from the interrogation, we met another prisoner or an interrogator," he notes, "I was stopped and had to stand with my nose to the wall, [and] not move or exchange any signs of recognition."[26] Preventing him from seeing others was another tactic intended to induce fear and uncertainty. When Dunda was forced to keep his face turned to the wall as other prisoners passed, his sense of isolation increased.

Alfred Delp's treatment at the hands of his Nazi questioners did not follow the good-bad pattern; there was only brutality. "They called me a liar while I was being beaten up," he wrote on December 31, 1941. "They accused me of lying when they found I mentioned no names except those I knew they already knew." Of these beatings, he says, "I prayed hard, asking God why he permitted me to be so brutally handled."[27]

As will be seen later, praying hard was a major source of inner strength not only during times of torture but throughout entire periods of incarceration. With prayer came a sense of the nearness of God and of doing God's will. Moyano Walker put it thus in his letter to the author of June 6, 1995: "What prevailed was the experience of God's presence and the acceptance of what he asked of me." Joseph Doan, too, reacted similarly to his imprisonment in Vietnam: "Father Arrupe had sent me on a mission and I accepted everything that happened as part of that mission," including, that is, his incarceration.

A form of psychological suffering prevalent in the twentieth century has entailed the deliberate stripping of personal identity by referring to prisoners as numbers rather than by using their names. Jean Moussé speaks of how, on his arrival at Buchenwald, he and his fellow French prisoners "ceased to be men and were soon to become mere numerals."[28] When John Havas wrote an account of his time in a Chinese prison in the 1950s, he called it "Four, Nine, Nine, Six," which was his number as a prisoner. In psychologist Viktor Frankl's story of his concentration camp experience, *Man's Search for Mean-*

---

[26] Dunda, unpublished memoirs, 1–2.
[27] Delp, *Prison Meditations,* p. 10.
[28] Moussé, "La Planète Buchenwald," 4.

ing, he observes: "A man counted only because he had a prison number. One literally became a number; the life of the 'number' was irrelevant."[29] Even though the earlier Jesuits, like the Elizabethans, suffered many torments, at least their identity, as defined by their names, remained intact. With the totalitarian regimes of the twentieth century, however, this vestige of human dignity was often wrested away by authorities who knew very well that the psychological impact of such an action would weaken a prisoner's will to survive.

Physical torture could assume a variety of forms. For Isaac Jogues, captured in what is now the northern part of New York State, it meant having his fingers crushed beneath the teeth of Iroquois warriors and being tormented on torture platforms as he and his fellow captives were taken from village to village. Night brought no respite: "At night, in a cabin, naked on the bare ground, bound with chains, [we were] exposed to the revilings of each sex and of every age. They threw coals and live ashes on our bare flesh—which, for us who were bound, it was difficult to throw off." Just as John Clifford was deeply troubled upon hearing the screams of the French priest, so too was Jogues pained at witnessing the sufferings of the Huron prisoners with whom he had been taken. "We . . . [were] tormented further by the sight of the torments which they inflicted upon our Huron companions, whose wrists they bound so tightly with cords that they fainted therefrom."[30]

While a galley slave, Pedro Paez lost sleep because of lice, not human malevolence. In contrast, intentional sleep deprivation was the lot of John Ogilvie in sixteenth-century Scotland. His keepers deliberately prevented him from sleeping for eight days and nine nights. "They forced me to keep awake with styles, pins, needles and pinchings," he writes in the brief personal story of his imprisonment, which he smuggled out page by page under the door of his cell to sympathetic visitors. But even in his initial interrogation after his arrest, which was conducted at the home of a Glasgow magistrate, Ogilvie was severely maltreated: "They shower their blows from all sides upon me, the hair is plucked from my beard, my face is torn

---

[29] Viktor Frankl, *Man's Search for Meaning* (New York: Simon and Schuster/Pocket Books, 1963), 83.

[30] Thwaites, *Jesuit Relations*, 39:193.

with their nails." He got no respite while in his cell: "I am fastened with two rings about a lump of iron of about two hundred pounds, shaped like a pole, so that I could only sit and lie on my back."[31]

In the sixteenth century, as in the twentieth, torturers were often careful not to leave incriminating marks on their victims' bodies that could later be used as proof of maltreatment. Prior to his execution in London in 1594 at the age of thirty-four, Robert Southwell had been tortured ten times during his three years of incarceration. When the judges at his trial challenged him to show the marks of his torture, he made his famous reply, "Let a woman show her throes"—that is, her birth pangs.[32]

Southwell did not live to tell of his torture, but John Gerard survived and, after his release, told the story in considerable detail. Like Southwell, Gerard was imprisoned for three years. Because he refused to divulge the name of his superior in England, Henry Garnet, the torture chamber of the Tower of London became agonizingly familiar to him.

His wrists bound in gauntlets, Gerard was forced to climb a set of wicker steps. His arms were then raised and an iron bar was passed through the gauntlets. The steps beneath him were removed, and he was left to hang for hours. "All the blood in my body seemed to rush up into my arms and hands," he writes, "and I thought that blood was oozing from the ends of my fingers and the pores of my skin." When he fainted, his jailers revived him and hanged him up again. The procedure was repeated three times the first day and twice the next, when he almost died.[33]

At one of the torture sessions, the experience assumed a spiritual dimension, which helps to explain how he and others were sometimes able to survive the severest forms of torture: "The pain was so intense I thought I could not possibly endure it. . . . Yet I did not feel

---

[31] Ogilvie, *An Authentic Account*, 27, 7, 19. In regard to the torture by sleep deprivation, Thomas Collins points out on pp. 157–58 of his biography of Ogilvie, *Martyr In Scotland: The Life and Times of John Ogilvie* (London: Burns and Oates, 1955), that doctors periodically examined him to determine how much more torture he could endure without dying. Only when they decided that death would occur in three more hours did the torture cease.

[32] Foley, *Records of the English Province*, I:364. Foley notes that he took his information from a manuscript account by Henry Garnet of Southwell's trial and execution.

[33] Gerard, *Autobiography of a Hunted Priest*, 36.

any inclination to wish to give them the information they wanted." He concludes, "The Lord saw my weakness and did not permit me to be tempted beyond my strength."[34]

This last sentence is a partial paraphrase of 1 Corinthians 10:13: "God is faithful, and will not let you be tempted beyond your strength, but with the temptation will also provide the way to escape, that you may be able to endure it." As Gerard's use of Corinthians suggests, passages remembered from scripture provided an important resource for captive Jesuits attempting to resist the pressure of their pain-filled environments.

Alexander Briant, Gerard's Elizabethan contemporary, experienced an equally powerful spiritual dimension when undergoing torture in the Tower. In a letter to his Jesuit brethren written before his execution, Briant first describes how he prepared himself for his visit to the torture chamber. "Before I came to the torture-chamber, giving myself up to prayer, and commending myself and all that was mine to our Lord, I was filled and replenished with a supernatural sweetness of spirit, and even while I was calling upon the Most Holy Name of Jesus, and upon the Blessed Virgin Mary . . . my mind was cheerfully disposed . . . and readily inclined and prepared to suffer and endure those torments." He goes on to say that when the racking actually began, he experienced no pain—a circumstance he believes bordered on the miraculous: "Whether what I am relating be miraculous or no, God knoweth, but true it is . . . that in the end of the torture, though my hands and feet were violently stretched and racked . . . yet, notwithstanding, I was without sense and feeling well nigh [free] of all grief and pain."[35] It is as if the very intensity of his prayer served as a powerful anesthetic.

During World War II, most Jesuits incarcerated by the Nazis were sent to Dachau, which by 1942 held approximately 2,500 religious. They were subjected to the same torments as other prisoners, including medical experimentation. Léo de Coninck speaks of a third-year theologian "who died after a month of atrocious suffering with his leg completely gangrenous; he received no treatment—he served as a standard of comparison for the gangrenous cases they *were* treating."[36]

---

[34] Ibid., 109.
[35] Foley, *Records of the English Province*, 4:357.
[36] de Coninck, "The Priests of Dachau," 119.

To withholding medical treatment were added various forms of gratuitous cruelty. In his article, de Coninck mentions a priest in his work gang who collapsed after spending the day laboring in the fields. While the priest lay "in tortured agony on a pile of hay . . . a young S.S. guard amused himself by setting his dog on him."[37] Being forced to watch such maliciousness was in itself a form of torture to the other prisoners.

Otto Pies, who became the spiritual father of the Jesuits in Dachau, writes that the overall suffering of the prisoners was "of a highly concentrated nature." He describes the various forms of suffering as follows: "First there was the physical suffering: the constant threat against a prisoner's naked existence, his lack of freedom, his paralyzing insecurity; and then the loneliness, the murders, the patched and ragged clothing, the hard, extremely hard labor that was the prisoner's lot, especially in view of his poor and wretched diet." But he observes that "the spiritual suffering was immeasurably greater. Each prisoner felt himself uprooted, robbed of all rights and dignity . . . [and] depersonalized."[38]

The pain of witnessing the torment of others was also experienced by Jean Moussé in another concentration camp, Buchenwald. In his 1985 article in *Etudes*, he tells of his own feelings as he observed the punishments to which others were subjected—punishments so severe that they could lead to death. Moussé was well aware that such punishments could be his lot as well:

> It sufficed for me to see a hanging during roll call to remember. . . that the next day I, also, could be led to the gallows. Another time, it was the sight of a man being subjected to the torture of 25 blows from a cudgel. The victim, kneeling with his chest stretched over a saw horse placed atop a mound of stones, was forced to count the blows aloud to a rhythm which two S.S. determined as they administered the punishment with full force. . . . Another time, a Pole, shivering from the cold, was attached like a horse to an iron ring near the main gate of the

---

[37] Ibid., 118.

[38] Otto Pies, *The Victory of Fr. Karl,* trans. Salvator Attanasio (New York: Farrar, Straus and Cudahy, 1957), 114. Pies notes on the same page, however, that for those in religious life who were assigned to special blocks, "religious life *was* experienced and lived in Dachau," and served as a life-sustaining source of support. The Father Karl of the title was a young diocesan deacon, Karl Leisner, who was secretly ordained a priest at Dachau by a French bishop who was also there because of his support of the French resistance.

camp. He carried a pouch filled with stones and wore a sign indicating that he had attempted to escape. I think that he stayed there until he died.[39]

In the book-length expansion of his article, *Libre à Buchenwald*, Moussé describes how the guards' cruelty to the prisoners had a contagious effect, leading some of them to inflict gratuitous punishments on one another. This was especially true of those who held minor positions of authority in the barracks. He speaks of one, a Frenchman like himself, "who became an assistant barracks leader, and was led by his position to inflict punishment on thieves [usually of food]." Moussé notes that although his French compatriot was a Christian, "one day I had the impression that he experienced pleasure in striking a defenceless man, and that to me was horrible." On the other hand, some were strong enough to resist such a deadly inner contagion: "A friend who did not allow himself to be perverted in this manner told me how much it cost him to strike an imprisoned comrade."[40]

Over the centuries, one of the most frequent forms of torture has been solitary confinement. After his arrest along with five other Jesuits who worked at the Aurora Prep in Yanzheou in 1951, Eugene Fahy and his companions were taken to Shanghai, where they were imprisoned separately. Because of his recalcitrance in answering questions during his interrogations—when an iron bar was placed across his arms to lock him into a chair—Fahy was confined in a dark, narrow coffin-like cell, measuring only four feet by eight feet. In his account of his imprisonment that later appeared in condensed form in *Life*, he speaks of his time in this cell as "a burial above ground in a vault of boards and bars . . . in the numbing cold." It was a burial made more onerous by shackles. As soon as Fahy was placed in the cell, the guard "dangled a set of ancient shackles before my nose. Bending, he snapped one of the irons about my ankle and linked its mate to a bar of the grill [of the cell door]." Because his foot was chained to the grill of the door, almost all movement became impossible, thus making it more difficult "to fight off the increasing winter cold." By January, snow lay outside the cell door itself.[41]

---

[39] Moussé, "La Planète Buchenwald," 338–39.

[40] Jean Moussé, *Libre à Buchenwald* (Paris: Bayard Editions/Centurion, 1995), 113.

[41] Fahy, "The Red Take-Over of a Mission," 21.

John Havas underwent similar brutal treatment in solitary confinement, again in circumstances that involved extreme cold. During part of his imprisonment in Shanghai from September, 1952 until May, 1954, he was confined in a windowless cell like a cave—another form of burial underground. So frigid was the temperature of the cell that the right side of his body became paralyzed. "They took me . . . to a 5' by 8' concrete cave which had no number. It was made of concrete [and] . . . it was so cold that I cried. The pain from cold is indescribably insupportable. My right side became paralyzed." The damage was permanent. Writing more than twenty years later, he said, "[M]y hip sometimes, even now, begins shaking with a reflexive shock."[42]

Havas was subsequently moved from solitary confinement to a cell with sixteen others. Several members of this group informed on him for uttering what they considered—in their desire to gain favor with their captors—disrespectful words about Mao Tse-tung. Guards appeared and punishment swiftly followed: "My hands were chained behind my back. No sleep!" To the chains were added deliberate humiliations: "Even the food placed before me was pushed far away from me. I bent for it like a dog." What food he did receive during his incarceration was of such poor quality that not only did he contract scurvy and beriberi, but he also lost a hundred pounds during the time of his captivity.[43]

In Albania, the Communists subjected many religious to torture in the post–World War II period. The ordeal of one of them, Daniel Dajani, who was eventually executed along with two other Jesuits in 1946, was described by an eyewitness, one of his students who was now a fellow prisoner. After a midnight torture session involving electric shock, Dajani was dragged back to a common cell in the basement. "His cassock and face were covered with blood which

---

[42] John A. Havas, S.J., "Four, Nine, Nine, Six" (unpublished, undated typed manuscript of 105 pages in which Havas recounts his experience in China preceding and after his arrest), 91. The manuscript was found in his room at Murray-Weigel Hall at Fordham University after his death on September 9, 1994. The description of his life in prison is limited to a dozen pages or so. The title refers to the number assigned to him in prison. Havas was a member of the Hungarian Province, even though he spent the last two decades of his life in the United States. Although his command of English was good, the fact that it was not his native language led to some non-English sounding locutions in the manuscript.

[43] Ibid., 96.

came even from his eyes," the former student wrote, adding, "It seems his interrogators had used electric shock because this torture has this effect on a person." But the torment was not yet over. "After a while, the guards took him and moved him under the stairs in that horrible dark place [the latrine] full of excrement and slime."[44]

The student, Myfit Q. Bashati, asserts that Dajani "valiantly preserved his dignity without giving in and without a broken spirit." Indeed, later the same day he saw moving evidence of Dajani's generosity. One of the prisoners in the basement cell had received some food from his family and offered Dajani an orange. Dajani, however, declined to accept it, saying, "No, my son, this is for you to eat. You are young and you need it more than I do."[45]

Giacomo Gardin, an Italian-born Jesuit who survived a decade of incarceration in Albania, managed to keep a diary during that ten-year period. In one 1950 entry he writes of hearing, through smuggled letters, of the various tortures to which members of the clergy were subjected. Those tortured included not only Dajani but also four scholastics: Mark Cuni, Gjon Shilaku, Gjergj Bici, and Pronk Lesej. He writes: "Most of them were beaten on their bare feet with wooden clubs; the fleshy part of the legs and buttocks were cut open, rock salt inserted beneath the skin and then sewn up again. . . . Electrical wires [were] placed in their ears, nose, mouth, genitals and . . . [they were] forced to drink their own urine and eat their own excrement."[46] Hearing of such torments, Gardin, though a prisoner himself, speaks of his anguish at being unable to help.

Although one would like to think that all Jesuits who were tortured

---

[44] Myfit Q. Bashati, "An Eye-Witness Account of the Last Days of Fr. Daniel Dajani, S.J.," *Albanian Catholic Bulletin* (University of San Francisco, Xavier Hall) 15 (1994): 32ff.

[45] Ibid., 33.

[46] Gjon Sinishta, ed., "The Diary of Father Ják [Giacomo] Gardin, S.J.," in *The Fulfilled Promise*, 148. The Italian-born Fr. Gardin wrote an account of an Albanian Jesuit, Fr. Gjon Karma, who after his arrest on Christmas Eve 1946, spent seventeen years in prisons and labor camps. He too underwent torture. "Among the preferred methods were beating his feet with metal rods, placing steaming-hot boiled eggs under the armpits, electric shocks . . . and the constant denial of adequate food and water." Gardin, who was in close touch with Karma until the summer of 1948, notes that the worst torture occurred in the summer of 1997. "The police would tie him to a schoolyard tree until he collapsed from heat exhaustion. His captors would then revive him by pouring water in his face, only to repeat the process. It was at this point that Karma felt closest to death." (Ják [Giacomo] Gardin, S.J., "Father Gjon Karma's Slow Road to Martyrdom," *Albanian Catholic Bulletin* 11 [1990]:57.)

would have been able to forgive their tormentors as another way of sharing in the passion of Christ, who forgave his own captors, a striking example of documented forgiveness concerns the Uruguayan Jesuit Luís Pérez Aguirre. A social activist arrested during a period of widespread repression, Pérez Aguirre—founder of the Uruguayan branch of Paz y Justicia (SERPAJ)—was tortured by the military authorities in the early 1980s. Several years after his release, he was interviewed by Lawrence Weschler who was preparing a two-part article on Uruguay, which appeared in *The New Yorker* in April, 1989.

Observing the cigarette burns that ran up and down both arms, Weschler asked Pérez Aguirre whether he could ever imagine pardoning his torturer. He replied that he had already done so and went on to describe a remarkable encounter in which he had approached the man on the street one day and engaged him in friendly conversation. His actions caught the torturer totally off guard. "I took the initiative," said Pérez Aguirre. "I called him over. I said hello, how was he doing. You see, I wasn't acting the way he expected." Pérez Aguirre then described the man's reaction: "He told me he was very depressed. He is one of the foremost accused [in a subsequent investigation of the period of government tortures]. He said that his life had become terribly complicated, that it was not good for him or anyone to live in this state of ambiguity." When asked about his own reaction to these comments, Pérez Aguirre said, "I showed him in a practical way that I was not angry. I told him if he needed anything to come to me. And I told him I forgave him." Summing up his reflection on his forgiveness of this man who was responsible for causing him so much pain, he added, "It's a personal, internal process that I went through from profound Christian conviction."[47]

When Lawrence Weschler expanded his *New Yorker* interviews with Pérez Aguirre (and others) into a book, *A Miracle, A Universe: Settling Accounts with Torturers*, he quoted Hannah Arendt on forgiveness: "In contrast to revenge, which is the natural, automatic

---

[47] Lawrence Weschler, "A Reporter at Large (Uruguay–Part II)," *The New Yorker* (April 10, 1989):95. John A. Havas also comments on his own lack of any desire for revenge. In his prison diary, "Four, Nine, Nine, Six," he writes: "I had no feeling of revenge, and I had no resentment then [after his release from his Shanghai prison on May 13, 1954] nor have I now, because with Christ we must become brethren in one family." (70).

reaction to transgression and which . . . can be expected and even calculated, the act of forgiving can never be predicted; it is the only reaction that acts in an unexpected way. . . . Forgiving, in other words, is the only action which does not merely re-act, but acts anew and unexpectedly."[48] As Pérez Aguirre noted, his manner of addressing the torturer "caught him totally off guard," and it was the very unexpectedness of his actions—approaching him in a kindly rather than a hostile manner—that allowed the process of forgiveness to assume concrete form.

This process, however, had entailed an inner struggle long before the actual encounter took place. Forgiveness, said Pérez Aguirre, is "not a very simple process. It takes a lot of internal effort." He adds, "You need a strong conviction of the power of pardoning—the power of love and reconciliation—and how it affects the other person. But it has to be true reconciliation. And it's something I have to do—the state can't claim to do it for me [in its investigation]."[49] It is perhaps not too much to suggest that many tortured Jesuits have undergone a similar process in their effort to make contact with "the power of love and reconciliation."

Pérez Aguirre underwent both physical and psychological torture. "They were very sophisticated in how they tried to break each person, through isolation and humiliation," he said in the interview with Weschler. He then cited an example of psychological torture by means of humiliation: "Once, in a Montevideo prison, I was brought into a public office and kept under the table, like a dog, with my legs cramping up, for hours on end, all day long, all the passersby seeing me like that."[50]

How did he endure such treatment and yet remain mentally intact? Like the Elizabethan John Gerard, he was able to tap deeply into his spiritual roots. "Religious people are trained for such situations," he commented in reference to the experience in the public office. On another occasion his strength through spiritual means became evident to his cellmate in a military barracks, who, upon return-

---

[48] Lawrence Weschler, *A Miracle, A Universe: Settling Accounts with Torturers* (New York: Penguin Books, 1990), 270. The quotation from Hannah Arendt is taken from her book, *The Human Condition* (Chicago: University of Chicago Press, 1958), 241.

[49] Weschler, "A Reporter at Large—Part II," *The New Yorker* (April 10, 1989):95.

[50] Weschler, "A Reporter at Large—Part I," *The New Yorker* (April 3, 1989):78.

ing from a torture session of his own, told him, "I was lucky, because I knew how to pray. All he could do, he said, was to count up to a thousand and back."[51]

Franz Jalics in Argentina was another Jesuit who found it in his heart to forgive. In his case, however, the process took years and was focused not on his immediate torturers, who were acting under orders, but on the man who had falsely accused him of being a terrorist. His bitterness was even greater because he had heard of the man's intention to denounce him to the military and had visited him to explain the peaceful nature of his work among the poor residents of the Buenos Aires barrio where he had been living. The accuser had promised to assure the military authorities that Jalics and another Jesuit were in no way connected with terrorists. But he did not keep his promise and denounced both Jesuits to the officers responsible for their arrest and subsequent maltreatment.[52]

In prison, Jalics tried to pray for his persecutors and in particular to be able to forgive the man responsible for his imprisonment. The effort continued after his release while he was living in the United States and then in Germany. Gradually, the rage diminished, but it was years after his arrest before he was freed of his anger and able to pardon his accuser and the others who were involved. The transformation occurred in the following way.

In preparation for serving as retreat director for a group of young Jesuits in Germany and guiding them through their tertianship year—the last phase of Jesuit formation—he decided to first make the full four weeks of the *Spiritual Exercises* of St. Ignatius on his own. (Jesuits are obliged to make the *Spiritual Exercises* only twice—as novices and, years later, after ordination, as tertians. Jalics thus made them a third time, by his own choice.) He describes how his interior release finally came about unexpectedly on the last day of his retreat:

> On the last day, while walking in the forest, I asked myself what changes or corrections were called for in my life. Suddenly the realization came to me that although I believed I had forgiven my persecutors, I nevertheless still kept in the closet of my room the documents that proved their guilt. Evidently, I still harbored the secret intention

---

[51] Ibid., 79.

[52] Franz Jalics, *Ejercicios de Contemplación*, 160.

of using the documents against them. I returned to the house and burned them. That was an important step.[53]

But the burning of the papers was not yet the last step. That did not occur until four years later when Jalics went in Rome to attend a meeting at the Jesuit curia [headquarters]. During a break in the meeting, Pedro Arrupe, the superior general, approached Jalics and asked if all was well with him. Considering the question as a sign of genuine personal interest, Jalics asked the superior general if he could have a longer, private conversation with him later. Only then did he experience the ultimate moment of release: "In this conversation, there arose in me for the last time a pain like nothing I had ever felt. It was not anger, it was sorrow. I could not hold back my tears before my superior general."

As the tears fell, the last bonds slipped away: "Since then, I have felt myself truly free, and I can say with all my heart, I have forgiven. Now I feel no resentment, rancor or sorrow for what happened. On the contrary," he adds, "I am grateful for this experience which is an indissoluble part of my life." The process of purification, as he refers to it, lasted eight years, from its beginning until "the last remnants of rancor disappeared." He concludes by suggesting that perhaps his account of the process might serve as a breath of hope "for those who have suffered something similar, and who find forgiveness very costly.[54]

---

[53] Ibid., 283.
[54] Ibid., 284.

SEVEN

Jesuit Brothers

BECAUSE OF GOVERNMENTAL FEAR of both their preaching as pastors and their influence on youth as teachers in high schools and professors in universities, priests have long been the special targets of repressive regimes uneasy over their ties with the Vatican. Brothers, however, were seen as less of a political threat. When the Jesuit priests from Aurora Prep were arrested on July 31, 1951, a Hungarian brother, Michael Fekete, wanted to be taken away with them. Learning that the Chinese authorities had crossed his name off the list, he "got down on his knees and begged the police to take him to jail." The police refused, saying that as a brother, "he did all the work and that the priests were lazy."[1] Instead of being jailed, Brother Fekete was expelled from the country.

Nevertheless, many brothers over the centuries have known incarceration in one form or another, and it has sometimes led to their torture and death. Besides Brother Constantine March Battles, more than thirty other brothers were detained and later executed during the Spanish Civil War.[2] During World War II, eight French brothers were forced to work as slave laborers in German ammunition factories. Others were at Buchenwald, and four Polish brothers died at Dachau—victims of the Nazis' combined hatred of Poles, Jesuits, and Jews.[3]

Following the war, the Albanian brother, Gjon Pantalija, was imprisoned by the Communist authorities that had assumed control of the country. He did not live to tell the story of his incarceration, but one of his students at the Jesuit-sponsored Saverianum College in Shkodra later wrote about him in a chapter of the book *The Fulfilled Promise: A Documentary Account of Religious Persecution in Albania*. The student, Zef Shestani, who later became a priest, states that the

---

[1] Fleming, *Chosen For China*, 150.

[2] Ignatius Echaniz, *A Symphony of Love: Stories of Jesuit Brothers* (Anand, India: Gujarat Sahitya Prakash, 1985), 3.

[3] Lapomarda, *Jesuits and the Third Reich*, 391.

brother's arrest took place in the fall of 1946. To extract information from him about other Jesuits, he was tortured by being "denied food and sleep, beaten with clubs, tormented with the application of electrodes to his body, and subjected to the insertion of wooden splinters under his toenails." After the Communist authorities converted the Franciscan monastery in Shkodra into a prison, Pantalija was sent there and held in a cell near the choir loft of the church.

Shestani reports that one night "Bro. Gjon attempted to escape by taking advantage of a considerate guard and jumping from the choir loft into the church." The effort was doomed, however, because not only was the church locked, but in jumping from the choir loft he broke both legs. He was found in the morning and taken to a hospital. Shestani says of this final stage of his life, "From a person who was present at the time of his admission to the hospital, I learned that his sufferings had reduced him to a mere skeleton, and yet he retained his serene smile throughout. I heard nothing more about him, except that he died in pain as a result of renewed police interrogations." He was probably buried outside the Catholic cemetery in Shkodra "along with the other Jesuits, Franciscans and priests who had been executed."[4]

One of the most remarkable brothers in terms of steadfastness in the face of torture was the seventeenth-century Japanese convert, Michael Nagascima. According to the story of his life in a mid-nineteenth-century account of martyrs in Japan, he was baptized at the age of eleven by an Italian Jesuit missionary, Giambattista Baeza. As an adult, once Christianity had been proscribed, Nagascima hid Baeza in his home for twelve years. When Baeza died, he offered hospitality to another priest, Manuel de Borges, and secretly brought Catholics to him at night to receive the sacraments. By the time he reached middle age, he had been received into the Society as a brother.

The local governor became suspicious of his clandestine activities, however, and in 1627 ordered him to be placed under house arrest. He remained confined at home for a year. Then one day preparations were being made for the execution of Christians, and as was the custom, the citizens were asked to contribute wood for the pyres. When

---

[4] Msgr. Zef Shestani, "Brother Gjon Pantalija, S.J., the Man and the Martyr," in Sinishta, *The Fulfilled Promise*, 136–37.

approached for his contribution, Nagascima refused. The matter was reported, and he was taken to a prison in Shimabara, where he was tortured in an effort to force him to renounce his faith.

His torturers tied him on his back to a trestle, stuffed a gag into his mouth, and pumped water into his body through his nostrils. Then they stamped on his stomach to force the water back out through his nostrils and repeated the process. In a letter he was able to write to Manuel de Borges during his imprisonment, Nagascima describes how he was also tortured by being exposed to the sun. During one such instance he spoke of receiving a particular grace. "As the sun was beating down on me, I prayed, saying: 'Lord, this sun is your creature, subject to your will. I pray to be released from its intense burning.' " When he finished this prayer, he writes, "[T]he air around me suddenly turned dark, creating a shaded area around me, and at the same time, a cool breeze sprang up that brought me relief."

Other forms of torture continued into the frigid winter, but again, despite terrible physical pain, Nagascima received supernatural aid through the medium of prayer, including prayer addressed specifically to Mary. Thus, in another letter he writes: "When the pain was at its most intense, I turned to Our Lady, asking for her intercession; and instantly I found myself without pain. . . . I understood that being able to bear the torments without denying my faith, was due not to my own strength but solely to God's grace." One is reminded of the experience of John Gerard, whose focused prayer all but blocked out pain during his torture sessions in the Tower of London.

Unable to make him abjure, Nagascima's torturers resorted to one final method, which resulted in his death. They thrust him into a spring of boiling sulfurous water. So hot was the water that the skin peeled from his naked body. His scalded flesh could endure no more, and at last, invoking the names of Jesus and Mary, he died on Christmas Day, 1628.[5]

As noted earlier, another brother who died while imprisoned in the East was the Portuguese Ambrose Fernandes, a fellow prisoner of Carlo Spinola. Arriving in Japan as a young layman, Fernandes joined the Jesuit order in 1577. In his old age, he and Spinola were

---

[5] Giuseppe Boero, *Relazione della Gloriosa Morte de duecento e cinque beati martiri nel Giappone* (Rome: Civiltà Cattolica, 1867), 145–50.

arrested in Nagasaki while both were being sheltered by a Portuguese during a persecution of Christians that had begun in 1614.

Crowded into an unprotected cage-like prison in Omura with Spinola and two dozen other Christians, Fernandes suffered greatly from the cold winds that swept over them in the winter months. A biography of Spinola, written in 1628 by Fabio Ambrosio Spinola, only six years after Fernandes's death, relates that he endured his suffering "with patience and happiness." Even allowing for pious hagiographical exaggeration, the phrase carries a ring of truth. Because hunger and the cold left him weakened, his death after a year's imprisonment was all but assured.[6]

During the English persecution of Catholics in the late sixteenth and early seventeenth centuries, several English brothers also endured periods of imprisonment that sometimes ended in death. Among the best known is Nicholas Owen, nicknamed Little John for his small size. Because he was admitted to the Society in 1588, when Henry Garnet became superior of the English Mission, he was chiefly associated with Garnet.

A carpenter, Owen was famous for building hiding places in English homes that allowed priests to elude government pursuivants. As one commentator notes, "With incomparable skill, he knew how to conduct priests to a place of safety along subterranean passages, to hide them between walls, to bury them in impenetrable recesses, and to entangle them in labyrinths and a thousand windings"—windings that frequently made the difference between capture and the apostolic freedom to continue ministering to Catholics.[7] His work and his prayer went together. The same commentator says that "when he was about to design one [i.e., a hiding place], he commenced the work by receiving the Most Holy Eucharist, sought to aid its progress by continual prayer, and offered the completion of it to God alone."[8]

Although Owen was most closely associated with Garnet, he also worked with John Gerard, who speaks of him often in *The Autobiography of a Hunted Priest*. Owen was imprisoned three times. The first occasion stemmed from his open praise of Edmund Campion after

---

[6] Spinola, *Vita del P. Carlo Spinola*, 136–37.

[7] Foley, *Records of the English Province*, 4:247. Foley quotes from Mathias Tanner, S.J., *Vita et mors Jesuitarum profide interfectorum*.

[8] Ibid., 4:248.

the latter's martyrdom.[9] In the second instance, he and Girard were apprehended together by London pursuivants after they were betrayed by a servant in the house where they were staying.[10]

During this second incarceration, Owen was tortured for the first time, along with another Jesuit brother, Richard Fulwood. The two were hung up "with their arms fixed into iron rings, and their bodies hanging in the air . . . but all to no purpose in terms of forcing them to provide information that would have incriminated other Jesuits."[11]

Though Gerard was in prison himself at the time and soon to be transferred to the Tower of London, he was able to procure Owen's release by means of bribes. Owen, now free, was thus able to facilitate Gerard's daring escape from the Tower, thanks to careful planning that included the securing of horses. Using a rope that had been smuggled in to him, Gerard swung down the wall to a boat waiting on the moat, which was manned by two other Jesuit brothers, one of whom was John Lillie. After crossing the moat, Gerard mounted one of the waiting horses and reached safety at Garnet's hiding place in the country.[12]

When Owen was arrested the third time, however, his apostolic work—and life—came to an end. Aware that Owen's carpentry skills and ingenuity had enabled many priests to slip through the government's fingers, William Cecil, Queen Elizabeth's secretary of state, was elated to learn of his capture. He ordered the keeper of the Tower to use any means to force Owen to reveal the locations of the hiding places he had constructed. Identifying the locations would not only deprive priests of refuge, but would also allow the government to arrest the owners of the homes that had sheltered them.

Owen was hung up once again, this time for as many as six hours a day. Perhaps he had incurred an injury during his secret construction work because he was found to have a hernia. Theoretically, English law prohibited the racking of prisoners with this medical condition; nevertheless, the torture continued. In fact, extra weights were added to his legs. Owen responded only by invoking the names

---

[9] Ibid., 4:248. Foley's source is again Mathias Tanner. Gerard does not mention this.

[10] Gerard, *Autobiography of a Hunted Priest*, 65.

[11] Foley, *Records of the English Province*, 4:51.

[12] Gerard, *Autobiography of a Hunted Priest*, 137.

of Jesus and Mary. At length, his body could no longer sustain the pressure; his intestines burst out and he died.[13]

Another remarkable brother serving on the English Mission around the same time was Ralph Emerson, who accompanied Edmund Campion to England in 1580. Like Owen, he was small in stature, leading Campion to refer to him affectionately as "my little man." Accordingly, during his years of imprisonment, Emerson used the name Mr. Homullus—a Latin diminutive for small man. While in the Clink prison, he for a time had both John Gerard and John Lillie as fellow prisoners. Emerson's cell was next to Gerard's. Again, using money supplied by Catholic supporters as a bribe, Gerard was able to hear confessions in Emerson's cell.[14] Directly above his own was Lillie's cell "whom Providence," Gerard writes, "had placed there to the advantage of both of us." Just as he was able to make use of Emerson's cell, so was Gerard able to use Lillie's cell, in this case as an impromptu chapel and meeting place for Catholic prisoners. As the cell walls only partially separated them, the three men formed what might be thought of as a small Jesuit community, a theme that will be dealt with in greater detail later.

Before becoming a Jesuit, Lillie worked as an apothecary in London, a somewhat more professional background than that of Owens, the carpenter. Because of his commitment to Catholicism, Lillie assisted priests in locating houses where they could live in relative safety; it was this activity that led to his arrest and imprisonment in the Clink. Since he and Gerard could maintain frequent contact, Gerard directed him in the *Spiritual Exercises*. This may have been the time when Lillie, still a layman, made his decision to become a Jesuit, although formal entrance into the Society would not take place for several years.

After being transferred to the Tower, Gerard—through messages secretly sent to sympathetic Catholics—managed to secure Lillie's release, as he had done for Owen. Thus, when Gerard attempted his own daring escape, Lillie was one of the rowers who brought him across the moat to the waiting horses and eventual safety.

Some time before Gerard's escape, Lillie, who was then free himself, showed extraordinary courage by serving as an escort to two

[13] Foley, *Records of the English Province*, 4:245–48.
[14] Gerard, *Autobiography of a Hunted Priest*, 90.

noblewomen, a mother and her adult daughter, who had begged to be taken to visit Gerard in the Tower. Gerard realized that to accept such a commission was indeed to place Lillie in the lion's mouth. Lillie, he humbly observes, "was running a great risk for a small gain."

Lillie ran an even greater risk when pursuivants raided the London house in which both he and Gerard were staying in July of 1599. As the searchers rushed into the house, Gerard barely had time to slip into a hiding place built into a gable of the roof. He tried to persuade Lillie to follow him. Knowing that the searchers had already found the room in which the equipment for a Mass had been laid out, Lillie refused. Instead, he deliberately allowed himself to be arrested and coolly let the government agents assume that he was a priest.

Even when he was taken into the room where the ladies of the house waited apprehensively as the search proceeded, Lillie continued to play his role so cleverly, with such gentlemanly authority, that Gerard described the ladies as "amazed and delighted and [they] almost laughed at John playing the priest, and doing it so well that he tricked those tricksters, who called off their search for [other] priests."

Lillie was then taken to the Tower and tortured in an attempt to force him to reveal the homes and families he had visited with Gerard. "Never with God's help will I do such a thing," he told the warden, adding, "True, I am in your power, but you can do with me only what God permits." Unable to extract information from him, they placed Lillie in solitary confinement for several months before transferring him to Newgate prison. His boldness was unabated. At Newgate, he met a priest-prisoner who asked whether he might be able to devise a way to escape. Lillie agreed to try, and together they fled successfully.

After remaining in hiding with Garnet for a time, Lillie crossed the English Channel and made his way to Rome. There, at the age of thirty, he officially entered the Society as a brother. Lillie stayed in Rome for six or seven years and then returned to the English Mission. He was never recaptured but died in 1609 of lung disease. In paying tribute to him after his death, Gerard observes that "during those five or six years he was with me . . . [he was] engaged in every kind of business on my behalf in places far and near, with people in every walk of life. . . . All that time he guarded his heart and soul with the utmost care. . . . He was an innocent soul if ever there was one. And he was so wise and prudent too."[15]

As for Ralph Emerson, he spent almost twenty years behind bars. Stricken with partial paralysis while at Wisbech Castle, his final place of incarceration, Emerson was banished from England. He spent the last years of his life at St. Omers, a college in Belgium where English youth were sent to obtain the Catholic education that was forbidden to them at home. There, he lived out his final months, "remarkable for his great patience, and especially for his piety toward the Mother of God."[16]

A lesser known but equally remarkable brother was Cuthbert Prescott, who was also imprisoned at Newgate. His assignment for the English Mission was to make the necessary arrangements for sending Catholic youth to St. Omers. As with Emerson and other brothers, Prescott was spared execution after his arrest, primarily because he was not in holy orders and therefore did not violate the law forbidding priests to minister sacramentally in England. But the *Records of the English Province* provides a moving description of the important services he was able to render to fellow prisoners at Newgate: "Here for some years he . . . actively and diligently exercised his vocation in serving the captive priests, in attending the dying, and in cheerfully rendering his services to all who were detained in prison . . . He liberally shared with his fellow captives the alms which were abundantly bestowed upon him by Catholics . . . so that they came providentially to many who would otherwise have died of starvation."[17]

Prescott's willingness to share alms with destitute prisoners was an act that could literally mean the difference between life and death for these people. Under the English penal system of the time, the day-to-day management of prisons was leased out to jailers who viewed those in their charge as objects of profit, and who consequently provided virtually no food or other necessities without payment.

---

[15] Ibid., 123, 151, 154–58. For more on Lillie, see also Foley, *Records of the English Province*, 5:440–55. In speaking of the various brothers with whom he had contact in England, Gerard refers to them in his autobiography as "servants," but their role was clearly akin to what we might now call companion-helpers.

[16] Foley, *Records of the English Province*, 3:17–37.

[17] Ibid., 3:100.

The above quotation's reference to attending the dying suggests that Prescott exemplified Ignatius's admonition in the *Constitutions* that temporal coadjutors, as brothers were then called, should "in their conversations . . . try to further the greater interior progress of their neighbors."[18] Prescott served his fellow prisoners at Newgate until, as the *Records* tell us, he himself "died in chains in London . . . worn out by his sufferings and the squalor of his prison, February 20, 1647, in his fifty-fifth year, and twenty-third in religion."

Instant death rather than a slow, agonizing one brought on by suffering and deprivation was the fate of René Goupil, the donné captured by the Iroquois along with Isaac Jogues. Because of his prior medical training in France, he had, according to Jogues, been of great assistance to "our Neophytes and Catechumens." During his captivity Goupil asked Jogues for permission to take vows as a brother. Jogues agreed; however, shortly afterwards, in 1642, Goupil was tomahawked by the uncle of a child to whom he had taught the sign of the cross—a sign that the uncle misinterpreted as an invocation of evil spirits. Aware that they might be attacked, Goupil and Jogues were praying the rosary together when the slaying took place. Once Goupil had been struck down, Jogues expected he would be accorded the same fate, so he fell on his knees to await the blow. The uncle said he had permission to kill only Goupil and told him to arise. As Jogues explains in his letter to his provincial superior in France, "I then arise, and give the last absolution to my dear companion, who still breathed, but whose life the Barbarian finally took away with two more blows." Goupil was thirty-five at the time, "a man of unusual simplicity and innocence of life, of invincible patience, and very conformable to the divine will."[19]

Half a century earlier, another French brother was taken captive and put to death for his faith, not in the new world but in the old. As was the case with Goupil and Jogues—and, one might add, with Lillie and Gerard—Brother Guillaume Saultemouche had an especially close bond with the priest with whom he worked, Jacques Salès. They functioned as a team, assigned to the Aubenas mission in France at a time when Calvinists (Huguenots) were vigorously persecuting Catholics.

---

[18] *The Constitutions of the Society of Jesus,* trans. George E. Ganss, S.J. (St. Louis: Institute of Jesuit Sources, 1970), #115.

[19] Thwaites, *Jesuit Relations,* 39:203.

While conducting a series of Lenten sermons, Salès was arrested and held in a cell at the Huguenot headquarters. There, Calvinist ministers disputed with him on the subject of the sacraments, referring particularly to Catholic belief in the real presence of Jesus in the Eucharist. The priest refused to depart from Catholic doctrine in any way and was accordingly condemned to death. Turning to Saultemouche, he said, "And you, my brother, what will happen to you? Take courage." Then he tried to persuade their captors that Saultemouche should be freed, a proposal to which the Huguenots were amenable.

However, Saultemouche was determined that they should remain together even in death and cried out, "I will never abandon you. I will die for the truth of the points you have disputed." One of the captors urged him to leave, claiming that the issue concerned only the priest. Undeterred, Saultemouche answered, "May God preserve me from falling into this fault. I will never abandon him to whom obedience has joined me as a companion." Thus, both men were led out, and after Salès had been shot and killed, Saultemouche was stabbed to death with the name of Jesus on his lips.[20]

Dominic Collins is another brother who ran afoul of the Calvinists. Born into a well-to-do Irish family in 1567, Collins became a soldier, enlisting in the army of Philip Emmanuel of Lorraine, who was fighting against the Huguenots in Brittany. Later Collins traveled to Spain, where, in his early forties, he entered the Society of Jesus. Three years later, he sailed with a Spanish expedition to Ireland, in what was regarded as a war in defense of the Catholic faith, and worked with James Archer, a Jesuit serving as chaplain to the Spanish forces. During the English siege of Domboy Castle, Archer managed to escape, but Collins was taken captive and held for four months in the prison in Cork. The documents pertaining to the cause for his beatification note that despite "tempting offers . . . of rapid promotion to honorable rank in the crown forces on condition that he renounce his Catholic faith," he refused to abjure and was condemned to death.

Collins was thereupon hanged, probably in his native town of Youghal. Why was Youghal chosen instead of the city of Cork? The documents suggest that the authorities may have chosen his native place deliberately, "in order to spread fear among the Catholics of the

---

[20] Carayon, *Documents Inédits*, 22:241–44. See also Jules Blanc, *Les Martyrs d'Aubenas* (Valence: Chez l'Auteur, 1906), 107.

place where his family and relatives were well known." According to reports of the time—which may or may not be accurate—he went to his execution wearing his Jesuit habit and told the onlookers that his sole motivation in returning to his native Ireland was to preach the Catholic faith in the context of a war that had the papal blessing. Collins was a simple man who saw no contradiction between his faith and the bearing of arms. The documents point out that whereas Archer was "both an intellectual and politically astute, Collins was neither." Consequently, his motives in taking part in the Spanish expedition "would have been quite uncomplicated and altogether religious."[21]

---

[21] Diocese of Dublin, "Cause for the Beatification and Canonization of the Servants of God Dermot O'Hurley, Archbishop, and Companions, who died in Ireland in defense of the Catholic faith 1579–1654" (Rome, 1988) v. 1, 387–400. See also Thomas Morrissey, S.J., "Among the Irish Martyrs: Dominic Collins, S.J., In His Time," *Studies* (Dublin: Autumn, 1992) 81(323):313–24.

EIGHT

Prayer in Prison

WHETHER FROM SCRIPTURE PASSAGES memorized long ago or through words spoken only in the silence of the heart, intense prayer has been a source of great strength and interior peace for many incarcerated Jesuits. Those who have written of their imprisonment refer again and again to prayer as the basis of what sustained them. Thus, Walter Ciszek discusses how, in Russia, he came to an understanding of his pain and suffering through prayer: "I learned it only by the constant practice of prayer, by trying to live always in the presence of God. . . . If I wanted to preserve my interior peace and joy, I had to have constant recourse to prayer."[1]

Like a number of his Jesuit brethren, Ciszek found that the efficacy of prayer had to be based on an unshakable trust in God: "In Lubianka [prison]," he writes, "I grew firm in my conviction that whatever happened in my life was nothing else than a reflection of God's will for me."[2] If God willed his incarceration, he reasoned, then that part of God's plan was to be accepted because the same God would stay at his side throughout the ordeal. "He would protect me," are the words Ciszek uses to conclude his reflection on Lubianka.

Paul Beschet, the French Jesuit who, like Jacques Sommet, was a scholastic during World War II, expressed similar feelings in *Mission en Thuringe,* his own autobiographical account of that period. Beschet had gone to Germany in 1943 with a group of Catholic students and priests connected with the Jeunesse Ouvrière Chretienne movement. Entering as voluntary workers, the group sought to provide support for Frenchmen conscripted as forced laborers in the Thuringia region.

Suspicious that they might be engaged in subversive activities, the Nazis arrested Beschet and his companions. During his detention at the Gotha prison in the spring of 1944, he describes the way in which

---

[1] Walter Ciszek, S.J., *He Leadeth Me* (New York: Image Books, Doubleday, 1973), 137f.

[2] Ciszek, *With God in Russia,* 133.

this experience filled him with a sense of happiness that became a part of what he called the fundamental prayer of desiring only God's will:

> Here I am in the disposition needed for an eight-day retreat, a prelude to a new step in our missionary witness. A feeling of happiness fills me: that of being with God now, at the bottom of the prison. . . . It only remains for me to let myself be led according to his pleasure. God chose this for me, placed me in this situation . . . in order that I might bring forth better fruit, and that it might endure. I bring all my companions into this fundamental prayer, and I sense that it is already heard by God.[3]

Beschet's trust in God's providence was often tested, particularly after he was moved first to the Flossenberg concentration camp and then to a forced labor factory at Zwickau. But, like Ciszek, he never lost the sense of God's sustaining presence.

Neither did Pedro Arrupe in Japan at the outbreak of World War II. He was jailed for thirty-three days on a charge of suspected espionage, which was later dropped. According to his biographer, Miguel Pedro Lamet, one day guards were escorting Arrupe through the street for his once-a-week bath in another building when he found himself in the midst of students from a nearby university where he had recently been teaching. Handcuffed, unshaven and dirty, he felt like a criminal, humiliated beneath the students' gaze; however, he realized that this painful feeling allowed him to have a deeper understanding of the humiliations endured by Jesus as He was taken to his judgment before Pilate—once again, an echo of the third degree of humility of the *Exercises*. And in the solitude of his cell, he was also able to reflect on Jesus' closeness: "How many times did I experience during this period the wisdom to be found in that silence, the interior dialogue with 'the guest of my soul.' I believe that it was the most instructive period of my whole life."[4]

Jean Moussé was another who felt this same awareness of God's abiding presence. Although he was not yet a Jesuit at the time of his confinement in Buchenwald in 1943, he intended to become one, according to his autobiography, *Libre à Buchenwald,* and in fact he

---

[3] Paul Beschet, *Mission en Thuringe au Temps du Nazism* (Paris: Editions Ouvrières, 1989), 117.

[4] Lamet, *Arrupe, Una Explosión en la Iglesia,* 157.

did become a Jesuit after the war.[5] Like Arrupe, Beschet, Ciszek, and many others, he found that trust in God both sustained him and brought him the peace that would help him survive the ordeal that he knew lay in store for him: "Cut off from the past, chasing the clouds of the future, I believed in God the eternal Present," he writes. "I tasted a peace which came from my faith; he in whom I put my trust was there, whatever might happen."[6]

In the midst of torments inflicted by his Iroquois captors, Isaac Jogues could similarly reflect that it was not his own courage that upheld him, but "that of him 'qui dat fortitudem lassis' "—the God, that is, who gives strength to the weak. These words referred to the terrible experience of having burning coals dropped on his naked body and cords binding him so tightly that he begged his captors to loosen them. The pain caused by the cords led him to focus on the greater pain Christ must have felt at being fixed to the cross: "I thank thee, O good Jesus, because I have learned with some little experience what thou didst condescend to suffer for me on the cross, where thy most holy body was not even sustained with cords, but hung . . . transfixed with hardest nails."[7]

The association of Christ's sufferings with his own was also part of the prayer of John Lenz at Dachau. While assigned to a heavy work detail at a gravel pit one day, Lenz had to push a wheelbarrow filled to the brim with gravel to the dumping site. With his strength all but gone and the palms of his hands covered with open sores, he felt he could not continue, even though he knew that the guard might shoot him if he stopped. He therefore prayed: "O Jesus, how Your steps must have faltered too after the terrible scourging when You had to carry Your cross!" Then, unable to hold onto the wheelbarrow any longer, he let it fall to the ground. The guard shouted, "You swine. . . . You priest! . . . I'll soon teach you," and he reached for his revolver. "O Jesus, mercy! Mary, help! I can't go on," Lenz prayed. As he waited for the bullet, however, a commotion broke out in another part of the work area, and the distracted guard ran off in that direction.[8] Lenz does not say that the guard's distraction was directly attributable to his prayer, but the implication is evident.

---

[5] Moussé, *Libre à Buchenwald*, 126.

[6] Ibid., 82.

[7] Thwaites, *Jesuit Relations*, 39:197.

[8] Lenz, *Christ in Dachau*, 47.

How important prayer was to his survival at Dachau is made still clearer at another point in *Christ in Dachau*: "Prayer was the only thing that saved us, not only in our physical but also in our spiritual need." Elsewhere, Lenz emphasizes that suffering itself became a kind of school for prayer. Indeed, he writes, only in this school of suffering is it possible to learn "the sort of prayer which pierces the soul like a sword . . . a blind submission to the divine will." Submission to God's will was even more necessary in the face of the Nazis' special hatred at Dachau of "Jews and priests [who] personified the worst kind of criminals in the eyes of those who knew no God."[9] This hatred resulted in the deaths of forty-three Jesuits in the various German concentration camps; another twenty-six died either in captivity or as a result of it.[10]

Also in the context of prayer, some Jesuits were able to see their suffering as purifying. Alfred Delp observes that the long hours spent manacled in his cell in Nazi Germany, harassed in both body and spirit, "must have broken down a great deal that was hard in me." As a result, "much that was unworthy and worthless has been committed to the flames." He even implies that without his imprisonment, he would not have come to know God as he did: "I have truly learned to know him in these days of trial and to feel his healing presence."[11]

The same theme of purification occurs in Franz Jalics's account of his eight-year effort to forgive those responsible for his imprisonment in Argentina in 1976. As he lay bound on the floor of his cell with a rubber "capucho" over his head, the only form of prayer he could utter was the repetition of the name of Jesus. This was the key to the purification process for him. In the days and weeks that followed, as his promised release was postponed Saturday after Saturday—delays that led to crescendos of rage, anxiety, depression, and tears of frustration—the single word, "Jesus," remained the sole form of prayer to which he could cling in his desperation. Together with his Jesuit cellmate, "as the days went by, from morning to night, we repeated this simple prayer."

During their three and a half months of imprisonment, always faced with the possibility of execution, Jalics and his companion ex-

---

[9] Ibid., 39, 47, 58.
[10] Lapomarda, *The Jesuits and the Third Reich*, 313–18.
[11] Delp, *Prison Meditations*, 11, 193.

perienced "a profound interior purification" by repeating the name of Jesus, and through it a measure of peace, however incomplete, entered their hearts. "By paying attention to Jesus," he observes, "we communicate with his saving power."[12]

Another in Latin America who was faced with the prospect of imminent death was Juan Julio Wicht. A professor of economics at the Universidad del Pacífico in Peru, he was among those taken hostage by guerrillas of the Movimiento Revolucionario Tupac Amaru (M.R.T.A.) on December 17, 1996, during a social gathering at the Lima residence of the Japanese ambassador. In an interview in *America,* he spoke of the intensity of his prayer during his four months of captivity: "I don't think I have ever in my life prayed as I did during those 126 days. A very long retreat!"

Wicht found traditional prayers to be particularly helpful in maintaining a sense of calm. "I managed not to think too much and just to pray, remembering some important prayers, such as [the] petitions from the Our Father, 'Thy will be done' or 'Forgive us our trespasses as we forgive those who trespass against us.' " As with other imprisoned Jesuits, his background in Ignatian spirituality was a further source of strength: "I also repeated the prayer of St. Ignatius, 'Take, Lord, receive all my liberty.' I paid a lot of attention to those first few words, 'all my liberty.' God helped very much."[13]

Basic, too, was the prayer of Francis Xavier Ts'ai. Packed into a small cell with twenty others after his 1953 arrest in Shanghai, he was forced to remain seated on the floor during the day with his back to the wall. Not only was talking forbidden, so too was prayer. The guards watched him to see whether his lips were moving. Thus, his prayer could only be a silent prayer of the heart with, like Jalics, the silent repetition of the name of Jesus, though the form of the prayer was expanded slightly.

"I used a prayer of this kind that came from the French Jesuit, Léon de Grandmaison, whose life was read aloud at the novitiate: 'Mon bon Jésu, glorifiez-vous, et le reste importe peu' [My good Jesus, glorify yourself, and the rest will count for little]," he said in an interview. "I used a similar prayer that was adapted from a Chi-

---

[12] Jalics, *Ejercicios de Contemplación,* 161–62.

[13] James Torrens, S.J., "Getting Out Alive: An Interview with Juan Julio Wicht," *America* (September 13, 1997):14.

nese poet: 'God is always Lord. There is no place that is not my home,' that is, even in prison."[14]

John Houle, an American Jesuit imprisoned for four years in Shanghai's Nantao prison—from June, 1953 until June, 1957—described his own prayer experience in equally crowded conditions. Referring to his 6:30 a.m. morning meditation, he cites the difficulties of focusing his mind and heart in the midst of the surrounding noise and physical distractions:

> Sometimes it [the meditation] is fervent, sometimes utterly distracted. Sitting on the floor, shoulder to shoulder with silent, suffering men, every movement, every whispered word, every noise in the corridor, is a distraction. Unremitting fatigue is wearing; no book or writing of any kind to suggest an idea; the old body snatches at anything, however small and cheap. Often the mind seeks to pass the steel bars, and I constantly seek to pull myself back from daydreams.

Houle expresses thankfulness, however, that these very difficulties caused him to grow in his love of prayer: "In this and the other hours of meditation during the day, I have really learned to love prayer, have felt gratitude to the depths of my being for little lights, little unexpected sources of strength."[15]

Under conditions of torture, the prayer stance of some prisoners might be based simply on not giving into demands for information; such resistance could thus lead to a prayer of self-offering. This was the experience of the Argentinean Juan Luís Moyano Walker following his arrest by the military in the 1970s: "While I was being beaten, my only reaction was one of concentrating on not giving in," he wrote in his letter of June 6, 1995. Once the beating stopped, however, "then . . . I could sustain a permanent dialogue with the Lord, of self offering and disponibility, rather than of petition." But in the same letter he added "[W]hen I believed I could not support much more time [imprisoned under such conditions], I prayed that it might end." Nevertheless, for the most part his was what he termed "a prayer of presence, of trust, and surrender."[16]

---

[14] Interview with Francis Xavier Ts'ai, S.J., May 20, 1995, at Our Lady of China Chapel, Queens, New York. (Fr. Ts'ai died in May, 1997.)

[15] John Houle, "Thoughts in Prison," *The Catholic Mind* (May–June 1958) 56(1137): 266. (Reprinted from *Jesuit Mission*, January–February 1958, 48 E. 48 St., NYC.)

[16] Juan Luís Moyano Walker, letter to author, June 6, 1995.

For Jesuits fortunate enough to have access to a Bible, or who had committed large portions of it to memory in the course of their studies and apostolic work, scripture yielded new and deeper meanings. Jacques Sommet at Dachau, for instance, speaks of discovering "a sort of connaturality between our situation and the cry of the psalms, or Job's love for the God who seems to abandon him to his suffering."[17]

The psalms were a strong source of support for William Bichsel, too. After one of several acts of civil disobedience at the naval base near Puget Sound, he was held for two weeks at the county jail in Seattle, Washington. There he was placed in a single cell with fifteen other men. During our telephone conversation of January 24, 1995, he spoke of the tensions caused both by the crowding (there was only one toilet for all sixteen men) and by the volatile ethnic and racial mix among the prisoners—Hispanics, whites, and African Americans who were Muslims. Bichsel mentioned two particular psalm verses that he turned to in the midst of these tensions. One was Psalm 40:1: "I waited patiently for the Lord. He inclined his ear to me and heard my cry." The other was Psalm 121:1: "I lift up my eyes to the hills. From whence comes my help? My help comes from the Lord, who made heaven and earth."[18]

The psalms were also a source of strength for Stephen Kelly. After completing his sentence in California, he was rearrested in 1997 for another antiwar action at a shipyard in Bathe, Maine. While serving time for this offense at Allenwood, the federal prison in Allentown, Pennsylvania, he described his method of prayer in an interview for *America* (October 17, 1998). Each day, he said, he chose three psalms that were meaningful for him and then used them in conjunction with praying the Benedictus in the morning and the Magnificat in the evening. His time in various jails and prisons, including Allenwood, has been alternately spent in solitary and dorm settings. Thus, he said prayer in the former was easier because he felt "hidden from society and obscure"—circumstances that created a retreat-like atmosphere. Praying in the dorm setting was more difficult because of the noise and movement; he compared the latter to a key meditation at the beginning of the second week of the *Exercises:* "The dorm

---

[17] Sommet, *L'honneur de la liberté*, 102.
[18] Telephone interview with Willliam J. Bichsel, S.J., January 24, 1995.

scene is like the meditation on the Incarnation . . . with the Trinity looking down on all creation and seeing the confusion, the people struggling in various ways, arguing and generally wandering."

This comment on the meditation on the Incarnation could be compared to the similar scene encountered by William Bichsel at his jail in Seattle, with its racially and ethnically mixed inmate population. To counter the commotion that surrounded him, Kelly would wait until everyone had eaten their early morning breakfast and gone back to bed. "That's when I'd sit on my bunk and pray, between four and five in the morning, when it was quiet."

As with Sommet, Bichsel, Kelly, and many others, Giacomo Gardin also found the psalms to be a particular help during his imprisonment in Communist Albania. He suffered especially from a sense of isolation, since neither his religious superiors nor his family knew where he was. For all the more reason, therefore, he said, "I found comfort in those parts of the Psalms that I still remembered, as I had not seen a book, not even a prayer book, in years. The verses from Psalm 23, 'The Lord is my shepherd, I lack nothing. Should I walk in a dark valley, I would not fear evil, as you are with me' . . . were fixed in my memory."[19] Again, evident in Gardin's words is the role of memory as a foundation for prayer.

The peace activist John Dear had to readjust his expectations in regard to prayer while serving time in his North Carolina jail in the 1990s. Prayer did not come as easily as he thought it would. "My inability to pray has been my greatest disappointment. I thought I could be a great contemplative in jail, a mystic. Alas for my dreams," he comments in his autobiographical book *Peace Behind Bars*. "I'm lucky if I sit still and say simply, 'Lord have mercy,' or 'Lord, I believe, help my unbelief.' "[20]

But Dear was by no means the only one to have found prayer in prison difficult. James Enda Thornton, in his unpublished recollections of his prison experience in China in the early 1950s, observes that "sitting there on my haunches [in my cell], I'd close my eyes and try to pray, but it was a prayer that was often sidetracked by vivid thoughts of food and medicine."[21] In Thornton's case, the body's

---

[19] Gardin, *Banishing God in Albania*, 85–86.

[20] John S. Dear, S.J., *Peace Behind Bars* (Kansas City, Missouri: Sheed and Ward, 1995), 175.

[21] Thornton, "The New Proletarian Man," 7.

unmet demands for food and needed medications posed the primary obstacle. For Dear, it was the psychological effect of his oppressive surroundings.

The rosary and other Marian prayers have been important sources of interior strength as well. In situations in which possessing rosary beads was forbidden, some Jesuits have resorted to ingenious methods of continuing this form of prayer unperceived. With a touch of humor, Eugene Fahy describes how his fellow Jesuit prisoner, James Thornton, was able to say the rosary by counting the bare toes of the Chinese prisoners who shared his cell: "Inside the cell . . . the general rule . . . was eyes on the floor. Fr. Thornton relates that, when his rosary was taken away, he found this convenient when saying the beads. He would use the feet of those crowded around him as markers for the decades and mysteries as he ticked off the ten on his fingers."[22]

Patricio Cariola's incarceration in Chile served as an avenue for recalling a Marian prayer from his early youth, the prayer beginning "Bendita sea tu pureza" [Blessed be your purity]. "While in my cell, I remembered this prayer, though I had not said it since my childhood. I realized I had forgotten Mary. She knows about virginal love. It was a good meeting with her." As this prayer is centered around Mary's purity and virginity, it led him to reflect on the liberating nature of his vow of celibacy: "Celibacy makes it possible to do what we [Jesuits] do. The father of a family cannot risk himself in this way"; that is, engage in human rights activities that could result—as they did in his case—in imprisonment.[23]

In his Nazi concentration camp, Jacques Sommet found himself turning to vocal prayer. Like Job on the dunghill, Sommet looked on it as a way to protest his situation and even blame God, while at the same time remaining faithful to Him. "Vocal prayer has a physical dimension," he writes, "tied as it is to the cry of God's grace. At the same time," he continues, "it is the giving over of oneself to the divine mercy through a medium which is to some degree biological." As an example, he cites a Chinese Jesuit, incarcerated for two decades, who once told him: "For five or six years I was alone in my cell;

---

[22] Fahy, "The Red Take-Over of a Mission," 12.

[23] Patricio Cariola, S.J., "Dos Meses," *Noticias Jesuitas Chile* (July/August 1976):5.

I forced myself to say my rosary aloud to the wall opposite me."[24] Employing his otherwise unused voice to speak aloud, even though no human was there to hear or respond, became an important part of the Chinese prisoner's prayer.

Prayer in the group setting of Dachau could also involve communal discernment. Sommet and others took part in a discernment process during a devastating outbreak of typhus. Any religious or clerics who fell ill with the disease were separated from the other prisoners and taken to a special set of barracks, which were surrounded by barbed wire. The discernment, therefore, revolved around the issue of whether some of those who were still uninfected should accompany their sick companions and thereby run the risk of contracting the disease themselves. Sommet describes the process:

> Imagine, in the life of the camp, these few days when we remained in a state of prayer over this question. . . . There was a mystical aspect involved in the decision: in the ones stricken with typhus, Jesus Christ is present with his wounds. . . . Here we are truly faced with the excluded, the rejected. In the new society we envision, what place will it have for the rejected ones of tomorrow? If we stand apart from them now, what hopes do we have to struggle later for the dignity of all people?

After several days of prayer, the discernment resulted in a decision to intervene in the situation immediately. The group selected an elderly priest to coordinate the process, which involved accepting the names of those who desired to accompany the ill members of the community into the quarantine barracks and to remain there with them. Sommet tells us what the well Jesuits faced: "The action consisted of immuring oneself in the barracks with those ill with typhus. To live among the living, and assist the dying to die, . . . to share the life of the dying person in such a way that his agony might truly be a struggle for life. . . . Some who went in could return, others would leave their lives there."[25] Of the prisoners who volunteered, including Sommet, only a certain number were chosen. He speaks with regret that he was not among them.

---

[24] Sommet, *L'honneur de la liberté*, 145. Sommet does not give the name of the Chinese Jesuit, but he dedicates the book to Vincent Chu, S.J., "in prison for life for the faith," so he may have been referring to him.

[25] Ibid., 105–6.

It is not surprising that the prayer of many Jesuits was often specifically Ignatian. Finally back in his cell after his torture in the Tower of London had ended, John Gerard turned to the *Exercises*. "Now, as in the first days of my imprisonment, I made the *Spiritual Exercises*," he writes, adding that each day he spent four or five hours on the various meditations, relying solely on his memory.[26]

Dominic Tang, too, during his twenty-two years of incarceration, faithfully made his eight-day retreat every year. As with Gerard, memory served him well: "Luckily, before my imprisonment, I often preached retreats; so I remembered the *Spiritual Exercises* of St. Ignatius and the order and matter of the meditations." Here, too, the element of purification through prayer under conditions of confinement was present. Tang notes that during his meditations, he tried to "find out my predominant bad inclinations . . . [and] after each retreat I made some resolutions to reform."[27] Even in prison, the desire to put on the mind and heart of Jesus remained strong.

During roughly the same period in China, Eugène Beaucé—a French Jesuit who was a member of the Aurora Prep community arrested with Eugene Fahy and others in 1951—also found interior support through making the *Exercises*. In his thirty-six-page unpublished account that parallels Fahy's in substance, he speaks of making an eight-day Ignatian retreat, which he lengthened to twelve days because of the interruptions caused by the brainwashing sessions he was forced to attend. He comments, "[I]t is good to make the *Exercises* of St. Ignatius in prison: each meditation stands out in relief there to reveal hitherto unsuspected truths."

Within the *Exercises*, Beaucé's favorite prayer—as was the case with Dominic Tang and others—was the so-called Suscipe: "Take, Lord, and receive all my liberty, my memory, and my entire will." For him, he observes, the concept of liberty is the key to the prayer: "If you lose memory, that suppresses many forms of suffering; if one's intelligence is lost, that suppresses everything. But if you lose your liberty [only], you have the leisure to savor all the others."[28]

---

[26] Gerard, *Autobiography of a Hunted Priest*, 107.

[27] Tang, *How Inscrutable His Ways!*, 108.

[28] Eugène Beaucé, "Quelques Expériences Communistes en Chine," unpublished account of his imprisonment in China, written in Manila after his expulsion from China, and dated July 8, 1952. The account was among the papers of Eugene Fahy (d. August 1996) in Taiwan and was sent to the author by Guilbert Guerin, S.J., October 12, 1996.

During his imprisonment in the Paris Conciergerie at the time of the 1871 uprising of the Commune, Pierre Olivaint wrote a series of letters to Jesuits on the outside. In several of them he speaks not only of making the *Exercises*, but also of extending them far beyond the traditional long-retreat period of thirty days. In a letter of May 5, 1871, for example, he comments on being on the thirty-ninth day.[29] The retreat continued virtually up to the day of his violent death three weeks later. As with Tang, who called them the center of his life, the *Exercises* for Olivaint served as a bulwark against the approaching maelstrom of violence that would soon engulf him and his companions.

John Havas was another who went well beyond the traditional thirty days of the *Exercises* when he made them by himself in China. Locked in his windowless, nine- by five-foot cell, without a bed or any other furniture except a wooden bucket that served as a latrine, he, too, relied on his memory as he embarked upon his retreat. He planned to extend the retreat from thirty to forty days to correspond to Jesus' forty days in the wilderness. Because the cave-like cell was in total darkness, he was unable to distinguish one day from the next. So judging the passage of time as best he could, he made a scratch on the wall to mark what he thought was the passage of each twenty-four-hour period. When he was finally allowed to have light in his cell, he counted the scratches and realized that his retreat had lasted not forty but fifty-five days in all—so deep had been his spiritual absorption and so fluid the passing of the days.

To help preserve his sanity while confined to his frigid, dark cell, which he called "this cage of living death," Havas also combined his prayer with a mental exercise intended to keep his faculties alert. The exercise consisted of reviewing his knowledge of Chinese shorthand, "using my fingers in formulating the symbols by way of sign language against the darkness of the pit." Observing the strange hand movements, his guards were puzzled, and, as noted previously, assumed that Havas was losing his mind—an ironic assumption, indeed, since it was these same movements of his fingers that helped him to retain his sanity.[30]

Also Ignatian was the prayer of Francis Hagerty in his Massachu-

---

[29] Ponlevoy, *Actes de la Captivité*, 5th ed., 109.
[30] Havas, "Four, Nine, Nine, Six," 99, 111.

setts jail. In our interview, he observed that when he rose at 5 A.M., long before the other prisoners, he based his morning prayer on the *Exercises,* especially the meditations on the two standards and the third degree of humility. He also meditated on the passion and death of Christ. Again as with both Tang and Beaucé, he wrote, "[M]y favorite prayer was an Ignatian prayer: 'Suscipe Domine': 'Take, O Lord, and receive all my liberty, my memory, my understanding and entire will, all that I have.' "[31] This deliberate self-emptying that allowed God to come into his heart may well have served as a counterbalancing and freeing antidote to the stripping of his physical liberty by the prison authorities.

In our own century, the sufferings of imprisoned Jesuits have tended to be of a more psychological nature than the kinds of physical torture that were commonplace for earlier Jesuits. One of the most prevalent forms of modern suffering has been the interrogation process, designed to break down resistance through fatigue, fear, and frustration.

In 1979, when Anton Luli was close to seventy years old and had already been under criminal justice supervision for thirty-two years—either in prison or in work camps—he was again subjected to grueling days of questioning over a period of many months: "For nine months there was the continuous pressure of being thrown against the wall, standing without the slightest movement with my hands tied behind my back all night from evening to dawn, the constant repetition of the same questions. The guards constantly repeated the same phrase, 'We know everything you have done, but we want you to confess.' "[32] When the interrogations were finally over, Luli was sentenced to twenty-five more years. He served ten of them before being suddenly released without explanation when the Communist regime in Albania collapsed in 1991.

The Czech Jesuit, Ján Korec, who later became Cardinal of Nitra following his release after eight years in prison, comments on his own long and exhausting interrogations in his autobiography, *La Notte dei*

---

[31] Francis O. Hagerty, S.J., interview, January 17, 1994. In his letter to the author of January 14, 1994, John Dear also speaks of this aspect of Ignatian prayer in regard to his incarceration in a North Carolina jail: "I feel Christ is answering my Ignatian prayer, 'Take, Lord, receive all my liberty.' Nowadays, I am concentrating on the lst part of the prayer: 'Give me only your love and your grace.' "

[32] Luli, "Dearest," 7.

Barberi (*The Night of the Barbarians*). To help endure the intense pressure that the interrogations produced, Korec, with a character from one of Franz Kafka's writings in mind, made a small circle on the wall of his cell with the burnt end of a matchstick. Gazing intently at the circle, Korec prayed: "In you, O Lord, I am strong! You give me strength! With you I am invincible. You have given me the health and the strength to exist."[33] Whereas Kafka's character acts without religious motivation, Korec was able to transport this circle-focusing method of seeking inner calm to a spiritual level.

Dominic Tang's interrogations were accompanied by thought infusion, a euphemistic term for brainwashing. Loud speakers in the prison blared propaganda, and Tang was ordered to read *The People's Daily*. During his seven years in solitary confinement, he was required to sit in a fixed position all day long. Although prayer was technically forbidden, he secretly recited the rosary as he held the communist newspaper in his lap. But any visible movement of his lips could bring repercussions.

Similarly, John Clifford describes one such incident during his incarceration in a Chinese prison. He writes of seeing "the peephole suddenly cracked open while I was completing my usual prayers." The guard summoned Clifford to the door and asked him why his lips had been moving. "I'm praying," Clifford replied straightforwardly. That answer prompted the guard to spew out a stream of abusive language.[34]

The rosary was an important form of covertly recited prayer to another Chinese Jesuit, George Wong. Writing of it in the London *Tablet* of May 5, 1994, Wong said he managed to fashion a rosary of "ten knots made from a torn rag like a five-inch string." The piece of rag had to be short, he explains, because "prisoners are not allowed to have any long string or cord in their possession for fear they might commit suicide with it"—a bleak reflection of the pressures to which those in Chinese prisons in the post–World War II period were subjected.

Wong notes in his article that he had been arrested for refusing to allow his name to be attached to a statement accusing his bishop, Ignatius Pei Kung, of being an "imperialist running dog." Wong was

---

[33] Ján Korec, S.J., *La Notte dei Barberi* (Rome: Edizioni Piemme, 1993), 198.
[34] Clifford, *In the Presence of My Enemies*, 90.

therefore considered to be "a dangerous 'propagandist' for the gospel." Even during his two years in solitary confinement, however, instead of becoming depressed, he became "the more joyful for being all alone," because he had "the spiritual company of Our Blessed Lord and Our Heavenly Mother and the angels and saints."[35]

The isolation of some Jesuits in solitary confinement was exacerbated by the awareness that they were under constant surveillance. In his memoirs, Tang speaks of warders who "would peep through the small hole to spy on what I was doing . . . [to see] whether I was keeping the rules."[36] He adds that the warders were careful to open and close the peephole door so quietly that he could not detect their presence by the sound. The psychological strain upon prisoners can well be imagined.

Eugene Fahy had a similar experience in his own bare ten- by ten-foot cell in China. "I was ordered to sit in a corner opposite the door. During the day and the following morning, guards . . . were continually at the slide of the door peering at me. . . . One of our memories is that unblinking, rolling eye that came and went both day and night, unnerving after awhile."[37] Rupert Mayer was also secretly observed. At the concentration camp at Sachsenhausen, his guards actually wore "straw sandals so that they might observe the prisoners without being detected."[38]

The pain of isolation could be heightened still further by a lack of communication with the outside world. Tang was not allowed to receive or send letters for most of his twenty-two years in custody. His relatives assumed that he was dead, as did his fellow Jesuits, who had Masses said for the repose of his soul. It was the same for the relatives of Ciszek.

As was the case with Léo de Coninck at Dachau and others who suffered greatly as they heard and saw the beatings of fellow prisoners, Anton Luli had a similar experience. When Luli arrived at the Albanian prison in which he was to undergo nine more months of

---

[35] George B. Wong, S.J. (a.k.a. Bernard Brown), "Candle in the Wind: a Prisoner's Testimony," *The Tablet* (London), December 24/31, 1994. In a letter dated March 17, 1995, Fr. Wong gave the author permission to use his actual name. At the time of this writing, he is residing at the Sacred Heart Jesuit Center in Los Gatos, California.

[36] Tang, *How Inscrutable His Ways!*, 115.

[37] Fahy, "The Red Take-Over of a Mission," 12.

[38] Koerbling, *Rupert Mayer*, 118.

interrogations, "weeping, lamentations, desperate screams, insults and moaning met my ears as soon as I set foot inside that place."[39]

Other Jesuits or their biographers have commented on the pain of witnessing or hearing the sufferings of fellow prisoners. Thomas Phillips, incarcerated in Shanghai from 1953 to 1956, had to listen to the moans of a Belgian priest in a nearby cell. The Belgian's hands were chained above his head to the bars of his cell as punishment for complaining about the small daily ration of hot drinking water, which served as a crucial source of warmth to stave off the cold.[40] Another who felt this psychological pain was Giacomo Gardin. In the autobiographical account of his imprisonment in Albania, he speaks of a gallows that was erected near the gate of his labor camp to serve as a warning to prisoners "tempted to be disobedient or rebel. We saw people hanging [there] from their wrists. . .bound with metal wire and they were just left there screaming."[41]

In the United States, Daniel Berrigan was also affected by the sounds of others' torment. Writing of his time at the federal prison in Danbury, Connecticut, he compares the noise of "cries, pounding, catcalls and screams" of men in the hole (punitive segregation) to the nightmarish scenes in paintings by Hieronymus Bosch.[42] Again, one wonders how Jesuits subjected to such inner suffering managed to maintain their sanity. Gino Belli, a long-time observer of the China scene who is personally acquainted with a number of Jesuits incarcerated there, noted in an interview: "It was their faith and their prayer that saved them."[43] The same could be said of other Jesuits who emerged from their ordeals mentally intact.

Occasionally, those with access to a Bible were struck by the scriptural accounts of persecution and suffering and came to view them in a new light. For Patricio Cariola in Chile, both the Gospel of Mark and Acts took on a deeper, hitherto unrecognized meaning. In "Dos Meses" he writes: "These [gospels] were books written for communities . . . whose members were frequently incarcerated. . . . The writers themselves, to judge from what we know of Paul, were as familiar

---

[39] Luli, "Dearest," 7.

[40] Kurt Becker, *I Met a Traveller: The Triumph of Father Phillips* (New York: Farrar, Straus, and Cudahy, 1958), 51.

[41] Gardin, *Banishing God in Albania,* 82.

[42] Berrigan, *Lights On In The House Of The Dead,* 25.

[43] Interview with Gino Belli, October 20, 1993. Belli is a pseudonym.

with the courts and prisons as we are with days of recollection and retreats."[44] Cariola then comments on the manner in which his fellow prisoners, for the most part men of little education, instinctively understood the biblical theme of persecution—not because of earlier catechetical instruction, which they seldom had, but because of what they were viscerally experiencing in their own flesh.

The same identification with the disciples in Acts entered into the prayer of Joseph Mulligan and served to sustain him during his time at the Sandstone prison in Minnesota. In one of his writings after his release, he says: "Working our way through Acts with other prisoners [in Bible study sessions], we were impressed by the apostles' principled disobedience to earthly authority (e.g. 5:29), and we used their prayer: 'Now, Lord, take note of their threats and grant that your servants may proclaim your word in all boldness' (Acts 4:29)." The impulse to proclaim the word of God "in all boldness," despite threats and retaliation, pervades the thought and writings of imprisoned Jesuits of other times and places as well.[45]

---

[44] Cariola, "Dos Meses," 3.

[45] Joseph E. Mulligan, S.J., "Reflections on Resistance against the War in Vietnam," *St. Luke's Journal of Theology* (Sewanee, Tenn.) 28(September 1985):21.

NINE

Mass

A CENTRAL COMPONENT of Jesuit prayer is the Eucharist, and in this regard, some incarcerated Jesuits were more fortunate than others. For example, two days after Patricio Cariola arrived at the jail in Santiago in 1975, the chaplain there saw to it that he had everything necessary for the celebration of the Eucharist. Although he had to celebrate it alone, it was the Mass, nevertheless; through it, he writes, "I felt myself more united than ever with the church"[1]—an important consideration given the isolation implicit in the conditions of his imprisonment.

In Walter Ciszek's case, and that of a number of other Jesuits as well, outsiders secretly sent in the necessary supplies. Nuns living not far from the Siberian work camp where Ciszek was imprisoned were able to smuggle wine in to him. Faithful prisoners then made sure that supplies of the wine, along with bread, were placed at strategic locations inside the camp precincts. As a result, not just Ciszek but other priests imprisoned with him were in a position to celebrate the Eucharist. There were distinct dangers, for if they were discovered, the priests were severely punished. But as Ciszek observes, "[T]he Mass was always worth the danger and the sacrifice." In his book *He Leadeth Me*, he adds, "We would do almost anything in order to say or attend a Mass."[2]

On the same page of his book, he provides an example of the personal sacrifice that he and the other priests exhibited: "I have seen priests pass up breakfast and work at hard labor on an empty stomach until noon in order to keep the eucharistic fast, because the noon break at the work site was the best time we could get together for a hidden Mass. I did that myself." And during the arctic summers, when the work days were longer and the hours for rest shortened, he saw both priests and prisoners deny themselves much needed sleep

---

[1] Cariola, "Dos Meses," 14.
[2] Ciszek, *He Leadeth Me*, 143.

in order to get up before the rising bell to share in a secret Mass before the day officially began.[3]

The same intense longing for the Eucharist pervades the letters Carlo Spinola wrote from his prison in Japan. In one letter, dated February 26, 1621, he observes that although "for many months we could not partake of the bread of life, by dint of stealth what was needed for Mass was brought in—even priestly vestments!" As a result, he could write, "[T]he greatest consolation we have is to be able to say Mass daily." He signs this and other letters "Carlo, incarcerated for the faith," in a deliberate allusion to St. Paul, who begins his Letter to Philemon, "I, Paul, a prisoner for Christ Jesus."[4]

In another letter written a year earlier, on February 18, 1620, he describes even more specifically just how much the Eucharist meant to him and his companions: "This holy bread gives us both bodily and spiritual strength. This celestial wine warms us, gives fervor, not only to make what we suffer seem small, but also makes us desire to see ourselves in even greater suffering."[5] The desire for greater suffering, common in the sprituality of the time, was granted many times over.

In mid-twentieth-century Albania, Giacomo Gardin writes in his diary of his happiness at being present for a clandestine Mass celebrated in another cell at the prison in Shkodra, after three years of eucharistic deprivation. The diary entry for November, 1948 reads:

> Through hidden channels, due to the inscrutable workings of Providence, we are able to partake of the Eucharist. . . . It is truly a great happiness. In just a moment, the reality of our suffering and isolation disappeared, and we now feel happy. I witnessed the fact which is a testament to genuine confessors of faith: a priest celebrating Mass in his prison cell. For altar, he has his lap. The host is a piece of bread and a few drops of sour wine, sprinkled upon it. The comrades partake of communion while going back and forth to the bathroom.[6]

Later in the same entry Gardin says that an informer—a scorpion, as spies were called—revealed the secret liturgies to the authorities.

---

[3] Ibid.

[4] Spinola, *Vita del P. Carlo Spinola,* 157.

[5] Ibid., 149.

[6] "The Diary of Father Ják Gardin, S.J.," in Gjon Sinishta, *The Fulfilled Promise,* 144.

The outcome was that "the priest is locked in a solitary cell, after being severely tortured."

Following his transfer from the prison to a work camp, Gardin himself was finally able to celebrate the Eucharist on Easter, 1952. At the time, the Albanian authorities were trying to establish a nationalistic form of the Catholic Church, one that would not have ties with the Vatican—somewhat like the so-called patriotic church in Communist China. To curry favor with the clergy, the camp commander granted Gardin's request and that of the three other priests in the camp to celebrate an Easter Mass and even allowed supplies to be brought in from outside: "We got everything we needed to celebrate the Mass from the sister of one of us who lived in Tirana. We received hymns and popular prayers, adorned the walls and altar with our best rags. . . . After five years of absolute void even I could finally celebrate Easter!"[7] The reader of his account senses the enthusiasm and joy he felt on this occasion.

By bribing the jailer at the Clink in sixteenth-century London, John Gerard was able to say Mass early in the morning, as well as hear confessions and reconcile fellow prisoners to the Church.[8] In our own time, the Catholic warden of Francis Hagerty's jail in Massachusetts allowed him to celebrate Mass for the prisoners during his incarceration for demonstrating in front of the Brookline abortion clinic.[9]

Through the intervention of the Catholic hierarchy in Germany, Rupert Mayer was given the use of a portable altar so that he could say Mass daily in his cell.[10] By a similar but broader arrangement with the Holy See, Jesuits and other priests at Dachau had the use of part of a cell block as a makeshift chapel. Léo de Coninck describes it in his account of his three years in Dachau: "The chapel was nothing more than a prisoners' room with a partition between eating and sleeping quarters removed. . . . The chapel had to be shared by the different denominations, and this was arranged with notable charity on the part of all concerned."[11] The parish priest of the town of Dachau donated the wine and hosts, and Mass was celebrated daily

---

[7] Gardin, *Banishing God in Albania*, 114.
[8] Gerard, *Autobiography of a Hunted Priest*, 78f.
[9] Interview with Francis O. Hagerty, January 17, 1994.
[10] Koerbling, *Rupert Mayer*, 160, 171.
[11] De Coninck, "The Priests of Dachau," 119.

before the official rising time. As was true for Ciszek in Siberia, the willingness to deprive oneself of sleep by getting up early for Mass represented no small sacrifice for the exhausted, half-starved prisoners at Dachau.

Although de Coninck says that both laymen and religious attended the services, their numbers would have been comparatively small because the size of the chapel was limited. To offset this limitation, a Czech Jesuit, Aloysius Koláček, went to other blocks to celebrate Mass. According to a brief description of his work in the *Woodstock Letters*, Koláček "often said Mass secretly and from memory for the inmates of the camp. He used only a plain table and a water glass containing a very few drops of wine . . . and a handkerchief covering the glass with a smuggled wafer in its folds for the ceremony, while prisoners kept watch at the door for approaching SS guards."[12] To make the Eucharist available to others was one of the most important functions that a priest could perform in ministering to fellow prisoners, as will become clearer in the chapter on ministry.

Although Alfred Delp's situation was characterized not just by isolation but by manacled isolation, he too deeply felt the need for the Eucharist. On the eve of the trial that would lead to his death, he writes: "Thank God, my fetters were so loosely fastened that tonight I could slip them off again. So I could celebrate Mass . . . with my hands quite free." This also meant that he could hide a consecrated host on his person during the trial itself: "This is the last night before the final stage and I am taking the Lord with me after all," he observes in his *Prison Meditations*.[13]

Rupert Mayer, too, had the consolation of having the Lord with him in the form of consecrated hosts. It was 1937, and Mayer had been arrested for ignoring the Gestapo's demand that he stop preaching. He received a visit from Augustin Rösch—his and Delp's provincial—who would himself be incarcerated after the war began. Mayer says that Rösch "handed me a book with the remark that the Gestapo had authorized its being given me. While he pressed the book into my hand he whispered in my ear: 'There are Hosts in it!' I hid the book in my breast pocket and went back to my prison cell radiantly happy."[14]

---

[12] "Varia: Germany," *Woodstock Letters* 74(4) (December 1945):361.

[13] Delp, *Prison Meditations*, 13.

[14] Koerbling, *Rupert Mayer*, 152–53.

Being able to celebrate a solitary Mass only hours before what he thought might be his last day on earth was a deep source of comfort for the American, Michael Evans. While working in Northern Sudan with the American Refugee Committee in 1989, he was arrested by the Sudanese secret police for "irregularity of papers." The real reason for his arrest was his persistence in trying to help a group of malnourished and often sick Ethiopian refugees.

Held under house arrest in his "tukul" (mud hut) with armed guards outside and cut off from all communication with people who might have been able to intervene for him, Evans describes the Eucharist which, under the circumstances, took on a special meaning: "I had smuggled a small bottle of mass wine into Sudan, something that was forbidden and punishable under *sharia* [the path to be followed in Muslim life], and I used the last of it that day to have a private mass. I received great consolation. I prayed quite a bit throughout the day, especially the rosary. I remember," he continues in one passage from a letter he wrote to the author that reflects the similar feeling of Jean Moussé on his arrival at Buchenwald, "not being so afraid to die—but being afraid that I would 'disappear' and no one would know what had happened." After being moved the next day and interrogated by both the military and the Sudan security police, Evans was eventually expelled from the country.[15]

Daniel Berrigan and his brother Philip were allowed to celebrate Mass twice a week in the chaplain's office at Danbury. They disliked both the chaplain ("a man subject to Caesar") and the arrangement because they were separated from other prisoners who might have wanted to share in their Eucharist. The office, with its "bookcases filled with dusty old tomes unread for years, the American and papal flags moldering in far corners," was "a place where literally no one comes or goes, the dead heart of a dead place." Nevertheless, Berrigan discovered that in celebrating Mass there, he and his brother found themselves "against all expectation strengthened to bear our lives one day more."[16] On other occasions, they were able to celebrate clandestinely with bread and wine brought in surreptitiously by friends when the defendants met with their attorneys prior to various court appearances.[17]

---

[15] Michael A. Evans, letter to author, December 7, 1995.

[16] Berrigan, *Lights On In The House Of The Dead*, 189–90.

[17] Interview with Daniel Berrigan, January 4, 1996.

Not all incarcerated Jesuits have been as contemptuous of their institutional chaplains as Berrigan. During his imprisonment by the Nazis, Rupert Mayer was grateful for the visits of the German chaplain. The chaplain, in turn, was so deeply impressed by Mayer that he subsequently wrote of his experience of hearing the latter's confession each week: "To be perfectly frank it required considerable self-control on my part. What could I offer such a one, spiritually so much greater than I? . . . But Father Mayer was so humble that he did not just receive every word, he even thanked me for it. As often as I was with him and we parted, he asked for my priestly blessing. Thus we always blessed each other: first I him and then he me."[18] But the circumstances of Berrigan's and Mayer's incarceration were very different.

In the farm-type labor camps of Communist China, Jesuits wrote to Gino Belli in Taiwan asking for ballpoint pens with tops—a seemingly innocuous request. The tops, however, were sought after for Eucharistic reasons. Under the less stringent regulations of some camps, prisoners could purchase flour and wine. The Jesuits used the flour to make tiny hosts, which they cut out with the tops of the pens. The hosts looked enough like pills to escape detection by the guards.[19]

Ján Korec faced far stricter conditions. At the Valdice prison, which held most of the incarcerated religious in Communist Czechoslovakia, he managed to make small quantities of wine from grapes; he then concealed the wine in medicine bottles. When he was held in a cell with other prisoners who were also priests, they could celebrate Mass with relative openness. But if lay prisoners were present in the cell, some of whom might be spies, "we celebrated . . . seated, with a book on our knees" to avoid suspicion.[20] Discovered once with a small bottle of the wine in his pocket, Korec was punished. Nonetheless, he continued to make communion available to lay prisoners. Concealing minute pieces of consecrated bread in a matchbox, he distributed them surreptitiously in the prison infirmary.[21]

For those unable to celebrate within their prison walls, friends on the outside were sometimes able to smuggle consecrated hosts in to

---

[18] Koerbling, *Rupert Mayer*, 163.
[19] Interview with Gino Belli, October 20, 1993.
[20] Korec, *La Notte dei Barberi*, 183.
[21] Ibid., 183, 189, 207.

them. Such was the case with Pierre Joseph de Clorivière—the last Jesuit to be professed before the suppression of the Society in France. Although a non-juror during the French Revolution, he managed to avoid arrest. He was arrested only after Napoleon came to power, when he was accused of complicity in an attempt on Napoleon's life and was sent to Le Temple. In his writings on the life of de Clorivière, Max de Bazelaire tells of two women who regularly brought him what appeared to the guards to be simply a basket of food. But "the ordinary basket they carried serves in effect as a tabernacle. Under a first layer of various provisions there is a little box of consecrated hosts."[22] As de Bazelaire notes, through this means de Clorivière continued to receive the "Bread of the strong" for the five years of his incarceration.

Similarly, later in nineteenth-century Paris, supporters on the outside also provided hosts to the French Jesuits arrested during the 1871 uprising. In a letter of April 13, 1871, Pierre Olivaint describes the strategy of a woman who brought what appeared to be a simple basket of food to the prison. However, the woman also carried two pots of cream in the pocket of her apron. Each pot had a false bottom, beneath which lay consecrated hosts concealed in three silk sachets tied with cords.[23]

Olivaint and two fellow Jesuits, Léon Ducoudray and Alexis Clerc, placed hosts in the sachets and hung them around their necks. The presence of the Blessed Sacrament on their persons was a source of strength to them. Just before being transferred from the Mazas prison to La Roquette—the prison for those condemned to death—they received a second supply of hosts. How much these hosts meant is evident in a letter written by Ducoudray: "I am no longer alone. I have the Lord as a guest in my little cell."[24] His words foreshadowed those of Alfred Delp almost a century later, when, with a consecrated host on his person, he was comforted and strengthened as he prepared to face the Nazi court that would condemn him to death.

For Jacques Sommet at Dachau, the secret distribution of consecrated hosts was more than a manifestation of God's presence to the

---

[22] Max de Bazelaire, S.J., *Le Père de Clorivière* (Paris: Societé de l'Apostolat de la Prière, 1966), 67–68. Following the restoration of the Society in 1814, de Clorivière was appointed superior of the French Jesuits and master of novices.

[23] Herbert, *A Martyr from the Quarterdeck*, 228f.

[24] Ponlevoy, *Actes de la Captivité*, 5th ed., 83.

recipients. The very process of distribution created what he calls a Eucharistic network, one that bound together all who received the body of Christ. It united them both to one another and to the Church as a whole. The network helped to create a sense of community that provided a level of support that would otherwise have been impossible.

To avoid discovery and punishment, those involved in the network sought anonymity. Sommet's first encounter with the network occurred soon after his arrival at the concentration camp. Lying on his wooden bunk one night, he found a small packet in the pocket of his tunic. "Someone put it there. Who?" he wonders. "I still don't know who. In this tiny packet, there was a small box, and in the box, a piece of ordinary bread and—a part of a host. How had I been marked out by whoever put the packet together? Whoever it was," he concludes, "never told me."[25] On this same page of his autobiography, Sommet reflects further on the meaning of this "revelation," as he terms it, this awareness of a Christ-centered linkage through the secretly given host as well as the gift of real bread. The latter was no minor gift either, in light of the prisoners' constant gnawing, physical hunger.

Finding the packet in his pocket also causes him to realize that he is not simply a prisoner alone amid hostile surroundings; rather, he is recognized for what he is, a believing individual. This realization brings a sense of comfort that suggests the near-miraculous: "Yes, in this terrifying and unknown universe, there rises up something that is awaiting me. A solidarity appears. Later," he goes on, "I myself will take part in this network which is epitomized by the Eucharist given in secret."[26] Like Ján Korec, he took part in the network by carrying bits of consecrated hosts—at his personal peril because of both the risk of contagion and the risk of discovery—to the quarantine barracks for newly arrived prisoners. Many of these prisoners were mortally ill. Thus, for them, receiving the host from Sommet was tantamount to receiving the viaticum.

Another Dachau prisoner, a German priest, consecrated the hosts used in the Eucharistic network long before dawn in a space at the end of their barracks that served as a chapel. One day an SS guard

---

[25] Sommet, *L'honneur de la liberté*, 75.
[26] Ibid.

conducted a sudden inspection as Sommet was holding the little box that he used as a pyx. The guard made him stretch out both hands, but ordered him to open only one; when he did so, it was not the hand that held the box containing the consecrated particles. Again, Sommet felt a sense of divine intervention.[27]

Jean Moussé had a similar experience. He, like Sommet, became a component in a Eucharistic network at another concentration camp, although it was not named as such. In December of 1944, Moussé was transferred from Buchenwald to Reichenau, a smaller camp northeast of Prague. On leaving Buchenwald, he had been able to take with him five hosts consecrated by one of the priests there. Instead of keeping them for himself, he shared them with others at his new location.

At Reichenau, he was assigned to a drafting office that was part of a factory connected with the camp. This gave him access to tracing paper. Moussé describes how he used the paper for apostolic purposes: "I divided the hosts into tiny pieces and wrapped them in little 'corporals' of tracing paper." Then, he says in a letter to the author, "I distributed them once a week to some Belgian and French prisoners and to four Poles."

The loss of one of the packets led him to a deeper understanding of his relationship with God: "On Sundays, when the factory was not in operation, some of us got together in little groups of three to recite the rosary while walking in the limited space of the camp. . . . One Sunday a packet with a host, part of which I had just shared, slipped from my hand and fell into the snow. I was desolate. I tried to find the white packet, but with the whiteness of the snow, it was impossible, and I had to give up. I said to myself that God is truly present in the depths of our afflictions."[28] The implication of this last line, verified in another letter from Moussé, dated November 25, 1995, is that the snow had become a symbol of the sufferings of the prisoners; but that Christ—the particle of the host—though hidden, was nonetheless present in their sufferings, as epitomized by the snow that covered the ground of the concentration camp yard.

As consoling as receiving communion might be, however, it could not entirely compensate for the inability to celebrate or assist at the

---

[27] Ibid., 108f.
[28] Jean Moussé, letter to author, November 7, 1995.

Mass itself. Léon Ducoudray describes this deprivation as a cruelty: "The isolation, the separation, the uncertainties, and especially the privation of being unable to celebrate the holy Mass, or even to be present at it, is truly cruel."[29] His companion in captivity in Paris, Pierre Olivaint, observes on May 14, 1871, that "it is now six weeks that I have spent in the shadows [of prison]. How many days without mounting to the altar!"[30]

Similarly, for Anselm Eckhart in his Portuguese prison at the time of the suppression in the eighteenth century, "our greatest privation . . . was the impossibility of celebrating the holy Mass." The conditions of confinement were so strict in this entirely Catholic nation that prisoners could hope for communion "only in the case of mortal illness, and even then it required a doctor's certificate;" that is, one attesting that death was imminent and that the communion would be considered as viaticum.[31]

The double deprivation of being forbidden to say Mass and of having no opportunity to receive communion was especially grievous for John Clifford. In the story of his three years of incarceration in Shanghai, *In the Presence of My Enemies,* he writes: "For me, the greatest punishment inflicted by the Communists was the brutal attempt to suppress my religion. I had not said Mass nor received Holy Communion for 888 days. . . . No one but a priest can fully realize the significance of that deprivation."[32] Ciszek's thoughts paralleled those of Clifford: "Those who have never been deprived of an opportunity to say or hear Mass do not really appreciate what a treasure the Mass is."[33]

Clifford, however, was more fortunate than some of the other imprisoned Jesuits, in that he eventually found the means to celebrate in secret. Toward the end of his three years of incarceration in Shanghai, he received a package from family members in California through the Red Cross. Along with other items, the package contained two little bottles marked "Pabulum Vitae" [food of life], a label whose hidden meaning was not understood by the Chinese guards who inspected all incoming packages. In one bottle was wine; in the

---

[29] Ponlevoy, *Actes de la Captivité,* 5th ed., 43.
[30] Ibid., 6th ed., 76.
[31] Carayon, *Documents Inédits,* "Les Prisons du Marquis de Pombal," (9):118.
[32] Clifford, *In the Presence of My Enemies,* 208–9.
[33] Ciszek, *He Leadeth Me,* 143.

other were hosts concealed between nickel-sized slices of sugar candy. The stopper of the wine container, which resembled a medicine bottle, became a miniature chalice when inverted. The labels noted that the company producing the products was the Domini Corporation in Los Gatos, California—Los Gatos was the site of the Jesuit novitiate of the California Province. The instructions on the labels said that a wafer and a teaspoonful of the liquid should be taken before eating.

At first, Clifford did not understand the meaning of the covert instructions. "I opened the wafers and found, to my disgust, that they were only . . . sugar candy. I suspected at once that the authorities had removed the legitimate vitamins for this pallid substitute." With similar skepticism, he then picked up the small bottle, whose glass stopper had been sealed with wax. "Scraping away the wax with an old toothbrush, I removed the stopper and sniffed. The odor was pleasing, if somewhat unidentifiable." Then came the moment of recognition: "I tasted it once, and then again. It was Mass wine! For a moment I sat on the cell floor trembling with such excitement that I almost dropped the bottle." Returning to the candy, he found the communion wafers inserted between the individual pieces. "There are no words to describe the glory of that moment," he writes.[34]

Although he suspected that the Chinese prison officials were not entirely ignorant of what the two bottles contained, Clifford decided to take the risk of saying Mass nonetheless, albeit with great circumspection. Certain that his cellmate was planted there to observe him, he waited each night until he was asleep; then, around midnight, he lay on the floor to celebrate his solitary Eucharist in the darkness. Having said one Mass, "after sleeping an hour or so, I would awaken and say a second Mass for the following day." Although strengthened by his secret Eucharists, he nevertheless felt the strain of engaging in a clandestine activity that at the least would mean confiscation of his Mass supplies: "I could never be sure that the guard would not burst in on me, or that my cellmate would remain asleep." But he was not caught, and by using only tiny amounts of the wine and hosts,

---

[34] Clifford, *In the Presence of My Enemies*, 207f. The phrase on the label, "the Domini Corporation, Los Gatos, California," was a play on the Latin word for Lord, "Dominus," and a sly reference to the California Province's novitiate at Los Gatos, on whose grounds grapes were grown for wine.

he was able to celebrate forty-one times before the supply finally gave out.[35]

Under similar circumstances, Thomas Phillips, who was incarcerated in Shanghai during the same period (1953–56), also received wine and hosts through the Red Cross. His two containers of "vitamins" had labels in both English and Chinese. The label for the container of wine said, "To be taken daily by those suffering from malnourishment. Dose: one cupful." The other container, a cylindrical glass tube with hosts, called for one "tablet" before breakfast each morning. In addition, the package contained what Phillips initially thought were handkerchiefs, but which were in fact altar linens with embroidered crosses. Although he and Clifford were in the same prison, they never saw each other until their incarceration ended in June, 1956.[36] It is probable, however, that since both Jesuits were from the California Province, their wine and hosts came from the same source.

Some who lacked the necessary supplies for a genuine Mass resorted to the dry Mass. In 1593, before being sold as a galley slave in a slave market on the Red Sea coast, Pedro Paez was held captive by a Turkish pasha in Yemen. There, each day before dawn, he and his Jesuit companion, Antonio Monserrate, recited the Mass prayers. A piece of bread was blessed at the offertory, and because they lacked wine, they raised a crucifix at the elevation.[37]

To John Gerard in the Tower of London, the dry Mass was a source of strength as well; he describes it as a "practice that brought me much consolation in my sufferings." Besides spending "four or sometimes five hours in meditation" every day, he writes in his autobiography that on a daily basis, "I rehearsed the actions of the Mass, as students do when they are preparing for ordination. I went through them with great devotion and longing to communicate, which I felt most keenly at those moments in a real Mass when the priest consummates the sacrifice and consumes the oblata."[38]

Centuries later in the county jail in Lumberton, North Carolina, John Dear used as his "oblata" a piece of supermarket Wonder Bread and a cup of cold water. As he awaited his trial for civil disobedience

---

[35] Ibid.

[36] Becker, *I Met a Traveller*, 166–69.

[37] Caraman, *Lost Empire*, 147.

[38] Gerard, *Autobiography of a Hunted Priest*, 116.

in a jail in Edenton, he received a container of grape juice as part of his weekly food ration. He carefully set the juice aside and used small portions of it for an actual daily Mass with his two codefendants, which was celebrated not at an altar but at a "barren stainless steel table."[39]

In China in the 1950s, John Houle was another who found the dry Mass to be a source of devotion and strength. After walking in a circle in his cell for an hour at 5:30 A.M. for exercise, he describes what happened next: "I begin my Mass, and I experience that 'peace which the world cannot give.' Plenty of distractions, annoyances, just from close contact with fifteen others; but over and under and through this hour is the intense realization that God is, that Christ's Church is offering up to the Father of us all the Holy Sacrifice of adoration and praise, of thanksgiving and expiation, and that all my needs, our needs, are being set before the Father who loves us and gives us life."

Houle then relates how—despite the distractions that surrounded him—reciting the Mass prayers, even without wine and hosts, is made possible by the gift of memory, which his guards had not be able to take from him: "Through our Lord's gracious gift, I know the Mass word for word, in English and Latin, the proper of the Feast of the Sacred Heart, and one of the Masses of our Blessed Mother for Saturday. If distractions throw me off, I turn from Latin to English to Latin until recollection comes again. This," he concludes, "is the really happy hour of the day."[40] The hour of happiness was his own, even though he had been without the real Mass for three months.

George Wong, who had also been in prison in China around the same time, remembers saying "in the privacy of my mind and heart a 'dry Mass' every day." In his article in *The Tablet*, he reflects, "My so-called 'dry Mass' was said without bread and wine, and of course without book . . . but I was blessed with a good memory in those days, as I could recite by heart all the fixed prayers of the old Latin Mass." After his seven and a half years in prison, he was transferred to a farm labor camp for another twenty years.[41] At the labor camp, a Catholic doctor was able to secretly give him wine concealed in a

---

[39] Letter to author, January 14, 1994, and Dear, *Peace Behind Bars*, 33–34.
[40] Houle, "Thoughts in Prison," 266.
[41] Wong, "Candle in the Wind: a Prisoner's Testimony."

penicillin bottle, in a manner reminiscent of the experience of John Clifford and Thomas Phillips—and, as we shall see, also of the experience of Joseph Nguyen-Công Doan in Vietnam. To obtain hosts, Wong included a code phrase in the once-a-month postcard he was allowed to send to his sister: "Remember what I like to eat the first thing in the morning before breakfast." His sister accordingly concealed hosts among the various food items that the authorities permitted him to receive. As was the case with many others, he celebrated the Mass itself at night while the rest of the prisoners were asleep.[42]

Letters to relatives also became the means through which a Lithuanian parish priest, Jonas Kastytis Matulionis, was able to obtain supplies for Mass. Secretly ordained in 1980, Matulionis was arrested and imprisoned in 1984 for refusing to obey an official directive not to accompany his parishioners to pray at a local cemetery on the Eve of All Souls. Since all letters were read and censored while he was incarcerated, he could not ask directly for hosts and wine. Instead, he managed to smuggle out a letter to his parents requesting hosts—or some form of bread that could be used as hosts—and raisins. They arrived in separate packages; the hosts came first and evidently were not recognized by the authorities: "The suspicious camp inspector looked through them against the light and broke them in smaller pieces, thinking that some secret correspondence or forbidden material might be contained in them." The raisins were admitted without question because the inspector did not guess their purpose. "It happened to be Holy Thursday," and Matulionis observes that he did not weep but "bawled for joy and gratitude." The joy and gratitude stemmed from his knowledge that by pouring hot water over the raisins, he would be able to create a wine of sorts and thereby "could say Mass in prison the evening of the day when Our Lord instituted that Holy Sacrament and Sacrifice."[43]

Another Lithuanian, Antanas Šeškevičius, who had worked with Matulionis, faced the same challenge of finding bread and wine for Mass. Soldiers arrested him at his rectory and took him to the KGB headquarters in Vilnius. Convicted of anti-Soviet activities because

---

[42] Interview with George B. Wong, May 5, 1995.

[43] Unpublished account of several incarcerated Lithuanian Jesuits sent to the author in December, 1994, by Anicetus Tamosaitis, S.J., of the Della Strada Jesuit Community in Chicago, Illinois, 5.

of his work with youth, he was sentenced to twenty-five years in a coal mining concentration camp. His job was to go down into the mines to measure the level of methane gas.

Despite the obstacles presented by concentration camp life, he commented during a 1994 interview in Lithuania, "I always said daily Mass." Like Matulionis, he had obtained some raisins. "Someone gave me a few bagels. I made communion wafers from the bagels and wine from the raisins." In Vorkuta, the camp population included 400 Lithuanians as well as German and Polish prisoners, and Šeškevičius was able to provide communion for many of them, as well as hear their confessions. However, he was punished for these two sacramental activities by being transferred to another camp. There, too, he persevered in saying Mass and distributing communion.[44]

Fellow Lithuanian Jesuit Gerardas Dunda followed the examples of Šeškevičius and Matulionis in obtaining wine or at least raisins from home. Again, the subterfuge of deliberately mislabeling the container as medicine was successful. When Dunda was transferred from the coal mining camp in Soviet Russia to a lumber camp in southern Tunguskaja, his mother sent him a 100-gram bottle of wine labeled "drops for the heart." He observes in his memoir: "When the packages would arrive and the guards on duty would check the contents and find the bottle, they would never confiscate it, but as necessary medicine would pass it down to me." A prisoner who was a former seminarian from Kaunas in Lithuania had been assigned to work at a lathe. With the appropriate tools at hand, he fashioned a small chalice

---

[44] Interview with Antanas Šeškevičius (b. April 14, 1914) in 1994 in Lithuania, by Edward Schmidt, S.J., translated by Ms. Ramuné Lukas, secretary at the Della Strada Jesuit Community in Chicago. In a telephone conversation on December 8, 1997, Fr. Schmidt, of the Chicago Province, said the idea for this and other interviews with aging Jesuits in Lithuania came to him after teaching a course in German to Jesuit novices in Kaunas in the fall of 1993. On his return to the Chicago Province, he decided to go back to record the memories of Jesuits who had lived through the German and Soviet occupations. With an ex-novice as his translator, he traveled about in Lithuania for three weeks in the summer of 1994 conducting the interviews, which Ms. Lukas in Chicago subsequently translated into English.

Eventually, after the death of Stalin, Fr. Šeškevičius's sentence was reduced by fifteen years, and he was released in 1956. He was later forced to do field work in the region of Osa. There, the KGB arrested him again and brought him to a prison in Vilnius, Lithuania. He was sentenced to seven years and assigned to work in a table factory, where he remained until 1969. Yet another arrest and another year of imprisonment followed. Finally, he was freed and went on to do parish work in Moletai.

and paten for Dunda. A group of Lithuanian women in a women's labor camp nearby sewed corporals and other Mass linens for him. Nevertheless, such amenities were rare among Jesuit prisoners; obtaining the wine was in itself no small feat.[45]

In Vietnam in the 1980s, Joseph Nguyen-Công Doan had no supplies at all with which to celebrate Mass for the first three of his nine years of imprisonment. While initially held with other political prisoners in Saigon, he prayed the Mass prayers from memory each evening. Of that difficult time, he said during an interview on April 11, 1995: "Even though I believed they would never release me, I felt peace, and was ready to spend the rest of my life in prison."

After his trial on June 29, 1982, however, Doan was transferred to the Saigon prison for ordinary criminals, a large, three-story octagon-shaped building built in a pavilion style. He shared a room with as many as eighty other men; each was allotted sleeping space on the floor measuring only twenty-five centimeters wide. In those cramped quarters, however, he was finally able to celebrate Mass. He described how the opportunity arose:

> It came about through another priest (himself a religious of another congregation) who was a prisoner on the same floor in the next pavilion. I met him in the courtyard when I came down for the twice-weekly bath. At that time I was living on the second floor. He was sent to do some cleaning work at the water pool. He approached and asked: "Do you have wine for Mass?" I said, "No, I don't know how to get it in." "I will send you some," he said, and he also told me how to get more into the prison. I already had some hosts with me from the first prison. They had been sent in with food provisions, together with wine—but the wine was discovered at the control station, and my cousin who sent it was blamed by the security men. The priest who promised the wine sent it the same day. That night, when the other prisoners were asleep, lying on the floor under my mosquito net, I celebrated Mass with tears of joy.

In the interview, Doan went on to speak of how he was soon able to obtain wine on his own from the outside, following the suggestion of the other priest: "At the next fifteen-minute monthly visit from my sister, I told her to bring me each time a supply of wet rice cakes, with a clear plastic packet of sauce that is used with them. Inside the

---

[45] Dunda, unpublished memoir, 6–7.

sauce packet, she was to put wine; the sauce and the wine are of the same color. As to a continued supply of hosts, all she had to do was to put them between some dry rice crackers. And from that day on, I got my 'Melchizedek material' regularly." Later, the use of the familiar subterfuge of a medicine bottle was substituted for the sauce packets: "A pharmacist friend of ours had a better idea, namely to pour wine into small medicine bottles and label them vitamins. Thanks to these regular supplies, for the remaining six years, every night from the darkness of the prison I could offer all the labors and sufferings of the prisoners and other human beings to God in the Holy Sacrifice. My altar," he concluded, "was my blanket folded as a pillow, with my daily clothes as priestly garments. But amid these difficult surroundings, I felt myself at the heart of humanity and of the whole of creation."[46]

An especially moving form of the dry Mass, even though it included communion, was experienced by the scholastic Paul Beschet on Christmas Eve of 1944. After their arrest and internment at the Gotha prison and then at a concentration camp, he and several other Jeunesse Ouvrière companions were working as forced laborers in a factory at Zwickau, near Leipzig. A priest there had hidden particles of consecrated hosts in an empty tin toothpowder container and gave it to a young Catholic factory worker named René, who in turn passed it on to Beschet to hold. For the three days before Christmas, Beschet kept the tin container in his pocket during the nighttime hours and returned it to René the following day for safekeeping when he began his own twelve-hour shift. Both knew that it might otherwise be discovered during an unannounced search on the factory floor.

On the night of Christmas Eve itself, Beschet and twenty others gathered at a prearranged time in the shower room of their block, which also served as the temporary repository for the bodies of those who had recently died of illness or exhaustion. In his autobiography, Beschet describes what happened then:

> Having come back to the block at midnight, Camille, Marcel, and some others gathered around the little box placed on my knees. I slowly read the midnight Mass. A Protestant, aware of what we were doing, offered

---

[46] Interview with Joseph Nguyen-Công Doan S.J., at America House, New York City, April 11, 1995, by the author.

to stand watch in the corridor. Just before communion, a young fellow
. . . whispered in my ear: "Paul, we're only lacking Him. . . ." "Another
moment, my friend, you'll have Him!" Amazed, tears in his eyes, he
received the host. Camille and Marcel received theirs. The Protestant
wept.[47]

The very bleakness of the scene—the young men half-starved, with
corpses only a few feet away in the cold, dank shower room—added
an even deeper significance to their receipt of the bread of life from
Beschet's hands in the palpable presence of death.

On another Christmas Eve six years later, in 1952, John Havas
longed to celebrate Mass in his Shanghai prison. Although his hopes
were unrealized, the brutal treatment he received as a result of his
request led him to an unexpectedly profound and joyous understanding of the meaning of Bethlehem. In a reflection written four decades
later as a 1991 Christmas letter to friends—just two years before his
death at the Jesuit infirmary at Fordham University in New York—he
recounted the story. If he had been willing to sign a "confession" and
to provide the names of students he had taught in China, he would
have been granted permission to celebrate a Christmas Eve Mass.
But he maintained the same position he had adhered to throughout
his ordeal:

> Two days before Christmas, the commissioner of the prison came to
> my cell. "So you would like to say your Mass tomorrow. We have no
> objection to your superstition, but I do not believe that you are a
> priest. I think that you are an imposter, a faker, an international spy.
> And you are a liar." Here he paused and read [stared at] the floor.
> "However, if you would sign the confession and give us the names of
> your students, our kind government might consider your request."

Havas's response was immediate. " 'No, thank you. Forget it!' I
said. He spun on his heels and disappeared." Two days later, after
Havas had gone to sleep on Christmas Eve night, the retaliation
began:

> Two of the guards barged into my cell, roused me from my uneasy
> sleep, and ordered me to get up. "Where am I going?" I dared to ask.
> One guard stuffed the question down my throat, while the other

---

[47] Beschet, *Mission en Thuringe*, 197. Marcel later died at the Mauthausen concentration camp.

grabbed me by the scruff of my neck and dragged me through the corridor, down the stairs, and dumped me into a damp, dark, and stinking cave. . . . The place reeked of cadavers, augmented by the stench of human excrement. I became nauseous.

So great was the degradation that he cried out against the God whom he had served all his life:

I had gone down into the pit. I prostrated myself and cried like a baby. "My God, my God, why have you forsaken me?" I bawled so loudly that one of the guards came and told me to shut up. If the purpose of my captors was to humiliate me, it worked. . . . My humanity cried out as I continued to harangue with the Lord. "I took a vow to serve you and trust you, and you treat me like this. I left everything behind to follow you and look where I ended up—abandoned."

Then, in the midst of this inner and outer blackness, came the Epiphany-like moment of understanding that totally transformed that night's horrors into a profound grace: "As I struggled with my feelings in this total darkness, and without any noise or light, the word 'Bethlehem,' perfectly formed, flashed in my mind." He kept repeating the word and then, ". . . Pow! My Lord and my God! What a fool I had been." He found himself suddenly begging for forgiveness in the realization that "it was on a night like this, in a cave like this, that You, the Almighty God, came down to earth to save a sinner such as me." He humbly concludes, "Your poverty and state were even worse than mine. Forgive my ingratitude."

Havas's final thoughts on this transformation in his outlook became suffused with thankfulness: "Thank you for not deserting me. Thank you for purifying me." As with Alfred Delp and others, he had come to recognize a purifying element in the extremity of the night's suffering that coincided, in his case, with the birth of Christ. What followed was intense elation: "Such an indescribable joy invaded me that I could not contain myself. At first I thought my heart would break because of my despair. Now I thought my pounding heart would break because of my unbounded joy. I had to do something physical to get relief from this overpowering emotion." The very chains that bound him and even the walls of the cell were transformed into sources of blessing: "I crawled on my knees in the darkness kissing my chains . . . until I bumped into the wall. I even kissed the wall. I felt the presence of the Lord. I experienced the wonderful realization that God, glowing in Holiness, was in me. It was my first transcendent experience."

The sense of rapture, of being seized by an immediate sense of God's presence, continued: "This was the happiest day of my life. I prayed for the whole world, especially for my captors. . . . Though a prisoner in chains, I knew that I was caught up in His will and no harm would come to me. I was prepared for anything and everything," he concludes.[48]

---

[48] This description of Havas's Christmas Eve in a Shanghai prison is not included in his autobiography, "Four, Nine, Nine, Six." It was written while he was living in retirement at Murray-Weigel Hall at Fordham University in New York, and was sent to friends by way of a Christmas greeting. The author received a copy from James F. Dolan, S.J., shortly after Havas's death. Dolan lived with him from 1972 to 1978, while both were on the staff of the Loyola House of retreats in Morristown, New Jersey.

TEN
Daily Order

WHILE PRAYER and trust in God have been two primary mainstays through which Jesuits have found the strength to deal with their imprisonment, some discovered a related strength in establishing a daily structure for their lives. Walter Ciszek resorted to an almost literal reconstruction of the daily order of his earlier life in the Society. During his long months in solitary confinement in Lubianka, he notes in *With God in Russia:* "I began to organize my day as if I were in a Jesuit house back home, and I made up a daily schedule for myself." He continues:

> After breakfast, I would say Mass by heart—that is, I would say all the prayers, for of course I couldn't actually celebrate the Holy Sacrifice. I said the Angelus morning, noon, and night as the Kremlin clock chimed the hours. Before dinner I would make my noon *examen* [examination of conscience]; before going to bed at night, I'd make the evening *examen*, and points for the morning meditation, following St. Ignatius' *Spiritual Exercises*.

The afternoon and evening also had prayer-based schedules:

> Every afternoon, I said three rosaries—one in Polish, one in Latin, and one in Russian—as a substitute for my breviary. After supper, I spent the evening reciting prayers and hymns from memory or even chanting them out loud: the *Anima Christi*, the *Veni Creator*, the *Salve Regina*, the *Veni, Sancte Spiritus*, especially the *Dies Irae* and the *Miserere*—all the things we had memorized in the novitiate as novices, the hymns we had sung during my years in the Society, the prayers I had learned as a boy back home.[1]

Others, who were denied breviaries but had access to Bibles, sometimes assembled their own makeshift breviaries. During his incarceration in East Germany in 1958, Josef Menzel speaks in his recollections of "the breviary which I put together from the Zurich bible

---

[1] Ciszek, *With God in Russia,* 75.

and the diocesan song book 'Laudate' of the diocese of Meissen, with little pieces of toilet paper as marks—how often would these be put in disarray."[2]

As Ciszek's words show, memory played a central role in the creation of the novitiate-like interior structure he had created for himself at Lubianka: "Sometimes I'd spend hours trying to remember a line which had slipped from my memory, sounding it over and over again until I had it right." Recalling lines of poetry was a help too, poetry learned in the juniorate—the two years of college-level study following the novitiate: "I would also recite what poetry I could remember: Wordsworth's 'We Are Seven,' or Shelley's 'Ode to the West Wind,' or Burns' little poem to a field mouse." Occasionally he made up "an extemporaneous sermon or speech on some subject . . . talking out loud just to keep myself sane."[3]

Those in religious life are not the only ones who have tried to create an order to their days in prison. In the *Mémoires de Madame Roland Ecrits durant Sa Captivité*, the writer, Manon Jeanne Roland de la Platière, who was executed in 1793 during the Reign of Terror in France, developed her own daily plan of activities in an effort to restore some sense of normalcy to her dire situation: "I divided my days with a kind of regularity. In the morning I studied English, by reading the excellent essay of Shaftesbury on virtue. . . . Then I sketched until the middaymeal. . . ." Like the Jesuits, she too made use of her memory—not to call to mind scripture or the writings of religious figures, but rather "the maxims of philosophy to sustain my courage."[4]

The Lithuanian, Sigitas Tamkevičius—later archbishop of Kaunas—was able to establish a sustaining connection between the prison schedule and the strict schedule he had known during his days in school, in the seminary, and finally in parish work. Arrested by the Russian KGB on May 4, 1983, in Kybartai, where he had been working as a parish priest, he was tried the following November and sentenced on December 2 to six years in a labor camp in the Urals region of Siberia. In a letter of May 10, 1985, he describes how the

---

[2] Menzel, "Recollections," 8.

[3] Ciszek, *With God in Russia*, 75–76.

[4] Manon Jeanne de la Platière Roland, *Mémoires de Madame Roland Ecrits durant Sa Captivité*, ed. M. P. Faugère (Paris: Librairie de La Hachette et Cie, 1804), 1:212–14.

regimented form of his earlier life had become a source of strength for him. After two years in the labor camp, he says, "I have become well acclimated to my new way of life. . . . Throughout my life, almost without interruption, there was one kind of regimen or another: For eleven years in middle school, I constantly heard the bell. . . . For five years in the seminary, I not only studied philosophy and theology, but observed external discipline of heart and conscience." Then, he continues, came two decades of parish work, "during which I also had to be exactly on time at the altar, in the pulpit or in the confessional. The bell of life summoned me over and over again"—that is, a bell that he came to know both in the seminary and later, unexpectedly, in a Soviet labor camp.

With such a background, he was able to think of the work camp's bell in Siberia, which summoned him "to work, to rest, to lie down and get up," as being "like the voice of the Lord: I go where he summons me and in my heart I am at peace because I know that the Lord is always with me." Every day, therefore, he was able to "offer God my incarceration, my longing for my dear ones, exhaustion, physical infirmities when they occur."[5]

James Thornton in Shanghai tried to establish a daily schedule "to hasten, be it ever so little, the monotonous oppression of slow-moving time." He says in his unpublished essay, "The New Proletarian Man": "I scheduled my day, reciting so many poems after breakfast, and so many after supper at 4:30. . . . Then I'd hold imaginary conversations with my relatives and friends. Almost every day I made a speech or two before both houses of Congress, giving them chapter and verse of what communism was all about."[6]

Much more meticulous was the schedule outlined by Léon Ducoudray, whose incarceration ended with his violent death at the hands of a Parisian mob. In an 1871 letter written from the Mazas prison, he describes in detail what he calls his little daily regimen: 5 A.M., rise, wash, and clean cell; 6 A.M., prayer; 8 A.M., matins and lauds; 8:45 A.M., rosary; 9 A.M., breakfast and office of the Virgin Mary; 10 A.M., spiritual sharing in the Mass celebrated at this hour in his

---

[5] *Chronicle of the Catholic Church in Lithuania*, no. 68, March 19, 1987; trans. Rev. Casimir Pugevicius (Lithuanian Catholic Religious Aid, 351 Highland Blvd., Brooklyn, N.Y. 11207), 26–27.

[6] Thornton, "The New Proletarian Man," 15.

community; 11:45 A.M. *examen;* noon, second rosary; and so on through the day until evening litanies before bed.[7]

One especially notable example of the ability to establish a daily order in painful circumstances involves Carlo Spinola. In his cage-like prison with two dozen others in seventeenth-century Japan, amid intolerable living conditions, he was nevertheless able to create a prayer-based order that was a key to the group's psychological survival. At his recommendation, the priests with him took turns assuming the role of superior for a week each and leading the rest in various spiritual exercises.

In addition to reciting the rosary together, "they spent time in holy discourse and other prayers. . . . Before supper they recited matins and the office of the Virgin." Then at bedtime, they spent a quarter of an hour making an Ignatian examination of conscience. Finally—and perhaps incomprehensibly to the modern mind, given the extent of their deprivations and their deplorable living conditions—they took the discipline, flagellating themselves as an act of penance. Spinola mentions the self-flagellation in a letter, dated February 18, 1620, to the superior general of the Society, Mutio Vitelleschi, adding that they administered it "every day except feast days."[8] This severe form of daily penance was part of their religious life prior to their imprisonment and therefore served as a bridge to the rhythms of life to which they had long been accustomed and which they now tried to replicate to help maintain their mental balance.

Although the circumstances of his incarceration were less harsh and penances of this kind had become rare, Ján Korec, too, following his arrest in Czechoslovakia in 1960, quickly established an order for the day, a day "subdivided into prayer, meditation, and the Holy Mass." The Mass was the dry Mass, the prayers of which he had long since come to know by heart: "I recited the Holy Mass every morning, but how exhausting it was to habituate myself to such an intense prayer! Luckily, I knew it all by heart . . . [including] the epistle of St. Paul and the gospel . . . 'You are the light of light—You are the salt of the earth and the light of the world.' "[9] Afterwards, he spent an hour or more walking in his cell, reciting the rosary and reading the few books at his disposal.

---

[7] Ponlevoy, *Actes de la Captivité,* 5th ed., 65–66.

[8] Spinola, *Vita del P. Carlo Spinola,* 149.

[9] Korec, *La Notte dei Barberi,* 117.

Besides prayer, Korec used his memory in other ways as well. "I began to repeat to myself a little history . . . [and] to go over in my memory various concepts of natural science, especially biology, which I had once studied. Then I turned to philosophy, and had dialogues with myself about it." In addition to these mental activities, he reviewed theology lessons in his mind, "and thus I fill the time day after day." Writing in his autobiography, he declares that singing to himself was also a help. "I set aside at least a half hour a day to singing, and thus I succeeded in going over many . . . sacred songs"— hymns like "We Welcome the Guest." He adds that he had to sing the songs silently in order not to be heard by the guards. Especially in the early days of his incarceration, mingling the sacred songs with his meditations "calmed my nerves," and he even "sang some popular songs to myself, for fifteen or twenty minutes a day. And thus I was able to pass the time for an entire day."[10]

Whether the songs were of the sacred variety or not, these "mental gymnastics," as he called them (one is reminded of how John Havas reviewed his knowledge of Chinese shorthand), were beneficial for John Clifford. While in his Shanghai prison, Clifford says in his autobiography, *In the Presence of My Enemies:* "I reread all my favorite books in my mind and struggled again with canon law. Through the long afternoons I went back through the principles of dialectical materialism, which I had studied years before in college." Even football memories were a help: "Quarter by quarter I replayed the twenty-game schedule of our star high school football team when, for two years, no opponent scored on us." He also mentally reviewed his high school and college debates, a period during which, "as a rebuttal specialist, I had acquired a reputation for backing any opponent into a corner."[11]

Similarly, Dominic Tang was aware of the need to have his own daily program: "Besides following the prison regulations and time-table, I also set my own time-table," he says in *How Inscrutable His Ways!* It began as follows: "Every morning, after rising, I recited the prayer of the Apostleship of Prayer, offering the day to God. Then I would say the 'Veni Creator' (Come, Creator Spirit) because every day there were many events which needed the light of the Holy Spirit. Then I would do half an hour of meditation." He particularly

---

[10] Ibid., 117.

[11] Clifford, *In the Presence of My Enemies*, 87–88.

liked the meditation on the passion of Jesus, and though he does not say so, this preference may well have stemmed from his living out a passion of his own in his solitary confinement in China. Each day, moreover, "whether I was brought for questioning or not," he recited the full fifteen decades of the rosary, with an additional five, "asking our Lady to protect our diocese of Canton."

Like Ján Korec, Tang found singing to be a help in the ordering of his prison life in China. "Besides my prayer and meditation, every day I sang some hymns in a soft voice: 'Jesus, I love you; Jesus, I die for you; Jesus, I belong to you. Whether alive or dead, I am for Jesus!' " He tells of learning this song to Jesus from a Protestant prisoner who shared his cell. One is reminded of the Protestant who stood watch at Dachau while Paul Beschet and his young companions said the Midnight Mass prayers in the concentration camp shower room with its corpses of prisoners nearby. Barriers caused by differences in religious traditions could quickly disappear under the pressures of incarceration. But there were other songs too: "At night, before retiring, I sang 'Good night, Holy Mary, my merciful Mother' " as well as Christmas carols—"Adeste Fideles" and "Silent Night," and similar hymns that he could call to mind. Together, "those short hymns gave me great spiritual strength"—an observation reminiscent of St. Augustine's remark that the person who sings sacred songs, like the psalms, prays twice.

Tang's day had other specific divisions as well. "At midday I made a short examination of conscience, and before retiring at night, I made another examination and an act of contrition and said: 'Jesus, Mary and Joseph, I give you my heart and soul. . . . Assist me in my last agony. . . . May I breathe forth my soul in peace with you!' " In view of the uncertainty of his own fate from month to month and year to year, the references to death in this prayer must have taken on a significance that they might otherwise not have had. Once a week, either on Friday or Sunday, "besides saying my usual prayers, I made the way of the Cross . . . [and] once a year I did my eight days' retreat. . . . Even in difficult times, I always made my retreat." Thus, week by week and year by year, "[e]very day I prayed, meditated and sang hymns, so that I had no free time."[12]

In addition to Dachau's regimen, John Lenz also set up a schedule,

---

[12] Tang, *How Inscrutable His Ways!*, 124–27.

but his was broad and philosophical rather than particularized. "I, too, did my best to make good use of my time. But not for the S.S.," he notes in *Christ in Dachau*. "I once set down my fundamental principles for daily life in the camp. Heaven knows what would have happened to me if the S.S. guards had found this paper." The paper served as a kind of manifesto for the incarcerated clerics, citing their duties and obligations from a clerical perspective:

As priests our life in the camp should be governed by the following:

1. Prayer and development of the spiritual life
2. Intellectual study—as far as this is possible
3. Work in the camp in the service of fellow-prisoners
4. Work in the camp which furthers respect and honour for the priesthood (e.g., good example)
5. Physical exercise in the interests of health
6. It is wrong to undertake more work in the camp than is demanded by the reasons above.
7. It is wrong, especially for priests, to undertake more work than is necessary and so neglect our spiritual life, intellectual study or health.

Dachau Concentration Camp, May, 1944

Given the brutal physical demands of their labors, one can see why the last two points of the document—in which Lenz in effect states that the work of priests should be limited—might well have enraged the camp authorities and brought down upon him severe punishment.[13]

Centuries earlier in Elizabethan England, Thomas Pounde also maintained a daily schedule of sorts. His biographer in *The Records of the English Province* describes it thus: "Prayer, the study of the holy Fathers, writing controversial treatises . . . in defense of the Catholic faith and its proofs, treating of the affairs of the soul with fellow-Catholics whom he might have in prison; these were his methods of spending the greater part of the night and the whole of each day."[14] Like Tang, Pounde was held three decades in prison, and, again like Tang, he steadfastly resisted the temptation to regain his freedom by abjuring his faith.

---

[13] Lenz, *Christ in Dachau*, 107.
[14] Foley, *Records of the English Province*, 3:610.

While under conditions that were less physically threatening, Daniel Berrigan, too, sought a sense of order in his noisy and chaotic surroundings at the federal prison in Danbury: "One resolves in the midst of this to continue his diet of prayer, reflection and reading."[15] The word *resolves* is a key to understanding the tenacity with which incarcerated Jesuits have tried to root themselves in a self-created daily order solid enough to withstand the destructive pressures surrounding them.

The much younger peace activist, John Dear, incarcerated in the jail in Lumberton, North Carolina, in late 1993 and early 1994, had his own schedule, rising at 5 A.M. to pray. Then, after breakfast he "checked in" with his two cellmates—Philip Berrigan (Daniel's brother) and another activist, Bruce Friedrich. Later came several hours of Bible study among themselves, followed by a dry Mass. In the afternoon there was letter writing; in the evening, in-cell walking (they were never allowed outdoors into the yard for exercise) and reading.[16] Throughout the history of the Society of Jesus, then, maintaining a sense of daily order based on early training and revived through self-established prayer, study, reading, and other activities— even the singing of hymns to oneself—has served as a sustaining force in the lives of many incarcerated Jesuits.

---

[15] Berrigan, *Lights On In The House Of The Dead*, 129.
[16] Dear, letter to author, January 14, 1994.

ELEVEN

Work

AS JOHN LENZ'S DACHAU MANIFESTO makes clear, priests and other religious in German concentration camps performed heavy labor; often it was so strenuous that, given the prisoners' inadequate food and rest, it could lead to death. But whether light or heavy, enforced labor has frequently been a part of the lives of incarcerated Jesuits in countries around the world. For American Jesuits serving time for acts of civil disobedience, the demands of the tasks have generally been minimal and seldom involved more than a few hours a day. Daniel Berrigan was assigned to the dental clinic. While at Sandstone, another federal facility, Joseph Mulligan performed janitorial duties in the prison kitchen. Despite his advanced age Francis Hagerty worked on the prison farm from noon to 4 P.M., gathering, washing, and stacking eggs while serving time for his abortion protests in Massachusetts.

But for Jesuits in other countries, obligatory labor has been far more physically burdensome and often devastating in its toll on body and mind. Even when the forced labor was onerous, however, some have been able to see it in a positive light because they believed it represented part of God's plan for them. This attitude is strikingly expressed in *He Leadeth Me,* in which Walter Ciszek says of his tasks at his Siberian labor camp: "I did each job as best I could. I worked to the limit of my strength each day and did as much as my health and endurance under the circumstances made possible. Why? Because I saw this work as the will of God for me." Viewing his work as God's will therefore led him to consider it as "not a punishment, but a way of working out my salvation in fear and trembling." In the same passage Ciszek asserts that his heavy labor "was ennobling, for it came from the hand of God himself."

Ciszek's fellow prisoners found his outlook on work bizarre and challenged him about it. "They could understand a man working to overfulfill a quota if it meant more food, but not out of a sense of pride or accomplishment . . . [and] they asked me how I could possibly cooperate with the wishes of the government, why I always did my best instead of sabotaging the work, how I could help to build a new society for the communists, who rejected God and despised everything I stood for." Perhaps the hardest questions of all to answer were those of Christian prisoners, who "even asked me if it were not sinful to cooperate with . . . communism."

Ciszek, however, was not swayed. For him, "all work, any work, has a value in itself. It has a value insofar as it partakes in the creative act of God."[1] The fact that he was able to develop skills in his years in Siberia and could see—in the factories he helped to build—uses that might benefit human beings in general, served to affirm his human dignity. Tzvetan Todorov discusses this theme of the relationship between work and the preservation of dignity in his book on World War II concentration camps, *Facing the Extreme*. Todorov relates the ability to do meaningful work while incarcerated to the maintenance of self-respect, an important aspect of the ability to survive: "Using one's skill or expertise to the best of one's ability can enable one to preserve a measure of self-respect."[2] Being able to find satisfaction in the use of their skills and expertise is what helped Ciszek and others to survive.

Nevertheless, unquestioning zeal in the performance of even "useful" tasks could bring self-destructive results. In *Libre à Buchenwald*, Jean Moussé tells of Père Louis de Jabrun, a French Jesuit from Toulouse in his sixties, whose zealous attention to the forced labor to which he was assigned finally cost him his life. He and Moussé were in the same work detail; their task was to cut wood. Aware of his own half-starved condition and consequent physical weakness, Moussé avoided as much of this heavy work as possible, in marked contrast to de Jabrun "who sawed logs conscientiously all day long while, for my part, I lost no occasion to do little and . . . worked at a snail's pace." Watching the elderly man's zeal, Moussé grew concerned and told him "that he was not obliged to wear himself out." The frail de Jabrun, however, "replied that sawing wood was useful for heating the barracks and consequently that nothing authorized him . . . to sabotage the work."

---

[1] Ciszek, *He Leadeth Me*, 117–20.

[2] Tzvetan Todorov, *Facing the Extreme. Moral Life in the Concentration Camps*. Trans. Arthur Danner and Abigail Pollack (New York: Henry Holt and Co., 1996), 66–67.

Moussé's gentle admonition had no effect, and he notes that for de Jabrun, attention to work was not only a question of providing wood to heat the barracks but also a matter of religious obedience. In his view, de Jabrun "had made a vow of obedience and the spirit of it led him to obey all orders that were not unjust." Because of his commitment to a type of labor that overtaxed his constitution, he fell ill and was taken to the camp hospital, where he died, "savagely killed around Christmas time by a capo who hated priests."[3]

Rupert Mayer was not required to do hard labor because of his disability; he had lost a leg in World War I. Still, like Ciszek and de Jabrun, he had the same desire to do his tasks well. However, if Mayer's attitude was less extreme than de Jabrun's, who viewed working diligently as a way of responding to the vow of obedience, he still exhibited similar overtones. Mayer's job was to paste together small paper bags, and he was intent on learning to do it with a certain degree of perfection:

> A guard, together with a prisoner who carried the material, came to my cell and showed me my work. The bags were small pharmacist bags. The guard showed me how to make the folds, but at such a rapid tempo that I could see absolutely nothing of what he was doing. I studied and experimented with a model and then tried to do it as well as I could. The next day he looked over my work and expressed extreme dissatisfaction with it. He said I was the most unskillful person he had met in his life.

Chagrined, Mayer asked the guard to show him the process at a slower pace, which he did. "But when I asked him if I might then try it while he was still there . . . he just turned on his heel and walked out." Mayer kept on as best he could, but the next day the guard "said that I just had no desire to work." At this point, stung that he should be considered a malingerer, Mayer "asked to see the warden to lodge a complaint, because I felt that as a priest I could not let such a reproach go by, namely, that I was guilty of neglecting my duty."

Always respected because, as a former chaplain in the German army, he had been decorated for valor in action during World War I, Mayer did in fact receive a hearing from the warden. Afterward, the

---

[3] Moussé, *Libre à Buchenwald*, 117–18.

contemptuous guard did not reappear. Instead, the head of the paper-working department himself explained the procedure, after which Mayer mastered the method and "spent every minute at the work." But the phrase, "guilty of neglecting my duty," helps to explain how this same sense—in a less balanced person under more rigorous conditions—could lead an overly conscientious person like de Jabrun to illness and, indirectly, to death.[4]

Despite the onerous conditions of their captivity, some Jesuits in forced labor situations responded with humor to accusations that the quality or quantity of their output was unsatisfactory. In Communist China, for instance, Francis Xavier Chu, whose three decades of incarceration ended only with his death, was often reprimanded for the alleged slowness with which he performed his assigned tasks as he neared old age. Replying to this criticism on one occasion, he said, "I am not slow—my pace is normal. It's just that the others are too quick!"[5]

Frequently concentration camp inmates were given tasks of a purely make-work variety deliberately designed to cause discouragement. In *Facing the Extreme*, Todorov tells of prisoners "carrying sand back and forth and digging a hole and filling it up again," a type of forced work that is "impossible to do . . . well," and therefore one through which it is "impossible to keep one's self-respect."[6] As noted below, the work of Dominic Tang and Jan Korec was not quite as meaningless, but it was not the kind that could provide any satisfaction whatsoever.

Tang's job was not unlike Mayer's assignment of assembling paper bags, but he was under constant pressure to meet a daily quota and had no sympathetic warden to turn to. "We had to paste together cardboard boxes in the cell. . . . My companion and I had to paste over ten dozen daily. Thus, apart from the time for interrogation and meals, we had to spend all our time pasting boxes. If the work was not well done, we had to re-paste them." Despite the demands of the heavy quota, there was no increase in the meager food rations, a diet of rice and sweet potatoes that left him with "great pangs of hunger and sometimes we would shiver all over with hunger and would

---

[4] Koerbling, *Rupert Mayer*, 158–59.
[5] Carmelite sister of Macao, *If the Grain of Wheat Dies*.
[6] Todorov, *Facing the Extreme*, 66–67.

break out into cold perspiration."⁷ Such a diet led to beriberi, but that did not lessen the quota to be filled and the food did not improve in either quality or quantity.

During his years of incarceration in Czechoslovakia, Ján Korec had several jobs. With the first, there was, as in Tang's case, a quota that was almost impossible to meet:

> My task consisted of threading pearls together to make necklaces, six and a half dozen a day. It was too much for me, and not only for me. We sat at a table, two or three of us in each cell, using big needles and heavy thread. It had to be done in the same order halfway on the thread, and then as in a mirror, in the opposite order from the other end. Eighty pieces a day! Sometimes the thread broke; then we had to pick up the pearls from underneath the beds.⁸

Although Korec's work was not physically exhausting, it involved both tedium and frustration in the struggle to fulfill the almost impossible daily quota.

Much more demanding was his later work assignment at the Valdice prison. Korec and other prisoners were herded outside to pick beets in fields a half-hour's walk away. Guards with machine guns and attack dogs surrounded them while they worked to ensure that they remained together as a group. "We worked like slaves, always under surveillance." The only positive aspect of these grueling work sessions occurred when they were permitted to accept food offered by civilians who occasionally approached them.⁹

After Korec was transferred from the prison to a factory that made glass products, his work became even more difficult. His task was to grind pieces of glass for automobile headlights. He had to hold a piece of glass in each hand and press them simultaneously against a rotating stone, which was pulled by a belt cooled by water. "As I worked, the blood literally trickled from my fingertips, because they were always brushing against the grinding stone which took the skin off, especially the index finger and the thumb." In addition, the water from the belt inflamed his fingers. "At night, adjusting the rough material of my blanket made my fingers sting, and I would often be awakened by the pain." Those who did not do the work satisfactorily

⁷ Tang, *How Inscrutable His Ways!*, 103.

⁸ Korec, *La Notte dei Barberi*, 173–74.

⁹ Ibid., 205.

were put in underground cells for ten days and given food only every three days. Korec summed up the brutality of such treatment with the dry observation, "It isn't necessary to whip or burn a man to torture him efficiently."[10]

At Dachau—the Nazi camp with the greatest number of Jesuits—the work was so heavy that it at times led to the death of prisoners from exposure or exhaustion, in a manner reminiscent of de Jabrun's sawing logs with excessive diligence. Otto Pies, the Jesuit who was the spiritual father for Jesuits in Dachau, comments in *The Victory of Father Karl* that the barracks in block 26 housed almost 2,000 priests and 60 Protestant ministers. The largest group of priests were Polish, and among them, every second or third died. All in all, about a thousand clergymen perished at Dachau. They were from twenty-five nations and represented forty religious orders, "among which the Jesuits stood highest with 95 prisoners."[11] In his own reflection on the Dachau ordeal, Léo de Coninck notes that although—again through an agreement between the Reich and the Holy See—religious at Dachau were technically exempt from heavy labor during the early years of the war, the reality was quite different.

He writes that in the winter, for instance, "the terrible job of removing snow from the camp was imposed upon them. All day long we were out shifting snow, piling it on upturned tables on long wagons and tipping it into a river at the edge of the camp." He adds that the work itself was only part of the misery the prisoners suffered: "The work, besides being hard and exhausting, was made more intolerable by being placed under the charge of *capos*—poor, degenerate brutes, worse than the S.S. and the cause of the death of many unfortunate people"[12]—again, like the capo who caused de Jabrun's death in the camp hospital.

At other seasons, "most of the priests were formed into gangs to work in what was called the 'plantation.' Medicinal plants and expensive flowers were grown there" for the financial benefit of highly placed officials of the Nazi party. Most of the priests who died at Dachau worked on the plantation. One can understand why, upon reading de Coninck's description of the conditions under which they

---

[10] Ibid., 215–16.

[11] Pies, *The Victory of Father Karl*, 113.

[12] De Coninck. "The Priests of Dachau," 117.

were forced to work: "Just to walk there was exhausting enough in their famished condition, and they had to work like slaves from dawn to dusk." Even the end of the day brought no relief: "They might return soaking and muddy, but there was no way of drying their thin working clothes—they had to put them on again, wet, the next day."

The priests were also assigned to land clearance details. "I was in one of these," he says, continuing: "I have seen unhappy men die in the fields, worn out by privation and maltreatment. And could I ever forget that poor priest lying in tortured agony on a pile of hay while a young S.S. amused himself by setting his dog on him?" Cruelty of this kind could reach a zenith of malevolence aimed specifically at priests: "Never before Dachau had I seen real hatred: eyes aflame with wickedness, mouths twisted in anger at the mere sight of a priest. To strike, wound or even a kill a priest seemed, with some of these men, a necessity of instinct." As another example, de Coninck cites an incident in which a Carmelite, who had been a professor at the University of Nymwegen, had been brutalized so sadistically by the capo of his block that he "survived only two months under the beatings this brute inflicted on him at every opportunity."[13]

One day John Lenz, too, came close to death because of a capo. At the gravel pit to which he was assigned, the capo yelled: "Hey, you priest, come here!" The capo filled an enormous wheelbarrow with gravel and ordered Lenz to push it to the dumping site. Great blisters began to appear on the palms of his hands, but the capo drove him on, kicking him from behind all the while. To make matters even worse, "he forced me to run up the gravel hill with a full load and would then push me over the side at the steepest point so that I fell and rolled down some 18′ together with my load of gravel. He did this several times."

His strength ebbing, Lenz cried out that he was working as hard as he could, but the capo simply looked at him "with his terrible eyes" and said, "Don't you realize, you miserable priest, that it's your turn to die like a dog today?" Using the last reserves of his strength to keep going, Lenz comments, "Never before was the image of Christ crucified so alive in my soul. Never before was His Passion so real to me as in that moment." But finally, because it was a Sunday, the

---

[13] Ibid., 117–18.

whistle blew for work to stop at five o'clock. "I had been saved," he writes, adding, "By six o'clock it would have been too late."[14]

The mere fact of being a priest was often enough to incite the SS guards to deeper levels of brutality. From his own vantage point within the walls of Dachau, Otto Pies observes that "the priests were free game for the SS; they were baited, beaten, literally whipped to death and assigned to the most backbreaking work details."[15] Lenz's experience at the gravel pit provides a concrete example of how the work details could be made even more horrific by the SS or the capos under them.

One Jesuit who asked to remain anonymous told the author that he arrived as a scholastic at Dachau and was ordered to perform what to him was especially painful labor: building another crematorium. He and others were first trained as bricklayers for construction work of various kinds. Fortunately, the crematorium assignment came late in the war, and because of a shortage of fuel, it was never put into use after its completion. The young Jesuit was thus spared the sight of this instrument of mass death, which he had been forced to help create, belching forth flames to destroy the corpses of prisoners.

Especially grueling was the work of Giacomo Gardin, whose treatment in a forced labor camp in Albania resembled that meted out to Jesuits in German concentration camps two decades earlier. An Italian, Gardin was a professor at Saint Xavier College and a spiritual counselor at the Pontifical Seminary, both in Shkodra. His arrest occurred on June 21, 1945, the feast of St. Aloysius, after he had spoken to a group of young workers and students who belonged to the Youth Association of Catholic Action. In his diary, he observes that his reflections on St. Aloysius—a patron saint of youth—gave him "the opportunity to set meditations about the spiritual life and the patrimony of the Christian man, in direct confrontation with the intellectual and spiritual degradation of the Marxist man." Since he had already been under observation by Communist agents, state security officers came to make their arrest that very night.[16]

After two years in the prison in Shkodra, Gardin was transported to the swamps around Lake Maliq in southern Albania. There, he

---

[14] Lenz, *Christ in Dachau*, 40–41.
[15] Pies, *The Victory of Fr. Karl*, 102.
[16] Sinishta, *The Fulfilled Promise*, 141–42.

says in his diary, "all day we are in water up to our knees, working to open the channel for irrigation." He and the other prisoners were allowed only five or six hours of sleep in the barracks, which were "devoid of beds or sanitary facilities." Six months later, in November, when the group was taken back to the prison for the winter, he said, "We have left more than one comrade there in the swamps . . . with a message in their dying eyes"—a message, it would appear, that the same fate might eventually be theirs.[17]

The following spring he was sent back to the swamps. This back-and-forth rhythm between prison and swamp continued for several years. So difficult was the work in the marshes that the return to the prison each winter came as a welcome respite; and no wonder, for Gardin had developed such severe arthritis from the swamp work that at times he could stand only with difficulty. In the book he later wrote as an expansion of his diary, he describes what it was like to work on the irrigation canals: "The waters would invade finished sectors, filling them with stagnant sewage that had to be manually pushed back to the river bed, and the shovellers often had to work in waist-high mud." In the hot summer weather, mosquito infestation meant that "the horrifying job . . . added more victims to the already high malaria death toll."[18]

Gardin was part of a special squad made up of clergy. Ironically, he writes in his diary, on one day in May, 1948, his squad worked so well that it was awarded a prize—a red flag.[19] The irony of awarding a red communist flag to one who had preached against communism must surely have struck him; but the priests' determination to work zealously again reflects a background of religious training in which work was considered a matter of obedience, a duty to be fulfilled, no matter what the circumstances. Ciszek, de Jabrun, and Mayer are three of the most extreme examples of this attitude, but they were certainly not the only ones.

Gardin and his companions worked effectively together for another reason as well, namely, as fellow priest-prisoners they had communal support. Twenty-nine priests were in Gardin's group, and "we would program our work carefully so that we often did more than required

---

[17] Ibid., 143.

[18] Gardin, *Banishing God in Albania*, 87.

[19] Sinishta, *The Fulfilled Promise*, 144.

and in less time."[20] Even the commander, who disliked them because of what they represented, and who frequently assigned them the most difficult tasks, begrudgingly commended them publicly in front of the rest of the workers.

Gardin and his clergy companions had an even more immediate reason to work diligently—not to meet the required quota led to denial of food as punishment: "If we haven't met the work quota by nightfall, we get no food (soup or bread), and we usually pass the night in a corner of the campground." Since they were already in a debilitated condition, death through hunger was as frequent as death from malaria: "Those whose food ration was denied the night before . . . fall down on the way to work. They die gradually, as they walk to work from the camp."[21]

Early in 1953, Gardin was sent to work in a brick factory. The high temperatures and air filled with dust and ashes contrasted sharply with the wet work in the swamps, though it was equally enervating: "The rough hot bricks had to be touched by hand. We would walk out of there exhausted, with sweat dripping from our bodies, dust in our mouths and noses, and our hands stripped of flesh. What a torment!"[22] As what might be considered a "dark grace," however, the extreme heat of the factory almost cured him of the arthritis he had contracted in the marshes. He was quick to attribute this unexpected turn of events to God's help: "How could I not consider this a fatherly intervention of Providence?"

The French scholastic Paul Beschet was assigned to a similar setting in his forced labor at Zwickau, in a factory that manufactured glass cylinders for thermos bottles. "We generally worked twelve hours a day, in an atmosphere that was both tropical and pestilential, with insufficient food. Without any respite, armed with a shovel, we had to carry the incandescent glass cylinders from the bellows to the oven."[23] He estimated that in the course of a single day he walked sixteen kilometers between the oven and the bellows.

Sigitas Tamkevičius, who was shipped as a prisoner to Siberia, tells of his own factory work in a 1988 letter printed in the *Chronicle of the Catholic Church in Lithuania*. "Here, they make ice-hockey

---

[20] Gardin, *Banishing God in Albania*, 87.
[21] Sinishta, *The Fulfilled Promise*, 145.
[22] Ibid., 122.
[23] Beschet, *Mission en Thuringe*, 147.

sticks, and I plane the handles." Along with the constant noise, he was exposed to dust. "My eyes, ears and lungs are full [of it]," he writes, in words reminiscent of Gardin's description of the dust-filled brick factory. Later Tamkevičius observes that in another camp he had worked at a loom, where dust had also been a problem. Nevertheless, he comments, "I did not forget to pray [and] I did not forget to laugh." And he is able to say: "For everything I am grateful to God. He grants me enough of everything."[24]

In his short memoir, Tamkevičius's fellow Lithuanian, Gerardas Dunda, describes what his work entailed at a Russian coal mining camp at Inta. (Of the 7,000 prisoners, 700 were Lithuanians, three of whom, in addition to Dunda, were priests.) After initially being assigned to help construct new quarters for the prisoners, Dunda had to go down into the mines themselves: "They 'invited' us to descend to a 120-meter depth. The coal beds shone in the darkness, and we had to blast them with dynamite and load the coal into wagons. The wagons were pulled to a lift and . . . transferred to the surface. There the coal was poured out into a permanently moving conveyor . . . [from which] stones were picked from the coal."

The work had one significant benefit for the prisoners, which was unknown to the authorities. The citizen miners who transferred the coal onto railway wagons were willing to accept letters from the prisoners, "put them into cloth bags, attach them to the wagon walls and cover them with coal." The workers who eventually unloaded the coal at the other end sent the letters on to their destinations. In return for a favor that involved such distinct risks, prisoners like Dunda would help the citizen miners with the difficult job of blasting the coal inside the mines.[25] Thanks to this mutually beneficial arrangement, Dunda observes that "I too . . . have sent many letters to my loved ones." Officially, he and the others were allowed to send only two letters a year; the ability to send more would thus have made a significant difference in maintaining family ties and morale.

---

[24] *Chronicle of the Catholic Church in Lithuania,* no. 79, October 15, 1988, 30.

[25] Dunda, memoir, 4–5. Dunda notes that for a time in the labor camp in Russia, he had a clerical job and worked at the same desk as Alexander Solzhenitsyn, of whom he says: "I remember how he would joke. 'I'll describe the USSR to you. It is "strana ciudes"—land of miracles—[because] everyone steals, from the highest official to the lowest collective farmer, and the country does not go bankrupt, everything goes on.' "

Jesuits interned at Los Baños in the Philippines, many of whom were American scholastics caught there at the outbreak of the war, did not perform slave labor in the same sense. Indeed, shortly after the war several of them jointly wrote a long article in the *Woodstock Letters*. The scholastic who wrote the section on work observed with wry amusement: "Our lot was not as bad as that assigned to prisoners of the Japanese in the comic strips. This is always a bitter disappointment to little boys, but," he adds, "the shameful truth must be told: we never pulled a plow through the muck of a rice field while the Japanese stalked alongside us, beating us with bull whips."[26]

What they did have to do was to operate their own area of the camp with little food and few supplies. "We cut wood, carried it, worked the fires, boiled the rice, tilled a garden, fought disease, nursed the sick, buried the dead . . . everybody had a job."[27] As the Japanese reduced food rations toward the end of the war, more deaths occurred among the camp's mixed population of religious and lay prisoners, men and women of all ages. The Jesuits built the coffins and opened the graves. "You will find this burial crew working even in the middle of the night," the same scholastic observes. "Men are dying two a day now and they cannot keep ahead of them."[28]

Philippine Jesuits were treated more harshly than the American internees. Writing in the same article, another American scholastic said with admiration: "During two full years of Japanese occupation, they [the Philippine scholastics] had lived with us starving, singing, working, studying. The Japanese had slapped them, questioned them, locked them up and tortured them."[29] One third-year Philippine theologian was "conscripted into a labor battalion by the Japanese [and] died of exhaustion." Two other Philippine scholastics, "trying to protect the sacred vessels and vestments in a church, were killed and their bodies burned." And "a fourth year [Philippine] theologian was given the infamous water cure three times . . . an ancient torture." What led to this special hostility to the Philippine Jesuit scholastics? They could have transferred to one of the Spanish seminaries that had remained opened and thereby would have been pro-

---

[26] "Philippine Jesuits under the Japanese," *Woodstock Letters* 74(3) (October 1945):217.

[27] Ibid., 217.

[28] Ibid., 219.

[29] Ibid., 205.

tected by Spanish neutrality. Instead, loyalty to their fellow Jesuits led them to remain with the Americans—and therefore they were considered to be consorting with the American enemy.

Two decades later, George Wong completed the last long segment of his sentence in a labor camp northwest of Shanghai that focused on farming. (Chinese labor camps performed three types of work: farming, factory work, and construction work.) Because of poor health, Wong was initially assigned to relatively light labor in the vegetable gardens. The day's regimen included two hours of obligatory indoctrination, along with lectures and required reading of the *People's Daily*. In a bizarre contrast to those Jesuits who found the singing of sacred and popular songs helpful in establishing a daily order for themselves, every morning before work Wong was obliged "to sing a song to Chairman Mao—almost like the Communist version of morning prayer." He added that during the winter months, when outdoor work was more limited, the length of the indoctrination sessions doubled from two to four hours. One prisoner was made to read aloud; an obligatory discussion of the material read followed.

"After two years," Wong said, "they decided that my brain hadn't been sufficiently 'washed,' because I continued to insist that religion was above politics. So I was punished by being transferred to the rice paddies." Physically unable to plant the rice as fast as his overseers wished, he was instead assigned to pull cords in straight lines across the paddies for others to use as guides in the planting. "But it was difficult just the same, because I had to work in ankle deep water and leeches would cling to my flesh—so deeply imbedded that I had to break the leeches into pieces to pull them off." The leeches led to a skin infection that left permanent scars.[30]

At the end of sixteen years—in 1976—he was allowed his first annual home leave. On this occasion, he surreptitiously brought back a New Testament, even though spiritual books were still forbidden. "One night I was reading it with a flashlight under my mosquito net in the dormitory. A guard who saw me demanded to know what it was, and I told him it was a book of Lenin's writings, but he found out and so I got a public scolding."[31] Finally, his total of twenty-seven

---

[30] During our interview of May 29, 1995 at America House in New York City, Wong pulled down his socks to show me the scars on his ankles.

[31] Ibid.

years of prison and labor camps came to an end, and he was eventually able to leave China and come to the United States.

Much of Francis Xavier Ts'ai's confinement—thirty-five years, beginning in 1953—was also spent in Chinese labor camps, but of the factory kind. After his 1960 trial, he was sentenced to fifteen years of forced labor. When the sentence was up, though, he was obliged to remain for an indefinite period. Part of the time, he worked in a brick factory. However, "I was older than the other prisoners, and not strong enough for the heavy work with the bricks, and therefore they had me work with tiles, from 6 A.M. to 6 P.M."—a twelve-hour day. In contrast to Léo de Coninck's description of the contemptuous treatment often accorded priests by some of the other inmates of Dachau, Ts'ai was treated respectfully and was even given help with his tasks.

Although Ts'ai's contact with them was infrequent, three other Jesuits—Vincent Chu, Joseph Cheng, and Gabriel Cheng (not related to Joseph Cheng)—worked in the same brick factory. In our interview, Ts'ai said that one of them, Gabriel Cheng, did not want to leave when his sentence had been served because in order to leave he would have had to 'repent' of his crime.[32]

In some cases—such as with Gardin who found fraternal support in being with other priest-prisoners performing forced labor in the swamps of Albania—work has had certain compensations, although hardly those favored by the prison authorities. In most situations, however, obligatory work was simply an unmitigated evil, robbing famished and exhausted Jesuit prisoners of the little strength that remained to them. The wonder is that so many survived it at all.

---

[32] Interview with Francis Xavier Ts'ai, May 20, 1995.

TWELVE

Ministry

PRISON LABOR, whether burdensome or light, has frequently served as an avenue for ministering. Daniel Berrigan welcomed his job in the Danbury dental clinic because it allowed him access to the prison's medical wing. There, he was able to provide support, along with such pastoral assistance as getting messages out to prisoners' families. As he describes his situation in *Lights On In The House Of The Dead*, the lack of tight security between the two areas meant that "the impending door often swung wide, and with no guard in sight . . . I was [therefore] able, from time to time, to prowl the corridors of the hospital; even to enter the cell of this or that ill prisoner, greet him, offer him whatever help I could, and learn something of his condition. . . . This was a great consolation to me." The purpose of the visits was to "lighten the burden of one or another of the men; a simple exercise in the truth that 'God is love.' "[1]

In addition, he and his brother Philip were given permission to conduct classes on great books, such as *Gulliver's Travels* and several Greek tragedies, along with the writings of Gandhi. The study of Gandhi sometimes led to an opportunity to minister in yet another way, through promoting peace and nonviolence at the time of the Vietnam War when a number of the young men at Danbury were serving sentences there for opposition to the war: "Class tonight took a good turn. We got from Gandhi to a discussion by two of the young war resisters of their feeling about being in prison—torment, meaning, community."[2]

Berrigan also exercised a ministry of what might be called the informal hearing of confessions. Describing his conversation with a young drug offender, a former seminarian who would not have responded to a traditional confessional format, he observes, "He has seen everything, tried some of it . . . and lives to tell it to the priest—

---

[1] Berrigan, *Lights On In The House Of The Dead*, 13.
[2] Ibid., 156.

not in the old way of confessional, but in a newly found friendship, with an unspoiled spontaneity."[3]

Commenting on what his ministry in prison had meant to him in Ignatian terms, he said in the interview: "Phrases like 'deeds not words' from the Contemplation to Attain the Love of God in the *Exercises* are in our bloodstream, and so much are we contemplatives in action that we continue to take our ministry seriously even in abnormal circumstances." He added that ministering in these circumstances helps to reduce the sense of abnormality that is endemic in incarcerational settings.[4] His observation could be applicable to the experience of other imprisoned Jesuits as well.

At the federal facility in Minnesota during the same period, scholastic Joseph Mulligan ministered to fellow prisoners by offering basic catechism classes and Bible study sessions. Informal counseling was also part of his ministry. In an interview in New York on July 12, 1994, he spoke of a man who was serving a sentence on a tax fraud conviction. When he was turned down for parole, the man became despondent. "We often prayed together," Mulligan said. "The encounter made me realize how much we're thrown back on faith in God when a lot of other supports fall away, because it's then that fellowship with the Lord can grow."[5]

Francis Hagerty was not a peace activist; his focus on civil disobedience took the form of protests at abortion clinics. A sympathetic Catholic warden granted him permission to move about freely in his Massachusetts jail, doubtless because he was impressed by the elderly priest's willingness to go to jail for his belief in a Catholic cause. Besides celebrating an early Mass for a small group of inmates in the library, Hagerty visited the men in segregation, who were confined to their cells for twenty-three hours a day. Listening to their problems, he, like Berrigan, provided informal counseling and encouragement. He also made contact with their families and was even allowed to bring them small gifts of candy from the commissary.[6]

At roughly the same time in the early 1990s, John Dear was helping fellow prisoners at the Lumberton County jail in North Carolina.

---

[3] Ibid., 29.

[4] Interview with Daniel Berrigan, January 4, 1996. The full phrase from the *Exercises* (#230) is "Love ought to manifest itself in deed, not in words."

[5] Interview with Joseph E. Mulligan, July 12, 1994.

[6] Interview with Francis O. Hagerty, January 17, 1994.

"I have been asked by one prisoner for some counseling and then heard his long confession," he said in a letter. Within the first few weeks, he was also "asked to pray over a person who had just been brought in and was quite broken [and] there is a person across the hall . . . with whom we pass notes. I write prayers for him and encourage him." Moreover, he was spending "much time translating for and speaking in Spanish with two different inmates, one from Cuba, the other from Mexico, neither of whom could speak English. . . . I was able to explain what was happening to them, when they might get to court, etc." Apart from this specific act of ministry, which came about because he was the only person in the jail who spoke Spanish, he felt that his most useful ministry was simply "listening to the others"— most of whom were "poor, uneducated African Americans in jail on drug charges." Since many of them were unbalanced and violent, "this ministry of listening and being present is very challenging . . . [and] calls us to love and serve 'Christ in the distressing disguise of the poor,' as Mother Teresa says."[7] For many other Jesuits behind bars in countries around the world, the service of listening played a large part in what they were able to do for others.

In contrast to those imprisoned for civil disobedience in America who could minister with relative freedom, in other countries ministry could be carried out only in secrecy, under conditions that called for considerable ingenuity. Once it became known that Ján Korec was a priest, several young Czech prisoners began to seek him out while they worked together. "Some were interested in religious thought and the spiritual life, even to the point of wanting to know how to meditate." To help them, Korec wrote short passages from the gospels on cigarette packs, which they then memorized. "At times," he says, "the result was conversion and holy confession."[8]

Every new encounter taught Korec something that he had not previously realized. He speaks of one young man named Zdeno P. who came to him wanting to know what prayer was. "I told him what I knew in concise and simple language." Then, to provide a concrete example of prayer, Korec began to recite the Our Father. He had barely begun, however, when Zdeno took his hand and became visibly agitated. "Stop!" he said, moving away from the machine at which

---

[7] Letter to author from the Lumberton jail, January 14, 1993.
[8] Korec, *La Notte dei Barberi*, 240.

Korec was working. But within half an hour he came back and, after a silence, explained why he had become upset. Because he had had a very painful relationship with his father, the very word "Father" in the prayer was too much for him. After this incident, Korec reflected, "For a person who has an ugly remembrance of his father, how can the Our Father be recited in a heartfelt way?" He had no answer for Zdeno's dilemma.

Some of the young men were interested not only in religious questions but also in foreign languages. Korec accordingly tutored them in French, English, and other languages. "I always found time for them, and they were grateful." Korec was grateful as well, because contacts of this kind resulted in friendships that sooner or later led these youths who had been reared in atheistic settings to inquire about spirituality.[9]

While he was at the Valdice prison, Korec was also able to minister to fellow Jesuits. One was Martin Viskupic. During a period in 1951 when Korec was in an isolation cell, Viskupic was a corridor helper whose job was to bring meals to the men locked in their cells. "Once he told me he wanted to make the *Spiritual Exercises,* and asked me to prepare some meditations." Consequently, they made an arrangement whereby when Viskupic brought the meal each day, Korec would give him a meditation written on a little piece of paper that was hidden inside a matchbox. When Viskupic returned with the next meal, another meditation was placed in the matchbox.

There was an initial scare, however, that could easily have resulted in the punishment of both Jesuits. After giving Viskupic the first meditation, Korec was later surprised to see the warder under whom Viskupic worked come to his cell—a Slovak who had himself been a prisoner for many years, and who, fortunately, was friendly. He had found the matchbox containing the meditation and, correctly deducing its source, returned it. Korec realized with alarm that Viskupic had lost it. Two hours later, Viskupic came to the cell saying he had searched everywhere for it. "I told him what had happened, and he promised to be more careful the next time. For the whole of the following week, he made the exercises with the meditations I joyfully wrote out for him each day."[10] Korec's happiness at preparing the

---

[9] Ibid., 241.
[10] Ibid., 210–11.

meditations reflects the life-giving nature of ministry, no matter how "abnormal" the circumstances.

Walter Ciszek, too, had to be cautious. Discovery of his priestly work could have brought punishment and an end to his ministerial efforts in Siberia. But in contrast to the close confinement of Jesuits like Korec and Tang, the comparative freedom of movement within his Siberian labor camp allowed Ciszek to minister unobtrusively in the midst of the daily comings and goings of his fellow laborers.

For example, in *He Leadeth Me*, he provides a long description of his method of giving retreats based on the *Exercises*. Noting that he could take only one retreatant at a time, he continues, "Points for each of the meditations were given . . . at 6 A.M., before all the prisoners left for work." It was difficult to give retreats, however, because he needed half an hour to explain the points for meditation properly, and at that time "the whole camp was in turmoil. Prisoners poured out of the barracks, rushing in all directions . . . [and] the camp guards, too, ran about like madmen from barracks to barracks, watching the prisoners and yelling at strays to return to their barracks and get ready for work." Amid this confusion, he had to find a quiet spot to be alone with his exercitant. In the evening, it was easier to do so because the workday was over and the two could usually find an hour to be together.

For the most part, Ciszek gave his retreats to other priests. They lasted anywhere from three days to a week, and, whenever possible, he tried to persuade them to help him—and thus acted as a coordinator for their own ministry. "Sometimes there were as many as three of us engaged in giving the individual retreats, so the others could have a choice of spiritual directors." Ciszek himself focused on the key meditations of the *Exercises*, having as his basic objective to help prisoners increase their trust in God and "to strengthen again their resolve to see his will in the events of every day—even such days as we were experiencing."

The days in Siberia were especially difficult for priest-prisoners; as was the case in German concentration camps, they were singled out for harsher treatment than the other prisoners. Ciszek states, for instance, that the older priests, unaccustomed to the hard physical labor required of them, were frequently ill and in need of medical attention. "Yet even the limited medical care available in the camp clinics was often denied them . . . because they were priests." They also suffered from the deprivation of the external practices of religion to which they were accustomed. The Mass, for instance, had to be said sitting down or reclining, because "the prescribed external rituals would only have called attention to what we were doing and brought the guards upon us quickly."[11] For many, this prohibition against visible rituals created a sense of despondency that made the retreats even more important for sustaining morale.

Ciszek adapted to the absence of external forms with less difficulty. He might hear confessions while walking with the penitent in the evening, as if they were engaged in ordinary conversation. "If there were a lot of confessions or communions, I would try to have the men get up early . . . and go to the various points around the camp. I'd meet them there, and under the guise of a morning greeting, distribute Communion."[12] Suspicious officials sometimes questioned him and warned him not to engage in religious work, but he was never deterred.

Although his retreats were primarily for the benefit of the other priests, Ciszek ministered to unschooled lay prisoners as well. In one moving account, he describes a thief named Yevgeny who took a liking to him and taught him "many a trick for scrounging food"—a necessary survival tactic. Although baptized a Catholic, "he had a primitive idea of religion, mixed with any number of superstitions." Once Yevgeny asked Ciszek to bless a little cross, but he wore it primarily as a good luck charm. He blessed himself with the sign of the cross as he put it on, "but he also pulled out a knife and warned the crowd around him, 'If anyone laughs at this cross, he'll get this knife right in the belly.' "

At last, after many conversations, Ciszek "brought him back to the point where he finally made a confession and received Communion." Thereafter, although Yevgeny still resorted to violence to settle disputes with other prisoners, he went to confession and Communion with considerable regularity. As head of a work crew, Yevgeny one day reprimanded two young Lithuanians for loafing on the job. One of them then split his skull open with a sledge hammer—a commentary on camp life that showed brutality was not limited to the labor itself and the harshness of the guards. Ciszek describes himself as

---

[11] Ciszek, *He Leadeth Me*, 158–59.
[12] Ciszek, *With God in Russia*, 198.

heartbroken by the murder, although he was consoled by the knowledge that just two weeks before Yevgeny's death, he had received the sacrament of reconciliation and Communion. Ciszek's reaching out to the young man was thus twofold: the ministry of friendship and the ministry of the sacraments.[13]

Yevgeny and others who came to Ciszek did so not only because they knew he was a priest, but also because they saw him as someone who lived out in his daily life the principles he professed. Ministry in prison, therefore, involved the concept of witness. He says in *He Leadeth Me:* "The key word, in fact, of our priestly apostolate in the camps had to be the word 'witness,' . . . [which] was not so much a matter of preaching God and talking religion . . . as it was a matter of living the faith that you yourself professed."

The prisoners had difficulty understanding why anyone would want to live a life dedicated to God that involved significant sacrifices, especially because the camp officials subjected the priest-prisoners to special harassment. But they were impressed at the sight of these same priest-prisoners making themselves "available to the sick and to the sinning, even to those who had abused or despised them," with little regard for their own comfort or safety. Their self-giving behavior so impressed some prisoners that they were inspired to try to establish a relationship with God. Understandably, then, for Ciszek and his priest companions, "to help prisoners return to a belief in a God they had long abandoned . . . was our greatest joy and consolation."[14] The same could be said of many other Jesuits who saw their ministry bring similar results.

Among these Jesuits was Gerardas Dunda. Just as Ciszek succeeded in bringing the former criminal Yevgeny back to the sacraments through their friendship, so too did Dunda offer his friendship to a fellow Lithuanian, leading him to rediscover a long-neglected faith. The prisoner's name was Jurgis (George) Polujanskas; he and Dunda were both in a Soviet labor camp. Before his imprisonment, Polujanskas had been a lieutenant in the Lithuanian army who was arrested for political reasons. He initially expressed little interest in religious matters, but as the months went by, the two became friends and "his indifference began to disappear."

---

[13] Ibid., 204–6.
[14] Ciszek, *He Leadeth Me,* 129–30.

One day at the end of April, 1952, he approached Dunda in a state of alarm; the right side of his body, along with his right eye, mouth, and tongue, was paralyzed. Dunda advised him to go to confession and to put himself into the hands of God. At first, he resisted the suggestion. However, some remnants of his childhood faith still remained, for Polujanskas had kept a promise to his mother to remember her and to say one Hail Mary every day.

A few days later, Polujanskas's name appeared on a list of prisoners who were to be moved to another location, and it was then that he decided to avail himself of the sacrament of reconciliation. Dunda describes what took place: "It was the Sunday after Easter, 1952. We climbed into my top bunk and he began to prepare for his confession. At the same time, concealed under a blanket, I offered the sacrifice of the Mass. When I finished Mass, he was ready for confession. Sincerely and candidly, he confessed his sins . . . [and] received the Eucharist." He then said that he wanted to pray alone for awhile and left the barracks. Two hours later, "he ran into the room shouting, 'I'm cured! I'm cured!' And really," Dunda writes, "he was cured. The paralysis had left his eye, his face, his tongue, his arm, his leg. All traces of his illness were gone. Embracing each other, we cried from joy." Without pressing the point, Dunda suggests that the sudden healing may have been a grace from the Virgin Mary to Polujanskas for having kept his promise to his mother. The next day, he was transferred,[15] and Dunda never saw him again.

At Dachau, too, Jesuits found ways to minister. Their spiritual father, Otto Pies, observes in *The Victory of Father Karl* that "in April 1943 it became possible for the priests to capture the stronghold of the hospital barracks, known as the Revier, which up to then had been the domaine [sic] of communist nurses and orderlies." The latter abandoned their patients after an outbreak of typhus. At that point, Pies continues, "the camp leadership then suddenly reminded itself of the priests [who] . . . were [consequently] required to assume nursing duties." Of the large number who presented themselves as volunteers, twelve were chosen. Their excellent care of the typhus patients lasted a year, after which the SS authorities removed them. But with a new outbreak of typhus, the authorities later summoned them back. Most contracted the disease in the course of their work.

---

[15] Dunda, memoir, 7.

Six died, "victims of their charity toward others," as Pies describes them.[16]

John Lenz was among the Jesuits who served typhus patients in the hospital. He describes his experience in considerable detail in *Christ in Dachau*. Although he voluntarily accepted the undertaking, he regarded it with trepidation. "Right up to the last moment I secretly hoped that God would not ask this of me. Yet all the time I kept telling myself that He had preserved me from such perils during the past five years: why should He not save me from typhus too?" Then, on an Ash Wednesday morning, he packed his few possessions in a cardboard box and made his way to the isolation block. What conditions did he find there? He tells us in the following passage: "I would make my way among the piteous figures, lying on plank beds, three tiers high, and on straw mattresses on the floor. The filth of these 'beds' was unspeakable . . . crawling with lice and covered with human excrement. . . . Since most of the windows were broken, the cold was intense. . . . The stench in the ward was almost unbearable—the terrible festering smell of pestilence."

Lenz moved among the patients, doing what he could to provide comfort through the daily actions of bathing and feeding. Eventually, he too fell ill but decided to keep on as long as possible. Besides helping with physical tasks, he administered the sacraments; among the last to receive them was a young Lithuanian. The Lithuanian's eyes were full of fear "that he would not be allowed to enter heaven." Lenz heard his confession, and then the young man "reverently and joyfully received Holy Communion." Lenz promised to return the next day, but the man replied in broken German, "I no more there, Father." And in fact, the next morning Lenz found him dead, "sleeping peacefully like a child on his miserable bed of rags," with a dozen other corpses on the floor nearby.

When Lenz became a patient himself, Otto Pies, as the spiritual father of the imprisoned Jesuits, was able to visit him frequently and "managed to obtain the drugs from outside which virtually saved my life." Lenz later learned that his friends had given him up for lost, and "had even decided who was to preach at my requiem!" Although the two weeks spent working in the hospital barracks added ten years

---

[16] Pies, *Victory of Father Karl*, 121–22.

to his age, Lenz nevertheless says that these weeks were "the most worthwhile days of my life."[17]

Priests were not the only ones to volunteer for ministry in the typhus block. A Polish scholastic, Jurek Musial, volunteered as well. An account of the Dachau experience by Peter van Gestel, another Dachau Jesuit, describes how Musial was infected with the disease but, unlike Lenz, did not recover. After Musial's death, he was "buried together with some ten thousand more, in one of the three collective graves outside the town of Dachau," rather than being cremated, because a shortage of fuel had caused the crematory to be closed down.[18]

As superior of the sixty-three Jesuits at Dachau, Léo de Coninck organized conferences and retreats, thereby helping to strengthen morale. He speaks of a series of 8 a.m. conferences he gave from January 1943 onward in one of the rooms in his block. Again, secrecy was essential: "We had some amusing adventures: the subject would have to be abruptly changed when the 'enemy,' as sometimes happened, popped in before our [own] guard, caught unawares, could signal to us. I repeated in these conferences the course of Pastoral Theology I used to give at Louvain."[19] He adds, "I had not a note to help me, only my memory," underscoring again the crucial role that memory played in the ability of incarcerated Jesuits not only to sustain their own morale, but also to bolster that of others.

During a secretly organized eight-day retreat, de Coninck gave three exercises a day in Latin; since priests of various nationalities were attending, they could all understand this common language. To avoid detection, they chose a different location for each exercise of the retreat, and those present stood or sat to avoid the appearance of a formal gathering. The retreat included "a daily Ciborium Benediction, with my spectacles case as the Ciborium and my knee as the Throne on which we placed our Treasure"—that is, the Blessed Sacrament.[20]

Although religious activities were forbidden outside the chapel, de Coninck and other Jesuits at Dachau refused to be deterred from

---

[17] Lenz, *Christ in Dachau*, 247–55.

[18] Peter van Gestel, "Jesuits in the Bonds of Dachau," *Woodstock Letters* 76(2) (June 1947):125.

[19] De Coninck, "The Priests at Dachau," 123.

[20] Ibid., 123.

sacramental ministry elsewhere in the camp. When he was able to obtain consecrated hosts, de Coninck broke them "into small fragments (twenty to a host), which I wrapped up in cigarette papers." One is reminded of Jean Moussé who, assigned to work in a drafting office connected with the Reichenau concentration camp, wrapped particles of hosts in the thin paper used for drafting. In this way de Coninck could carry his fragments with him night and day so that he could distribute them as the occasion arose, "and even on many occasions to give [them as] Viaticum to those on their way to execution."[21]

For most of his ten years in Albanian prisons and the labor camps where he was obliged to work in swamps, Giacomo Gardin was unable to exercise a sacramental ministry; consequently, there were times when he developed feelings of uselessness. In his diary for March, 1950, he writes: "Oppressed by fatigue and malnutrition, I am assaulted by the feeling of being a priest who does not exercise his vocation, feeling completely lost. Doubts circulate through my mind, as to why I was ordained a priest."

But later in the same entry, he acknowledges the fact that his very presence as a priest and Jesuit, together with his ability to show small acts of kindness and compassion to his fellow prisoners, was in itself a form of ministry:

> I realize that I can do much through my mere presence and my name, in my capacity as a priest and Jesuit, here, in this place of torment and martyrdom. . . . A word of relief, of consolation, in passing by someone, whose strength sapped, has fallen down not only physically, but spiritually as well. . . . The tenderness in a small piece of bread, taken from my daily portion and given to a fellow prisoner whose bread has been denied—all these excite my soul in the monotonous passage of days and months, and are brightening the image of a new ministry.

The realization that words of consolation and the sharing of a mouthful of bread with someone whose food ration had been denied as a punishment amount to a "new ministry," leads him to conclude this passage in *Banishing God in Albania* with a statement of hopeful self-affirmation: "So I am not lost after all." Others also sought him out because they knew he was a priest and that he would listen and

---

[21] Ibid., 122.

grant absolution: "On our way back to the barracks . . . there was always someone who would look for the priest to talk about his inner crises and seek to make peace with God." Then, he continues, "all the hard work, the humiliation, that horizon always blocking our hope, all these things showed these friends of mine and me the way to God."[22]

Jacques Sommet, too, found other ways of ministering besides taking part in the eucharistic network. On the train to Dachau from the holding camp at Compiègne, while still wearing his soutane, he overheard someone asking if a priest were present. "A man called out to me asking that I hear his confession—he was an unbeliever. But finding himself on the very margins of life, he felt the need to speak to someone." Although Sommet would have made it clear that he was a seminarian, not yet a priest, he was willing to be a listener. At Dachau, however, the same man avoided Sommet, as if he regretted having revealed a painful part of his inner self to another.[23]

Occasionally at Dachau, unexpected opportunities for evangelization arose. In *L'honneur de la liberté,* Sommet describes another encounter with an unbeliever, a young French Communist prisoner who one day

> found on the side of his bunk—no one knows where it came from—a page torn from a gospel pamphlet. Thus, he read the beatitudes without knowing what they were. He was overwhelmed. He did not know what churches were. In his eyes, they were only monuments, like museums or bank buildings, and for him, all that belonged to the past. But after what he read, he discovered that there were Christians in the camp. He had never met any.[24]

Something in the gospel text had stirred the young Communist. Sommet spoke to him "of the community that embodies this gospel, and of the Church. For someone who knew only the language of the party," he adds, "it was not easy for him to comprehend that the Church was community, communion." We are not told anything further about this prisoner. But, in contrast to the man on the train, it is clear that the Communist's discovery of the beatitudes and his subsequent conversations with Sommet—who says "we made a journey together"— were the beginnings of an inner growth that might otherwise have been impossible.

---

[22] Gardin, *Banishing God in Albania,* 143.

[23] Sommet, *L'honneur de la liberté,* 67.

[24] Ibid., 99.

James Thornton, the Jesuit from the California Province who was incarcerated for a year in China in the early 1950s, was another who, like Gardin, discovered ministry in humble forms he would never have dreamed of prior to his imprisonment. Three months after his arrest on July 31, 1951, as the October weather was turning cold, two nursing mothers with their babies were placed in the cell he was already sharing with several others. His response was immediate: "I decided to sleep on the damp brick floor and give the two mothers my one and only blanket." One mother had insufficient breast milk for her baby, who consequently cried continuously from hunger. Realizing her plight, he took turns with her "masticating a bite of the Chinese pancake we used to get each morning and coax[ed] the baby to swallow the mash." He thus found himself sharing with the mother in a ministry that was literally life sustaining: it helped to save the baby from starvation. Nor was this all he did for the two women and their children. "Each morning I used to pace back and forth between the cell door and the opposite high wall while the two mothers used the toilet tub. Then I would take it and clean it in the public lavatory."[25] One can imagine few forms of service more humble and humbling than this one.

In another form of direct service, John Robinson and Henry Morse, two Jesuits incarcerated together in York Castle in 1627, collected alms from Catholic supporters on the outside; as in the case of Brother Cuthbert Prescott, they used them to buy food for impoverished prisoners who might otherwise have starved to death. Besides assisting with material needs, Robinson and Morse also administered sacraments and reconciled prisoners to the Church. One night they heard a man and his wife uttering oaths in the dungeon reserved for those scheduled to be executed the next day. Morse managed to enter their cell and spent the rest of the night speaking words of comfort, which led the couple to request absolution in the hours before their death.[26] As a result, "they died devoutly these good thieves, professing themselves openly to be Catholics." Even the judge who had condemned them was impressed: "This was the couple that the other day had vowed vengeance on me and I don't know who else. When they came to die they were praying for us all."[27]

---

[25] Thornton, "The New Proletarian Man," 7.

[26] Caraman, *Priest of the Plague*, 56.

[27] Ibid., 56–57.

Similarly, although John Gerard's first jailer in London's Clink prison "had a fierce temper and took care to see that all the regulations were observed," his successor, a younger and more flexible man, was quite open to accepting bribes. With "a little coaxing," this second jailer "was induced not to pry too closely into our doings." Consequently, Gerard observes, "With this concession I was able to take up my apostolic work again [and] I soon heard a large number of confessions and . . . reconciled many people to the Church." Just how successful his efforts were is suggested a few pages later in his autobiography, when he states that "so many Catholics came to visit me, that there were often as many as six or eight people at a time waiting their turn to see me in Brother [Ralph] Emerson's room next door."[28]

At Wisbech, one of several castles used for Catholic prisoners a quarter of a century earlier, William Weston, who went by the name Mr. Edmunds (not only as a form of disguise but also in memory of the recently martyred Edmund Campion), ministered with even greater freedom after six years of close confinement, thanks to another willing and easily bribable warder. In fact, in his autobiography, he says of himself and the other three dozen Catholic prisoners, "You might have imagined that we were almost living in our own free house."

Weston speaks of establishing actual classes along the lines of an English college: "Catholics daily came to see us, and we were able to give them spiritual succor. We now set out to model our life on the pattern, as it were, of a college, arranging study classes and every other form of humanistic exercise. Days were fixed for cases of conscience, controversies, Hebrew and Greek classes, disputations, and lectures." Weston himself taught Hebrew and Greek. Not the least remarkable aspect of the situation was that visitors from the outside could also attend the various classes, lectures, and disputations. "As soon as it became known that we had been given freedom to see and speak with people outside, practically no day passed without some visitors." Not surprisingly, officials in London became concerned at the degree of freedom enjoyed by the prisoners: "The throng of Catholics of every condition in life was so unending that it gravely alarmed the Queen and her Councilors. They duly upbraided the keeper for

---

[28] Gerard, *Autobiography of a Hunted Priest,* 74, 79, 90.

allowing it."[29] But London was far away and, as Weston notes, "once a way had been broken through the barrier [regarding visitors], it could be blocked by the keeper only with great trouble." Consequently, people continued to come, even from distant places, "some as to a holy place, undertaking a kind of pilgrimage," while others "came for Communion, Mass and the sacraments so that the prison was scarcely ever empty, or we unoccupied in this work." This intense level of ministry continued for five years, until Weston was transferred to the far more secure Tower of London.[30]

Although it was more elaborate, the arrangement at Wisbech offers parallels with the classes on great books that Daniel Berrigan gave at the federal prison in Danbury, Connecticut, during the time of the Vietnam War. Experienced teachers, Jesuits have known how to apply their pedagogic skills in both classrooms and prisons in Weston's time as well as in the twentieth century.

For some, however, confinement was so restrictive that active ministry of any kind was impossible. At his concentration camp at Oranienburg-Sachsenhausen, Rupert Mayer speaks regretfully of having "no opportunity for apostolic action aside from prayers and sacrifices for others." We are not told what form these sacrifices took—perhaps corporal penances. But Mayer was able to perform small acts of generosity that could be considered a form of ministry. The camp had a canteen where prisoners could buy items like a type of sweet pastry: "I always bought a good supply in order to be able to do something for the faithful fellow prisoner who brought me my meals and did other little favours for me. . . . It all had to be done quite secretly."[31] Even generosity toward other prisoners had to be concealed from the guards.

In India, Roberto de Nobili seized upon the slightest opportunity for ministering. Despite his sixty-three years, his near blindness and other infirmities, and the harsh conditions that prevailed during his four months in the Madurai jail, he practiced the one form of ministry open to him: preaching about God's love to non-Christian visitors. "The gentiles come to visit us from morning to night," wrote Sebastian de Maya, the Jesuit incarcerated with de Nobili, in his letter of

---

[29] Ibid., 167.

[30] Weston, *An Autobiography from the Jesuit Underground,* 166–67.

[31] Koerbling, *Rupert Mayer,* 168, 170.

August 8, 1640, to their Malabar Jesuit provincial. "Far from insulting us, they show us some sympathy and even a certain amount of affection. Father Robert," he continues, "is constantly preaching the gospel to them; and all go away pleased with his discourses and charmed by his polished courtesy." The latter phrase, "polished courtesy," reflects de Nobili's aristocratic upbringing in sixteenth-century Rome. But the earlier phrase, "force and energy of will," suggests again the steadfast determination with which imprisoned Jesuits have persisted in their efforts to minister, no matter how adverse the circumstances of their incarceration.[32]

De Nobili's preaching to non-Christian visitors calls to mind the incarceration of the Japanese scholastic, Paul Miki. When he and others were being taken under guard from their prison in Miyako, the capital, he preached to bystanders along the way during the grueling 600-mile journey to Nagasaki, the place of his martyrdom.[33]

Just as the prospect of imminent death did not daunt Miki and others, neither did it deter Bartolomeo Arbona's impulse to minister. In July 1936, during the Spanish civil war, the house in Barcelona in which the Jesuit was staying was searched. A host wrapped inside a piece of folded paper was found in one of his jacket pockets. The searchers asked whether he was a priest. After Arbona acknowledged that he was, they took him to the San Elias prison, a former Poor Clare convent. When the prisoners at San Elias learned that a priest was among them, several sought him out for confession during the three days prior to his execution at the age of seventy-four.[34] His final ministries had thus been twofold: before his arrest, distributing Communion—using the hosts hidden inside the folded paper—as he walked through parks and other public places; and after his arrest, hearing the confessions of other condemned prisoners.

Miguel Pro's final ministries during the days before his execution on November 23, 1927, were focused on raising the morale of his fellow inmates in cell number one of the Mexico City jail. One of them, Jorge Núñez, described this cell as "a damp, cold hole, five feet wide by ten feet long . . . [with] a horrible smell [that] reached it from the lavatories." It was here that Pro "tried his best to entertain

[32] Rajamanickam, "De Nobili in the Madurai Jail," 92.
[33] Tylenda, *Jesuit Saints and Martyrs*, 41.
[34] Ibid., 430–31.

the other prisoners, and sang all the hymns, popular songs etc. he could remember." Each morning, "they prayed together and said the Rosary. It was cold, so they did their best to get warm by clapping their hands. His confidence in God did not waver all through the five days they spent in prison."[35]

Although—as with prisoners like Dominic Tang—the rule against speaking was strictly enforced in Chinese prisons, it did not always deter Jesuits from exercising a sacramental ministry in ways that escaped the guards' detection. In his Shanghai prison, the Californian, Thomas Phillips, and other prisoners were occasionally allowed to go into an enclosed yard for brief periods to exercise and to wash their clothes. Phillips came to realize that some of his fellow prisoners were secretly trying to attract his attention, although at first he did not understand the message they wanted to convey. His biographer, Kurt Becker, describes what happened once Phillips realized that what they were seeking from him was the sacrament of reconciliation. "A prisoner would be kneeling, scrubbing away at his colorless laundry, and then would shake his hand to dry it, and put it on his breast for a moment, as if to scratch. The sign was unmistakable: the kneeling man beating his breast, a penitent in the act of confessing his faults, wanting absolution."[36] "It was a wonderful thing for Shen Foo," Becker continues, "as out of a full and priestly heart, he was able to wipe away a man's sins." (Shen in Chinese means spirit, foo means father.)

After twenty-six months in the Loukawei prison, Phillips was transferred to the Massenet, a former French fortress in Shanghai. There, another opportunity for sacramental ministry arose. Among the prisoners with whom he shared a cell was a Chinese man who had received a life sentence. Because of the crowded conditions, it was difficult for the guards to enforce the prohibition against speaking. Consequently, when the man began to pose questions about the Catholic faith, Phillips was able to respond.

The prisoner eventually requested baptism. But realizing that the man would probably never be able to take part in the Eucharist or any other aspect of Catholic life, Phillips was uncertain about granting the request. He was persuaded to do so one day when the man

---

[35] Dragon, *Blessed Miguel Pro*, 130–31.
[36] Becker, *I Met a Traveller*, 133f.

asked him about the significance of the third glorious mystery of the rosary—the descent of the Holy Spirit on the apostles. Taking the question as a definitive sign pointing toward baptism, Phillips proceeded with the sacrament the next morning. Using a wet rag, he squeezed a few drops of water on the convert's forehead. That same evening Phillips was transferred to another cell and never saw the man again.[37] One is reminded of the occasion when Gerardas Dunda heard the confession of his Lithuanian fellow-prisoner, Jurgis Polujanskas, who—after receiving absolution and communion and being mysteriously healed of his paralysis—was transferred the next day.

Francis Xavier Ts'ai also secretly administered the sacrament of baptism while in prison. For a time, he, two other Jesuits, and two fellow priests shared a cell with five young Chinese prisoners who had been deliberately placed there to spy on them. But they, too, inquired about the Catholic faith and, after receiving instruction, were baptized.[38]

During his imprisonment in China, John Havas, like Phillips, gave general absolution through signs. Once, however, a prisoner's desire for confession took a new and dangerously specific form: "One of the 'penitents' passing before my cage, threw a tightly folded paper through the bars. It almost hit me as I stood in silence," he says in his autobiography. When the others who had received the sign of absolution passed by, Havas picked up the note. "I then hurriedly opened it to find [that] it was a written confession and signed. What a problem! Not only did I not know to whom I should give the absolution, but how I could destroy this . . . 'criminal' note and how could I get rid of the pieces!"

Havas realized that if an informer had seen the penitent throw the crumpled paper into the cell, he would be severely punished for failing to report the incident. He took care to rub the name off the note to protect the writer should it be discovered. "What if they question me?" he asked himself. "No, even if they kill me I cannot tell the name." He prayed to his patron, St. John Nepomucene of Bohemia: "Seal my lips, that I shall never disclose any information." It was an appropriate prayer, given the tradition that the martyrdom

---

[37] Ibid., 155f.

[38] Interview with Francis Xavier Ts'ai, May 20, 1995. Three of the young Chinese prisoners were later shot.

of John Nepomucene (d. 1393) resulted from his refusal to reveal the contents of the queen of Bohemia's confession to her jealous husband, Wenceslaus.

But where should he hide the note? "Then I got an idea. Since my toes were so sore, I patched them with the written 'sins.' " Soon after, a secret policeman and two soldiers came to his cell. "Where is the paper?" they demanded. "Here it is," Havas replied; but instead of the confession, he gave them several sheets of toilet tissue on which he had written what he called his "innovative hieroglyphics," the Chinese shorthand he practiced for mental stimulation. But the searchers did not understand what he had written, and assuming that the hieroglyphics might simply be a symptom of what they considered Havas's mental instability, they finally left.[39]

Sacramental, too, was Joseph Doan's ministry in Vietnam in the 1980s. After his sentencing, he was transferred to the Saigon prison for ordinary criminals. Once there, he realized that other Catholics were confined on the upper floor of the three-story octagon-shaped building. As soon as they became aware of his presence, they sought him out for absolution, as had been the case with John Havas and Thomas Phillips. During an interview, Doan described what happened:

> They would approach my cell door when they came down for their twice-weekly baths—there were tanks of water for that purpose on the ground floor where I was. We were forbidden to talk, but it was possible to communicate through signs. For example, with confession, if someone wanted absolution, he would bow his head and touch his heart while looking in my direction. I would then place my hand on my ear as a sign that I had understood. Then I bowed my head to show that absolution was granted.

Doan added that because he feared being observed by the guards, he could not even make the sign of the cross; nevertheless, the penitents understood that the gesture of bowing his head was a sign that absolution had been given.

Within the shared cell, the prisoners had greater freedom among themselves, particularly the young men in their twenties. "They would come to me and tell me their stories. I helped them to think

---

[39] Havas, "Four, Nine, Nine, Six," 101–4.

about the gospels [and] heard their confession." From his supply of secretly consecrated hosts, Doan was also able to give them communion. These young men would, in turn, become "apostles" by bringing others confined in the large cell to him. " 'That one over there is a Catholic,' they would say, 'bring him to the father,' and in this way, many returned to the faith." Doan added that the prisoners in general were protective of him. "They kept the guards from noticing what I was doing, and when someone wanted to talk to me, they would make space so that we could be a bit apart."[40]

For Isaac Jogues, living among the Iroquois in what is now New York State, the desire to minister was so deeply imbedded that he preferred to continue serving other captives rather than to take advantage of frequent possibilities for escape. "I have often enough the opportunity to escape," he informs his superior in France, "but I will not do so while I can help, console, and confess the French or Barbarian captives, assist the dying, baptize the children, etc." In the same letter, he underscores this resolve, declaring that "if it be necessary to live here even to the end, *flecto genua mea.*"[41]

Instruction in the faith followed by baptism was especially important to him. Even as he and the other Huron and French prisoners were being dragged from village to village, tortured on raised platforms at each, he gave instruction to his fellow captives, "baptizing these prisoners—two upon the stage itself, with the dew, which I found quite abundant in the great leaves of turkish corn, the stalks of which they gave us to chew." He baptized two others as they were crossing a brook. Whether the dew on the stalks of corn or the water in a brook, when water for baptism was at hand he lost no opportunity to make use of it.

Later on, when he was being held in a village in what he called his condition of "free slavery," new captives were brought in from another tribe. Among them was a woman who was to be burned alive as a sacrifice to one of their gods, Aireskoi. After they tortured her, the Iroquois "threw her, still alive, into a great fire, to make her die therein." Once again, unnoticed by his keepers, Jogues used a stratagem to administer baptism. "I, not having been able before,

---

[40] Interview with Joseph Doan, April 11, 1995.

[41] Thwaites, *Jesuit Relations* (39):221–22. The Latin phrase means "I bend my knees"— an act of submission to God's will.

baptized her in the flames, on occasion of giving her to drink;" and thus "this woman died a Christian" as she received from Jogues's hands what the captors assumed was only a sip of water.

Despite the harsh treatment he had received, Jogues—like de Nobili—exercised the ministry of preaching. Having learned enough of the Iroquois language to be able to communicate with them, at the beginning of an October stag hunt, "I began to announce to them a God, a Paradise, and a Hell." Jogues was pleased to observe that they initially listened, but their interest soon dwindled, "and because the chase was not successful, they began to accuse and persecute me . . . nor would they longer hear me speak of God."

A few months later, however, an Iroquois woman whose son had recently died "began to take some care of me," a practice similar to an informal adoption.[42] In his account of their captivity, Gabriel Lalemant explains that the Iroquois "are accustomed to give prisoners, whom they do not choose to put to death, to the families who have lost some of their relatives in war."[43] While staying with the adoptive family, Jogues intensified his study of the language. Then, as his ability to communicate improved, the people were better able to understand his preaching. In particular he aimed his preaching at the leaders: "Because I was in a place where all the councils were held—not only of our Village, but of all the country—I had opportunity to instruct the chief persons of the nation in our holy mysteries, and to preach to them the Faith." Recognizing that his knowledge of the outside world was wider than theirs, the leaders had already been asking him "a thousand curious questions" about the planets, the earth, the ocean; "and because I contented them in some manner, they admired me, and said that they would have made a great mistake in killing me, as they had so many times resolved." But as he states in the same letter, when he tried to move "from the creatures to the Creator, they mocked me with the fables which they relate of the creation of the world,— which originated, by their saying, from a tortoise."[44]

Their reluctance to believe in the God Jogues portrayed stemmed, in part, from his contemptuous attitude toward their pagan gods, an

---

[42] Thwaites, *Jesuit Relations* (39):195, 207–9, 213, 221.

[43] Ibid., (31):53.

[44] Ibid., (39):213.

accepted mindset among missionaries working among non-Christians in that era. For example, Jogues described the Iroquois god, Aireskoi, as "no other than a lying demon, who, driven out by virtue of the Cross from the rest of the world, had taken refuge among them, in order to receive from them some particle of that honor which was now everywhere denied him."

Nevertheless, although most of his listeners did not accept Jogues's words about the God of the Old and New Testaments, baptisms continued, "not only many children, but many sick people, and adult captives, who I think are now in heaven." He had enough freedom, moreover, to journey to other villages "in order to visit our captive Neophytes; to console them, and to administer to them the Holy Sacrament of penance; to assist the dying, and baptize them." He was thus able to see some concrete results of his evangelizing efforts, efforts that included leaving visible signs of his belief in nature itself. One spring, as he traveled on a four-day journey with an old man and an old woman to a fishing area, he literally carved these signs on the trunks of trees: "On how many oaks did I carve the most holy name of Jesus, to expel from them the terrified demons! On how many the most holy Cross!" This took place during Holy Week, a circumstance that led him to "meditate at the foot of a tall pine . . . where I had carved a great Cross."[45]

Just as Jogues regarded their forms of worship as evil superstitions, so did his captors view signs like these as equally evil. Thus, when he erected a large cross near the village at a spot he had chosen for his personal prayer, the Iroquois tore it down. In Lalemant's account of their captivity, we are told that "they cast reproaches at him that he was a wizard; that his prayers were sorceries, which prevented the success of their hunting."[46] In the same Relation, Lalemant notes that "the Algonquins and the Hurons—and next the Hiroquois [sic] . . . have had, and some have still, a hatred and an extreme horror of our doctrine. They say that it causes them to die, and that it contains spells and charms which effect the destruction of their corn, and engender the contagious and general diseases wherewith the Hiroquois [sic] now begin to be afflicted. It is on this account that we have expected to be murdered."[47] This same fear that Christian symbols

[45] Ibid., (39):213–17.
[46] Ibid., (31):73.
[47] Ibid., 121.

and gestures were forms of sorcery led to the killing of René Goupil for teaching the sign of the cross to a child.

Jogues's ministry among the Iroquois extended beyond the sacramental. On one occasion, he risked his life by going to the aid of a pregnant woman who was carrying a small child. At the time, he was accompanying a group of old men who were returning to their village; the woman and child were attached to the group.

> As they came to cross a small stream, very deep and very swift, and which had no other bridge than a tree thrown across, this woman, swayed by her burden, fell into the torrent. The Father, who was following her,—seeing that the rope about her bundle had slipped to her neck, and that this burden was dragging her to the bottom,—plunges into the water, overtakes her by swimming, disengages her from her burden, and takes her to the shore, saving her life and that of her little child.[48]

But here too, as soon as he had rescued the pair, Jogues's thoughts again turned to the sacraments; seeing how ill the child was, he proceeded to baptize it. The child, however, died two days later.

Jogues allowed himself to be rescued only when he learned of a plan to put him to death. Dutch settlers who were on friendly commercial terms with the Iroquois undertook the rescue. Given the hostile mood of the Iroquois, Jogues realized that further work among them at that time would be useless; he felt "without power and beyond hope of being able to instruct them." He also saw that his now considerable knowledge of their language and culture "would die with me if I did not escape."[49]Aided by the Dutch, he sailed on one of their ships and at length reached his native France, where he could have lived out the remainder of his life in peace. But his desire to continue ministering to the people he had come to know well was so great that within a year he returned to New France. Once again he was captured and tortured, but this time he was put to death. His escape had thus been only an interlude in his service to those to whom he had dedicated his life.

In the twentieth century too, this same fierce commitment—a commitment so intense that it outweighed the opportunity to leave prison after lengthy sentences have been served—has characterized

---

[48] Ibid., (31):73, 81, 121.
[49] Ibid., (25):53.

the attitude of a number of Jesuits incarcerated in China. During
our interview, Gino Belli declared that several had actually asked
permission to stay on in their labor camps when the time of their
release arrived, so that they could continue to minister to the prisoners who remained.

The anonymously written booklet, *Jesuits in China, 1949–1990*, for
instance, tells the story of a group of unnamed Jesuits, all former
prisoners, who refused an offer to leave the country in 1989. In their
statement, they said: "Our place is here, in prison, in camps or whatever place they allow us to stay." They then added: "We have a lot of
work to do, even if only by our presence, and we are happy to be
privileged to give witness to our faith." The prospect of freedom in
another country could not deter them from their resolve to remain
near those whom they had served when they themselves were prisoners.[50]

John Havas expressed similar sentiments at the time of his expulsion from China after spending almost two years in prison. He told
the Chinese guard who escorted him to the border: "I am not happy
that you are expelling me from China. . . . I have loved your country
and your people more than my own, because I sacrificed my own for
yours! If I could go back in the prison cave again, and know that I
would die there, I would rather choose death in your prison than
freedom in Hong Kong because I love you."[51] The desire to continue
to serve their fellow prisoners even when their own freedom was at
hand is another aspect of the prison experience of many Jesuits. As
Havas's words imply, this desire is based on love—a love that origi-
nates with the love of Christ which allowed them to see Christ's face
in the faces of their companions behind bars.

In some ministerial situations, Jesuits faced agonizing decisions as
to whether they should jeopardize their own survival to aid prisoners
who, without help, would perish. Near the close of World War II, the
young Paul Beschet and hundreds of other captive laborers were
evacuated from the factory at Zwickau in mid-April and forced to
begin what for many would be a death march. SS guards simply shot
those who were too exhausted and weakened by hunger to keep up
with the rest.

---

[50] *Jesuits in China, 1949–1990: Ignatian Year,* 20.
[51] Havas, "Four, Nine, Nine, Six," 15.

One day as the marchers began to climb a hill, a Frenchman named Perret, whom Paul had known as a worker in the French resistance, cried out for help as he began to fall behind the others: "A friend to give me his arm!" Ignored by scores of fellow marchers, he fell farther and farther behind. Finally he came abreast of Beschet and called him by name.

> Totally exhausted and ready to drop to the ground myself, I pretended not to hear him. . . . "Paul, your arm!" "If I give you my arm, I'll fall down with you." "Paul, I've no one to give me his arm. They're going to kill me." He makes the sign of the cross on himself, slowly letting his hand drop. I sense his hand searching for my arm, which is already tired from having sustained others. His fingers touch the fabric of my sleeve.

Perret continued to plead, speaking of his wife and children. His lungs were barely able to bear the strain of climbing the steep hill. Beschet tried to encourage him to keep walking:

> "Come, you're doing better," I say, without looking at him. "Keep going!" "Paul, give me your arm." . . . "You want to see your kids again, so march, take one step at a time, like me." "No, I'm going to die." "If you take my arm, I'll fall with you." Finally, Perret abandons his plea for Beshet's arm, and asks only for his hand: "Paul, just give me your hand, I won't pull on it."

Wordlessly agreeing to this compromise between arm and hand, Paul does take Perret's hand, which he describes as "soft and moist, like that of a dying person. I squeeze it very hard. He responds. Later, I gradually let it go." The saving action of the grasping of hands allows Perret to complete the day's march.[52]

During the same death march, another act of ministerial generosity on Beschet's part exhibited a strong communal element. At dawn, a Jeunesse Ouvrière companion, Chabert, was so chilled after spending the night in a field that he could not get up. Both men realized the danger—if Chabert could not rise when ordered to by the SS guards, they would shoot him. He asked the barely awake Beschet to warm him by rubbing his back. " 'Paul, warm me.' I turn over . . . [but] I no longer have the strength to rub his back." Unable to assist Chabert by himself, he asks another French youth, Olivier, to help.

---

[52] Beschet, *Mission en Thuringe*, 210–11.

"With Olivier, we clasped him between our chests to give him a little warmth." The life-giving help of both of them, holding Chabert in their arms as the three lay together on the cold, damp ground, restored sufficient warmth to Chabert's body for him to be able to rise to his feet.

But this action was not enough because Chabert was so weak. Again, Paul supplied what was needed: "Taking from my shirt the last piece of bread I had, I broke off a piece. 'Eat,' " Paul commands. "You're crazy," Chabert replies, "I don't want to. It's like taking your life." "Eat," Paul insists, adding: "I had to force him, though not for long. 'Eat, or else. Look what's happening.' " As they glanced around, they saw SS guards beginning to walk among the inert forms on the ground, shooting those who could not get up when commanded.[53]

Although the circumstances were quite different, Carl Hausmann also risked his life—or rather relinquished it—over the sharing of food, as noted earlier. Held prisoner in the hold of a Japanese ship off the Philippines, Hausmann died of hunger after consistently giving away his own limited rations to fellow captive Americans. But he had been risking his physical survival by reaching out to others long before this. After his capture, he was sent to a penal colony at Davao to work in the rice fields. The prisoners faced constant hunger, and the long days of work in the broiling sun with no clean water to drink or basic sanitary conditions led to outbreaks of dysentery.

As he worked in the rice fields, Hausmann felt compelled to lighten the burdens of those in worse physical condition than he was by taking their labor upon himself. Theoretically, each man at the camp was given periodic days of rest. Eventually, however, one American "noticed that Carl was always in the fields [because] on his rest days he was substituting for other men." The American was a major who had been given the task of assigning the men to work details, and who thus felt that he had evenly distributed the labor among them. He went to Hausmann, therefore, to question him about those workers whose place he was taking. "They're sick," said Carl, "and they can't stand the hours in the sun." Months later in the hold of the ship, the major remembered, "He said they were sick, and my God, you should have seen *him*! His body was a mass of festering scabs."[54]

---

[53] Ibid.

[54] Duffy, "He Kept Silence in Seven Languages," 343.

John Lenz was involved in a similarly life-threatening incident at Dachau, in this case aiding a Jewish prisoner who had "been subjected that morning to 'special treatment' in the gravel pit." The capo of the work crew had beaten him badly, covered him with wood shavings, and then set fire to him. "The man was a pitiful sight, his hair and eyebrows singed and his face quite black. . . . Worst of all, it must have been clear to him that this cruel game at his expense was only [the] prelude to his certain murder later on." Lenz became involved as the man limped along after them, barely able to stand. The guards were jeering at him and "making fun of his obvious terror." Lenz realized that the tormented prisoner was in immediate danger of being shot. At this crucial point, he says, "I broke out of the ranks and, running back to him, grasped him firmly under the arms and half-dragged him along with me." With notable understatement, Lenz observes that he did not know "how we managed to get away with it," but, he concludes, "God was there."[55]

---

[55] Lenz, *Christ in Dachau*, 38.

THIRTEEN

Guards

WHEREVER THEY WERE, in cells or in forced labor camps, incarcerated Jesuits—like all prisoners—have had to contend with those who exercised direct control over their daily lives, namely, the guards. The treatment could vary from the considerate to the brutal; often, the latter approach predominated. In unusual circumstances, such as those of Isaac Jogues and his companions, the guards were collectively the Iroquois inhabitants of the villages in which they were held. By and large, however, guards have been individuals working singly, in pairs, or in small groups. Although they held various ranks and were responsible to higher authorities that the Jesuits seldom saw, they wielded great power in terms of their ability to make the prisoners' lives more—or less—miserable.

Whether prisoners lived or died was, in many instances, of no consequence to guards who not infrequently put them to death in what might be considered casual executions. Speaking of his seven years in a Soviet labor camp, Gerardas Dunda describes the guards in a punishment barracks as killers and with good reason. The guards there "had their own caste. Prisoners were killed with and without warning. Some were killed in their sleep, others when awake . . . the dead prisoners were buried behind the barracks."[1]

As various examples have already shown, the SS guards in German concentration camps were notorious for gratuitous cruelty that focused particularly on priests and Jews. Léo de Coninck tells of a guard who ordered a young Tyrolese priest to twist a piece of rusty barbed wire into a crown and then forced him to clamp it onto his own head. Several Jewish prisoners working nearby were made "to dance around the priest, leer at him, strike him, insult him, spit on him," in a perverted parody of the crucifixion of Jesus.[2]

Working under the SS guards and answerable to them were the

---

[1] Dunda, memoir, 5.
[2] De Coninck, "The Priests of Dachau," 119.

capos, prisoners themselves who regulated the daily activities of the barracks and labor sites. Frequently no more than "poor degenerate brutes," as de Coninck calls them, they literally had the power of life and death over their charges. John Lenz's narrow escape from death at the gravel pit is just one example. But Lenz acknowledges in *Christ in Dachau* that there were a few capos who maintained a sense of decency in the midst of the inhumanity of the camps. "Not all were murderers," he writes. "Had this been the case, scarcely anyone would have come out alive." He mentions one capo who, at considerable risk to himself, managed to smuggle in fresh vegetables for the sick and who volunteered for work on Sundays because by so doing, "he could procure pig-swill for the hungry priests and Jews in the punishment block."[3]

Alfred Delp experienced one small act of kindness at the hands of the Nazi guards as he sat in his prison cell awaiting his trial and execution. On the last day of 1944, he reflected that "this is the first New Year I have ever approached without so much as a crust of bread to my name." He then observes that "the only gesture of good will I have encountered is that the jailer has fastened my handcuffs so loosely that I can slip my left hand out entirely. The handcuffs hang from my right wrist so at least I am able to write."[4] The guard thus displayed a trace of humanity.

Eugene Fahy encountered precisely the opposite with regard to his guards in China in 1951. Shackled with his hands behind his back in his underground cell, he was under constant surveillance by two teenage guards. In pain because the handcuff on his right wrist was too tight, he tried to work it into a less uncomfortable position. When one of the teenagers noticed what he was doing, Fahy asked him to loosen the handcuff. Instead of loosening it, however, he maliciously tightened it another notch. "Then, taking the left [handcuff], he pressed it in two notches to even things up." The other guard "thought it great sport to order me to remain in an off-balance position on a roll of matting" as Fahy lay on the floor with one ankle shackled to the door. But other guards did not seek ways to inflict gratuitous cruelty, and Fahy was thus able to observe that "on the whole the guards were decent enough to me," even though "some of them took delight in verbally tormenting other prisoners."[5]

---

[3] Lenz, *Christ in Dachau*, 41.
[4] Delp, *Prison Meditations*, 11.
[5] Fahy, "Red Take-Over of a Mission," 18, 21.

The fact that guards in Communist governments were heavily in-
doctrinated helps to explain not only the cruel behavior of the two
who watched Fahy, but also the particularly vituperative language of
one of John Clifford's guards during the same post–World War II
period in China. Because the guard had sharp features and a promi-
nent nose, Clifford nicknamed him the Mole; "hate and suspicion
smoldered in his slitted eyes." One day the Mole was watching him
through the peephole of his cell door as he was eating his meal of
rice. A grain fell from his chopsticks to the floor. "You American
capitalist-imperialist," the guard shouted. "You are wasting the blood
and sweat of our poor farmers. Pick it up!" In an act of defiance,
Clifford picked up the grain of rice, but then instead of putting it
back into his bowl, he deliberately dropped it into the latrine bucket.
"The Mole roared again . . . and cursed me with every slogan he
could recall." Eventually, however, the shouting stopped and he
went away, leaving Clifford to drift back into the memories of his
earlier life that helped him to maintain his mental balance.[6]

During the persecution of English Catholics in the time of Queen
Elizabeth and her successor, guards could—like the pursuivants—be
motivated by greed. Under the penal system of the time, prisoners
had to pay even for necessities. In his biography of Henry Morse,
Philip Caraman notes that at Newgate prison, for example, "for every
favor or comfort, payment was exacted." There was even a scale of
charges whereby a prisoner would have to purchase what Morse in
his own account of his incarceration calls "a sleeping hole a little free
of vermin . . . or wholesome air enough to keep the lungs from being
choked up."[7] Similarly, while imprisoned in Wisbech Castle—a principal holding place for Catholic prisoners—William Weston in his
Autobiography from the Jesuit Underground speaks of having to pay
the warder "twenty-four reals [silver coins] for his cell. When this fee
was paid by thirty or more, occasionally even by forty of us, it was a
substantial income for a shocking and sacrilegious service done by a
man who deserved nothing."[8]

Among the American peace activists of the late twentieth century,
Daniel Berrigan in *Lights On In The House Of The Dead* cites the

---

[6] Clifford, *In the Presence of My Enemies,* 80, 89.

[7] Caraman, *Priest of the Plague,* 128.

[8] Weston, *Autobiography from the Jesuit Underground,* 165–66.

harassment he received at the hands of the officer in charge at the federal prison in Danbury, Connecticut, in 1971. "In spite of [my] ill health . . . he has ordered me to do work for which I am physically incapable, under threat of 'a bust.' " But there were other lower-level functionaries who maintained a sense of the prisoners' right to dignity. Berrigan describes an incident in which, as he was subjected to the usual humiliating strip search after a visit, another inmate said to the guard conducting the search, "Don't you feel how wrong it is to treat priests this way?" The guard replied, "I don't feel good treating *any* inmate this way." Commenting approvingly on the reply, Berrigan writes, "Which wasn't, all considered, so bad."[9]

Under the Communist government of East Germany in 1958, Josef Menzel, after his arrest and incarceration for alleged espionage, found similar variations in the behavior of those who exercised control over him. He speaks in his recollections of "the master sergeant who took away my bible with the remark that 'others needed it too,' and of the sympathetic lieutenant who returned it to me."[10]

At times, guards' dealings with prisoners could be entirely positive. Writing of his 1975 experience in the Capuchinos prison in Santiago, Patricio Cariola—imprisoned for having helped a wounded leftist fugitive to obtain medical care—likens his experience with them at his Chilean jail to that of the apostles in Acts: "The guards have not changed. They are good. They have never struck a political prisoner." Even though he wanted to be treated the same as other prisoners, Cariola found that the prison personnel in general treated him "with singular kindness"; he was allowed more visits and greater freedom within the jail than the ordinary prisoners.[11] This was an example of captors perceiving a priest in a relatively positive light, which was in marked contrast to the way religious were treated in Communist countries. But as the experiences of Juan Luís Pérez Aguirre in Uruguay, and Juan Luís Moyano Walker and Franz Jalics in Argentina show, the fact that a priest is arrested in a primarily Catholic country is no guarantee that he will receive kinder treatment at the hands of guards and prison administrators.

---

[9] Berrigan, *Lights On In The House Of The Dead*, 196.
[10] Menzel, "Personal Recollections," 8.
[11] Cariola, "Dos Meses," 2, 8.

FOURTEEN

Becoming a Jesuit in Prison

GINO BELLI said in our interview that he knew some Chinese who had begun their Jesuit training while incarcerated. Because political dissidents and members of groups like the Legion of Mary were usually confined together, the older Jesuits were in a position to instruct young men seeking entrance to the Society—in effect creating a novitiate behind bars.

A similar situation occurred in seventeenth-century Japan. A Portuguese Jesuit, Francis Pacheco, along with four catechists, was betrayed by a former host who had apostatized after the shogun's decree forbidding Japanese Christians to practice their faith. The catechists and Pacheco, who was provincial superior for the Jesuits working in Japan, were imprisoned for six months, from December 22, 1625, until the time of their execution the following June. During this period, Pacheco admitted the four into the Society and created a minicommunity with set hours for rising and prayer.[1]

If he did not become a Jesuit while actually in prison, Louis Shen might be said to have entered the order between periods of incarceration. Having studied in a preparatory seminary closed by the Communists in 1955, Shen was arrested in 1958 for the "crime" of membership in the Legion of Mary. After three years of imprisonment, he was transferred to a labor camp, where he remained for twenty-five years.

Following his release from the labor camp, he entered the Society in 1981. Shen did not have time to pronounce his first vows, though, because he was arrested again toward the end of the same year. Seven months passed before his release for this offense. Eventually he obtained a visa and was enrolled in the Jesuit School of Theology at Berkeley, California. His ordination took place in 1993. Recount-

---

[1] Tylenda, *Jesuit Saints and Martyrs*, 185–87.

ing his own story, he speaks of what sustained him during his long years of confinement: "How did I keep my faith all that time? . . . I prayed and prayed. Even though I had no opportunity to attend Mass or to receive the sacraments for almost twenty years, I had the experience of belonging to the Church, which is a sacrament by herself, as Karl Rahner said, and God's self-communication offered to me always."[2] Again, prayer—"I prayed and prayed"—and the sense of belonging, both to the Society and to the Church as a whole, are two of the most important factors that have helped to sustain incarcerated Jesuits over the centuries.

George Wong, imprisoned in China at the same time as Shen, was a key person in introducing a fellow priest-prisoner to the Society. The priest, who was sentenced with Wong in 1967, had been procurator of the diocese of Shanghai. Already familiar with the *Spiritual Exercises,* he learned about the Society's *Constitutions* from Wong.

Discussing their relationship, Wong says, "Later, we met again when we were both transferred to the same labor camp. Although we were on separate work teams, on holidays we had an opportunity to walk and talk together. Through my underground superior, he made formal application to be admitted as a Jesuit. Eventually," Wong went on, "when we'd both been released, he pronounced his final vows in my sister's house in Shanghai in the late 1980s."[3]

Although his conditions were far more desperate, René Goupil was received into the Society while a captive of the Iroquois. He had been a novice in France but left because of health reasons and went on to study and practice medicine in Paris. However, his desire to be associated with the Jesuits remained strong, and so he allied himself with them as a *donné*—what we would call today a volunteer, working in an unsalaried capacity and living the identical life of poverty, obedience, and chastity as the Jesuits themselves.

Goupil and Isaac Jogues were held in the identical village, where they were both tortured. In a letter to his French superior on August 5, 1643, Jogues describes how the thirty-five-year-old donné was eventually tomahawked by the relative of a child to whom he had been teaching the sign of the cross—a sign that the man assumed to be a form of sorcery. He then describes Goupil and how he took the three vows of religious life:

---

[2] Shen, "Growing Up in the Church," 11.
[3] Interview with George B. Wong, May 29, 1995.

He was a man of unusual simplicity and innocence of life . . . [and] worthy to be acknowledged by Your Reverence as yours, not only because he had been . . . for several months in our novitiate, but also because here he had consecrated himself, under obedience to the Superiors of the Society, in the service of our Neophytes and Catechumens,—to whom, with the art of Surgery, he was of great assistance; and finally, because a few days before, he had consecrated himself with the vows.[4]

Jogues himself received Goupil's vows making him a full member of the Society as a brother, and Jogues was with Goupil when he was killed less than a week later. He expected to die at the same time, but his life was spared. The next day he searched for the body, which he eventually found "by the bank of the river, half eaten by the dogs." Covering the remains with stones, he intended to return to dig a grave. However, heavy rains caused the river to rise, and the body washed away. He found the bones in the spring. "These, together with the head, having reverently kissed, I then finally buried as best I could."[5]

Several young men during the Elizabethan period also became Jesuits while held in bondage. Henry Morse, whose ministry among plague victims was discussed earlier, had been ordained in Rome as a secular priest. In 1642, he was sent to England; but after working for a year among Catholics intent on remaining true to their faith despite government pressure, he was arrested and imprisoned. While incarcerated in York Castle, Morse had as his cellmate the Jesuit John Robinson and eventually told him of his desire to be a Jesuit as well. Richard Holtby, founder of the Jesuit mission outposts north of the Humber River, accordingly appointed Robinson as Morse's novice master.[6] Robinson guided his cellmate through the thirty days of the *Spiritual Exercises* required of all novices. In his life of Morse, Philip Caraman observes that the soundness of his vocation had already been tested "in the streets of Newcastle and among the poor of Durham." What took place in prison, Caraman adds, was therefore "a deepening of vocation. . . . [There was] not any difficulty in choice of life: that had been made."[7]

---

[4] Thwaites, *Jesuit Relations* (39):203.
[5] Ibid., (39):207.
[6] Caraman, *Priest of the Plague*, 34.
[7] Ibid., 58.

Banished from England after four years behind bars, Morse returned in 1632 and began the work for which he became famous—
attending to the needs of plague victims. Imprisoned again, he
pronounced his final vows before Edward Lusher, a Jesuit coworker
among the plague-stricken, who visited him at Newgate. Morse
writes in his journal: "Tuesday in Easter week, 23 April [1637], in
this very prison I was more closely bound to the Society, making my
solemn profession of the three vows of religion." He speaks of the
event, his grim surroundings notwithstanding, as "this signal and unexpected blessing"[8]

Morse was released once more, but after serving as a chaplain in
Flanders, he returned to England in 1643. Arrested a final time, he
was condemned to death the following year. His execution was carried out in the usual manner for English-born priests convicted of
treason: he was first hanged and then cut down and hacked into quarters. Finally, his heart was torn out and his entrails burned in the
sight of the spectators. Such gruesome scaffold scenes were becoming less frequent, however. By the middle of the seventeenth century, Protestantism had become more widely accepted as the
children of Catholic parents grew up accustomed to the new forms
of worship; thus, the government was not anxious to create more
martyrs out of Catholic priests.[9]

For Alexander Briant, some forty years earlier, the situation was
similar in that he, like Morse, was already a priest at the time of his
arrest. He, too, wanted to join the Society of Jesus. In an extraordinary letter to the English Jesuits written shortly before his execution
with Edmund Campion, Briant asked to be admitted to the Society.
In the letter, he relates how his private vow to seek admission had
helped him to bear the tortures to which he had been subjected, and
how it had been, in fact, "a source of great comfort to me amid my
worst trials and sufferings." He continues in these words:

> Since not the slightest hope is left to me of meeting you again, good
> Fathers, in the liberty which we formerly enjoyed. . . . I humbly ask
> you to decide my case according to whatever seems good to you in the
> Lord. If it is the done thing to admit anyone in his absence, I would

---

[8] Ibid., 135.

[9] Edwards, *The Jesuits in England*, 70. 73, 79. See also Gerard, introduction to
The Autobiography of a Hunted Priest, xxiii.

beg to be admitted with all the insistence I can muster. I promise by this letter obedience before God . . . and all of those placed in authority or already constituted my superiors.[10]

Visitors to the Tower were able to provide Briant with writing materials, and they conveyed the letter to the superior of the English Mission, Robert Persons. In the *Records of the English Province*, Henry Foley observes that "the Superiors of the Society . . . now had full evidence of his fervor and constancy as expressed in the . . . letter, written by his own mangled hands." As a result, "it seemed good to all of them to admit him into the Society." [11] At his execution, Briant was treated even more cruelly than Morse. Morse was at least allowed to die before his body was butchered in the sight of the crowd. Briant, on the other hand, was cut into quarters while still alive. The pain of his hanging was prolonged because the executioner had adjusted the noose so poorly that it slipped from its place, leaving Briant suspended by his chin alone. "Hence, when cut down he was still living, and made great efforts to raise himself on his feet; he was nevertheless thrown down by the officers, disemboweled and quartered, while yet alive and conscious."[12]

Another Elizabethan who was received into the Society during his imprisonment was Robert Middleton. According to Foley's brief account,[13] Middleton was initially educated at the English College in Seville and then sent to the English College in Rome. After his ordination there, he was assigned to the English Mission. Some time later, he was imprisoned in London. While incarcerated, he petitioned Henry Garnet, the superior of the Jesuits in England, to be admitted to the Society. Garnet wrote to the superior general in Rome, Claudio Acquaviva, to say that he had "sent to tell him [Middleton] that his desire had been granted, and I hope that the news reached him for his own and our consolation." Subsequently, Middleton and another priest, Thomas Hunt, were condemned and remanded to Lancaster in Yorkshire, where both had done their apostolic work. Middleton was thirty years old at the time of his execution. How he dealt with his incarceration in terms of issues like

---

[10] Edwards, *The Elizabethan Jesuits*, 132.
[11] Foley, *Records of the English Province* (4):358.
[12] Ibid., 367.
[13] Foley, *Records of the English Province* (8):962–63.

prayer and ministry is unknown, since little detailed information is available.

Another Elizabethan received into the Society while incarcerated was Thomas Pounde, who spent upwards of thirty years in and out of English prisons—ten of them with William Weston at Wisbech Castle. A man of wealth and distinguished lineage—his mother was a sister of the Earl of Southampton—he was popular at the court of Queen Elizabeth in his youth. But at the age of twenty-nine, he underwent a profound conversion and returned to the Catholic faith. He was open in his efforts to help Catholics, so his eventual arrest was all but assured.

Like others previously described, Pounde accepted his incarceration joyfully. One of the prisons in which he was held was Bishops-Stortford, a partially ruined castle that had belonged to the bishops of London—hence its name—but which was then being used as a prison because of the large number of incarcerated Catholics. As a blacksmith riveted the shackles on to his legs, Pounde bent forward and tried to kiss them. Angered, the blacksmith struck him on the head with the shackles, opening a wound. Pounde responded, "Would that blood might here flow from the inmost veins of my heart for the cause for which I suffer."[14] The blacksmith, astounded by the response to what was, after all, an unprovoked physical attack, asked him what was the source of such great faith. Influenced by Pounde's steadfast faith, the blacksmith eventually became Catholic and was himself imprisoned.

Because of his incarceration, Pounde, like Briant, was unable to petition for admission to the Society in the normal way. He consequently asked a close friend, Thomas Stephens, to go to Rome on his behalf to make the request of the superior general, Claudio Acquaviva. In his prior letter to Acquaviva, Stephens notes that Pounde had come to know of the order "in consequence of having letters of ours from the Indies, and hearing the good fame of the Society." Stephens continues: "He begs of your Paternity that (since he has for so many years had it in heart . . . to enter the Society, and seeing that he cannot get out of prison) you will be satisfied with such his desire

---

[14] Henry Foley, *Jesuits in Conflict or Historic Facts Illustrative of the Labours and Sufferings of the English Mission and Province of the Society of Jesus* (London: Burns and Oates, 1873), 64. Foley's identical account also appears in *Records* (3):567–657.

... and although absent and unknown, having regard to the longing and zeal for souls that is in him, you will be pleased to admit him to the Society."[15] Not surprisingly, Stephens also became a Jesuit and served for forty years as a priest in the Canary Islands.

Responding to Pounde in a letter dated December 1, 1578, Acquaviva said that although the Society admitted no one "unless well tried by many trials," he was willing to accept "as a long probation your labours and sufferings of so many years," as fulfilling the requirements, and therefore accepted him into the Society "as a true member engrafted into the whole body."[16]

A small but telling detail of his imprisonment involved Pounde's manner of dress: "His dress was rather a gay one, not for vanity's sake ... but rather by way of protest, that to a captive for the profession of the faith in Christ . . . every day was a solemn feast."[17] Pounde's festive apparel, in other words, was his way of highlighting the difference between the ways of God and the ways of a world bent on persecuting believers unwilling to be daunted by incarceration.

In Japan around the same period, Carlo Spinola—in the name of his Jesuit provincial—received into the Society a Japanese Christian who was a fellow prisoner. Peter Sampo had worked as a catechist with the Jesuits before the persecution began in 1614, and he shared Spinola's four years of incarceration. During their time together in the cage-like prison at Omura, Sampo was deeply impressed by Spinola's patient behavior under inhuman conditions. In a letter written toward the end of their imprisonment, he "affirmed that he had never known a man of more illustrious patience and penance, . . . not for one or two months, but for the entire space of four years." He marveled at Spinola's evident happiness and his ability to "accommodate himself to all. . . . He regarded his own suffering as if it were nothing." His admiration for Spinola makes his desire to be admitted into the religious order of which Spinola was such an exemplary member all the more understandable, particularly since they did not have long to live.[18]

One of the most dramatic instances of becoming full members of the Society shortly before being executed occurred in a Japanese

---

[15] Ibid., 39ff.
[16] Ibid., 54.
[17] Ibid., 82.
[18] Spinola, *Vita del P. Carlo Spinola,* 146–47.

prison a quarter of a century earlier. In 1597, two catechists, John Soan de Goto, a youth of nineteen, and James Kisai, a man in his mid-sixties, had asked for admission to the Society. Their admission took place on the very eve of their crucifixion with Paul Miki, along with the Franciscans and their lay helpers. The Jesuit Francisco Passio—who had not been arrested and who, with another Jesuit, John (João) Rodrigues, was allowed by Japanese officials to be present for the executions—received the religious vows of both catechists on behalf of the Jesuit vice-provincial.[19]

Not only have candidates been received into the Society while imprisoned; in some prisons those who were already members have been able to continue the studies leading to their ordination. Even in Dachau, Jesuit formation secretly went on. In his article, "Jesuits in the Bonds of Dachau," Peter van Gestel notes that because the camp held "professors of every type of secular and sacred learning," it was possible during the last year of the war to teach "our Scholastics some philosophy and theology, which saved them a year after they got home." In addition to scholastics, there were also novices, one of whom took his vows in the camp.[20]

Similarly, during World War II, scholastics interned by the Japanese in the Philippines were able to carry on their studies in surroundings that, though difficult, were far less onerous than those at Dachau. Among the facilities used for their internment was a Dominican university, San Tomas. One scholastic half-humorously described their classes in this way: "Moral theology class was held on the grass, under a tree, with Father Thibault presiding. Even if little children were playing all around us, and even if their paper planes did land on our open books, we can still say this: we studied in a Dominican university." Nevertheless, it was prison with—especially at the camp at Los Baños—"the real torture . . . of hunger" and the resultant beriberi.[21]

Several then-scholastics interned by the Japanese were still living and were active in various ministries at the time of this writing, two from the Maryland Province and one from the New York Province—

---

[19] Michael Cooper, S.J., *Rodrigues the Interpreter*, 136–38. See also Giuseppe Boero, *Istoria della Vita e del Martirio dei Santi Giapponesi Paolo Michi, Giovanni Soan de Goto e Giacomo Chisai* (Rome: Civiltà Cattolica, 1862), 115–17.

[20] van Gestel, "In the Bonds of Dachau," 116, 125–26.

[21] "Philippine Jesuits under the Japanese," 209–10, 231.

Clarence Martin, Richard McSorley, and Joseph Kavanagh. Along with other scholastics at Los Baños, they were able to complete two years of theology while behind the barbed wire fence that encircled the camp. "It was a time of great grace," said Martin during an interview early in 1994. "There was a sense of being in God's hand, and great peace came out of it."[22]

Also during World War II, several scholastics of the California Province completed their theological studies in the missionary compound at Zikawei, Shanghai, where they were being held. A dozen were ordained there: Thomas Carroll and James Enda Thornton in 1942; Robert Dailey, William Klement, and Edward Murphy in 1943; Louis J. Dowd and Philip Oliger in 1944; and Ralph Brown, Morgan Curran, Eugene Fahy, John Gordon, and William O'Leary in 1945.[23]

In the 1970s, Joseph Mulligan was able to continue his studies while serving two years at the federal prison in Sandstone, Minnesota. At the time of his arrest in the early 1970s, he had already completed his first year of theology at the Bellarmine School of Theology in Hyde Park, Illinois. His teachers sent him the required reading for three courses: the letters of St. Paul; the thought of Paul Tillich as reflected in his writings during the early days of Nazism; and a course titled "The Theology of Protest and Revolution."[24] During my interview with him, he observed that the books sent by his Jesuit teachers at the Bellarmine School of Theology had to pass through the hands of the institutional chaplain, and some of them, with words like "revolution" in the title, "blew the chaplain's mind." Since they were considered to be seminary texts, however, he could not validly refuse to pass them on to Mulligan.

He also said that the course on St. Paul was particularly meaningful because of Paul's own imprisonment as described in Acts. The Tillich course was important to Mulligan too. Tillich's criticism of Nazism's insistence on absolute authority "was nourishing to us . . . in our promoting disobedience against a warring government which seemed to receive unquestioning submission from most Christians"—submission, that is, concerning the war in Vietnam.

---

[22] Interview with Clarence A. Martin, January 7, 1994. Joseph Kavanagh died in June of 1999.

[23] Fleming, *Chosen For China*, 393.

[24] Mulligan, "Reflections on the War," 20.

FIFTEEN

Community in Prison

BECAUSE THE SCHOLASTICS AT LOS BAÑOS were confined with other Jesuits, they not only had an opportunity to continue their studies but also had the strengthening support of community life. The same phenomenon has been true of incarcerated Jesuits elsewhere. Communal activities with fellow prisoners, both religious and lay, improved incarceration situations that might otherwise have proved unbearable. At Dachau, John Lenz began a rosary confraternity. He observes, "This communal prayer gave us all new strength and inspired us with a greater love of prayer."[1] Even Christmas, a particularly desolate time there, was transformed into a joyous celebration one year when they shared what little they had. Lenz describes the transformation as follows:

> Christmas Eve came. . . . We sat there in our grim cell, hungry, lonely and homesick and thought nostalgically of past Christmases. . . . Our supper was brought in, no different from the same dreary prison supper we got every evening. There was nothing whatever to remind us that this was Christmas, the feast of Christ's Nativity. As the door slammed behind the departing warder these grown men suddenly began to cry like children. . . . I sat there with tears streaming down my cheeks. I tried to find a few words of comfort, but it was no use. The bitter reality was too shattering.

But Lenz and another prisoner had been fortunate enough to have received Christmas parcels from home, and as they distributed their contents, "all of a sudden our misery was forgotten in true Christmas joy, a joy which was all the greater for our own helplessness." Suddenly, the dark mood was transformed into a brighter one; Lenz read aloud the Christmas gospel "and we sang Silent Night. Soon we were as happy and hilarious as children under the Christmas tree."[2]

What is especially remarkable about Dachau, where most of the

---

[1] Lenz, *Christ in Dachau*, 96.
[2] Ibid., 16–17.

religious arrested in German-occupied camps were held, is that community life among the Jesuits not only existed but flourished to an astonishing degree, even in its formal aspects. This occurred through the leadership of a number of Jesuits in addition to Lenz and the superior of the Jesuits, Léo de Coninck. Notable among them was Otto Pies. In his book *The Victory of Father Karl,* Pies speaks of the Nazis' belief that "the black danger"—priests who were considered a threat because of their influence on other prisoners—had to be kept separate. To accomplish this goal, the camp authorities ruled that "the 800 priests were to live in isolation [in three blocks] within the camp itself, in a state of double imprisonment . . . so that as little contact as possible could be established between them and the other inmates. Their influence was to be restricted as much as possible."[3]

Ironically, however, deliberately assigning religious to certain blocks actually facilitated the formation of a tightly knit community: "The expectation of the S.S. to the contrary," Pies observes, "it was a special gift of grace . . . that the very isolation of the priests in their own blocks . . . enabled them to pray together and to live in a genuine Christian fellowship [and] . . . protected them from being swallowed up by the surrounding mass."[4] Earlier in his book, Pies speaks more broadly of the way in which this "Church in chains, . . . with hundreds of priests behind a doubled barbed wire enclosure," exerted a spiritual influence that reached "all parts of the camp through confessions, the administration of extreme unction to the sick and dying, communion, religious exercises, and even an extensive welfare activity."[5]

The large Jesuit community at Dachau was formed almost by chance as Jesuits came across one another unexpectedly in the same camp. As one of them, Peter van Gestel, puts it, "It was in the summer of 1942 that three or four of us discovered each other and laid the foundation of a regular Jesuit Community, or rather formed the nucleus from which it was to develop in the course of two years."[6] The gatherings were initially informal in nature. In the same article in the *Woodstock Letters,* van Gestel describes one way in which the gatherings took place: "Some three or four of us slipped away every

---

[3] Pies, *The Victory of Father Karl,* 107.
[4] Ibid., 117.
[5] Ibid., 114.
[6] van Gestel, "Jesuits in the Bonds of Dachau," 109.

Sunday morning and met somewhere, in a corner or on the crowded camp street, in order to help each other to guard a larger mental and spiritual outlook, and to meet each other on the common ground of our religious convictions, trying to look through the external curtain of our daily life and to analyze the spirit by which it was inspired from the other side."[7] Just how crucial such gatherings were can be deduced from Pies's observation that the aim of the SS in regard to the Dachau prisoners "was to shatter and destroy completely the very core of personality and of all human dignity."[8] As previously noted, the SS treated priests with special malice; one Jesuit—the one who was forced to help build a crematorium—told me that the SS treated "Juden und pfaffen [priests] with equal cruelty."[9]

As the group of approximately sixty Jesuits assumed a well-defined structure, Pies, formerly the master of novices for the Eastern Province of Germany, became its spiritual father. The Belgian, Léo de Coninck, was made superior; his appointment came about "through secret channels," according to his own account of this time. The reference to secret channels of communication indicates that links with the Jesuit curia on the outside remained intact.[10]

In van Gestel's description of the installation of de Coninck, one is again struck by the Jesuits' determination to maintain as many of the formal aspects of the Society's structures as possible. It was yet another way of strengthening their sense of a common identity. As van Gestel puts it: "There was some emotion as Fr. Pies installed the new Superior and with very appropriate words referred to the deeper meaning of this event; and as Fr. Superior assumed the office, with great loyalty and conscious of his responsibility, we all together recited the Litanies of our Saints, especially composed for this and other occasions."[11] The awareness that they were all indeed together—sources of mutual support for one another in the context

---

[7] Ibid., 110–11.

[8] Pies, *Victory of Father Karl*, 99.

[9] Interview, July 17, 1996, at Fordham University. As noted earlier, the Jesuit who was interviewed asked to remain anonymous.

[10] De Coninck, "The Priests of Dachau," 123. De Coninck was able to contact the bishop of Munster in regard to the need for a superior for the Jesuits at Dachau, and the bishop agreed. In due time "we received the appointment of a superior by secret channels." However, De Coninck does not explain the workings of these secret channels.

[11] van Gestel, "Jesuits in the Bonds of Dachau," 115.

of their shared Ignatian spirituality—meant that they "had lost that embarrassing feeling of being scattered atoms, cut loose from the body to which they connaturally belong."[12]

Once de Coninck became superior, the Dachau Jesuits "thenceforward led a true community life. Each month we had a full reunion; our spirit was fortified by an exhortation from the Spiritual Father (Father Pies) and an address from the Superior, and then we all assisted at Mass celebrated by one of us." In addition, there were "regular Renovations of Vows, preceded by the customary Triduum." Members of other religious orders established similar communities at Dachau, and, therefore, says de Coninck, "we were all happy to be able to tighten thus the bonds uniting us among ourselves and with those from whom we were separated by our prison exile."[13] Consequently, whether intentionally or not, the use of the word *bonds* in the title of van Gestel's article, "The Bonds of Dachau," makes it clear that the external bonds imposed by the SS were counteracted by the life-sustaining spiritual bonds of communal Jesuit life.

According to van Gestel, moreover, a deliberate effort was made "to concentrate on the fundamental ideals of St. Ignatius and his spirituality, for these ideals brought home to us again and again that we were not living in vain." Little wonder that he should exclaim: "Can you understand what these stolen hours meant to us?" Being left to their own devices to create a meaningful structure for their lives together actually had the unexpected effect of strengthening their sense of vocation. "It is no rhetorical after-thought to say that we never felt so forcibly and gratefully the grace of our vocation to the Society as when we were detached from her outward frame-work and were thrown back on . . . the foundation in mind and heart, received from our Society, which we never felt so much to be a Mother."[14]

The sheer diversity within the Jesuit community at Dachau is striking. It was a source of wonder for van Gestel himself, writing, as did de Coninck and Pies, only a few years after the war while the memories and details were still fresh in their minds:

> It was a marvelous community when we think about it now, marvelous in its component members. There were novices (one took his vows in

---

[12] Ibid., 115.
[13] Ibid.
[14] Ibid., 111.

the camp), philosophers and theologians. We had professors of every type of secular and sacred learning. There were Rectors and Superiors, a Master of Novices and more than one Spiritual Father. Procurators and Ministers we had amongst us, Prefects and First Prefects, famous preachers and simple parish priests, University students and Retreat Masters, Directors of Sodalities and of the Apostleship of Prayer, Cooks and Porters.[15]

Jacques Sommet—writing in the 1980s—speaks of the way in which, on a larger level, the incarceration of so many religious at Dachau had the opposite effect of what Hitler's regime had hoped to accomplish, namely, mastery over the Catholic Church in Germany. As he points out in his second book on the experience of Nazi incarceration, *L'Acte de Mémoire: 50 ans après la déportation,* the malevolent intentions of his captors were thwarted and in fact were transformed into the realization of a "power of weakness" on the part of the prisoners: "Dachau became like a reserve of the Christ-like future of humanity. In this place where everything was organized to destroy, to degrade, life was reborn, through union with Christ, in the great collective body of believers. . . . The city of death became the city of God."[16] Other Jesuits, too, had such faith and intense relationships among themselves as well as with other prisoners that they could view prisons that were "cities of death" as almost life-giving. It was a life always threatened by physical violence but at the same time one that sustained them in spirit and which could lead to remarkable acts of daring in the service of others.

Among those who performed selfless acts of daring at Dachau was Otto Pies. Although he does not mention it in *The Victory of Father Karl,* Pies himself undertook a bold mission, which was cited by John Lenz in *Christ in Dachau.* In March, 1945, shortly before the end of the war, Pies was released from Dachau and made his way to Munich, where he secretly worked as a liaison between the diocesan administration and those who were still incarcerated. As the Allies approached the camp a month later, the SS decided to evacuate it, forcing the prisoners into a death march similar to the one endured by Paul Beschet and his companions. Hearing of the march, Pies and

---

[15] Ibid., 116.

[16] Jacques Sommet and Albert Longchamps, *L'Acte de Mémoire: 50 ans après la déportation* (Paris: Les Éditions Ouvrières, 1995), 71.

another Jesuit, Franz Kreis, disguised themselves as SS officers. They then went to a military depot in Munich and obtained a thousand loaves of bread and three hundred cans of meat, as well as a supply of schnapps and cigarettes.

The two men loaded the food, drink, and tobacco into a truck and—after locating the marchers on the evening of April 28—convinced the unsuspecting SS guards that the bread and the meat were for the prisoners, so that the townspeople would not be dismayed at seeing them so clearly underfed. The schnapps and cigarettes were for the guards themselves. Later the same night, Pies and Kreis hid ten priests in the empty truck and drove them to safety. They returned the next night and took away another nine, along with three Protestant pastors.[17]

Another who came to know the supportive effects of community was Paul W. Cavanaugh, a chaplain with the American forces who was captured on December 19, 1944. During his captivity at a prison camp in Hammelburg, a group came together under his guidance: "We formed a Catholic study club which was very much appreciated by the Catholic officers and some non-Catholics alike. At daily meetings we discussed the dogmas of the Apostles' Creed and the sacraments." Although the material for the discussions was dry, given their circumstances, those attending the meetings developed a sense of togetherness that helped to sustain hope.[18]

Cavanaugh's camp had about a thousand officers, and he mentions that at the request of several of them who were Catholic, "we recited the prayers of the Novena of the Miraculous Medal after Mass daily."[19] For Cavanaugh and for those he served in the camp, the opportunity to rely upon the comforting routines of daily communal prayer led to a measure of inner calm in the midst of a situation full of uncertainties. Just how great the uncertainties were can be seen in his report to the military ordinariate two months later, in April, 1945. As the Allied troops drew near on yet another march through

---

[17] *Christ in Dachau*, 264. The story was told to Lenz by a Father Reiser, one of the priests on the march. In *Jesuits and the Third Reich*, 57, n. 69, Lapomarda mentions another source for the same story: Alfred Roche, "P. Otto Pies," *Mitteilungen* 19 (1960–62): 397–402.

[18] Paul W. Cavanaugh, "Monthly Report of Chaplain to the Military Ordinariate," February 1945.

[19] Ibid.

Bavaria, American planes bombed the group of 500 prisoners, killing 25; five bombs fell on the area where Cavanaugh and others were resting. Nevertheless, he quietly went about the business of ministering among the dead and seriously injured.

For Ján Korec in Czechoslovakia during the postwar Communist period, the communal aspect of imprisonment was of help too, because the Valdice prison held a number of priests with whom he could feel solidarity. They were able to go to confession to one another and to engage in conversations not only about the current political situation, but also "about fundamental matters, like the state of the Church in our country, the faith of modern man and Christianity in the world." He adds that many of the lay prisoners were also interested in these discussions, so the sense of community extended to them as well.[20] Similarly, the priests at Walter Ciszek's Siberian labor camp helped him both sacramentally and through the shared bond of their priesthood.

In sixteenth-century England, the relative freedom of movement that prevailed in some Elizabethan prisons enabled John Gerard to become part of a small lay community in the Clink. "I had Catholics praying in the next cell," he writes in his autobiography, describing how they did more than pray for him:

> They came to my door and comforted me, then they showed me how I could have freer dealings with them through a hole in the wall, which they had covered over and concealed with a picture. Through this hole they handed me, the next day, letters from some of my friends, and at the same time gave me paper, pen and ink, so that I could write back. In this way I was able to send a letter to Father Garnet [his superior in England] and tell him the true story of all that had happened to me.

He adds that the same opening in the wall also allowed him to make his confession and to receive the Blessed Sacrament.[21]

But this secretive means of communicating with other Catholics in the Clink was not needed for long, because some prisoners managed to have a key made that could open Gerard's door. Before the warder was out of bed, they would come for Gerard and take him to another part of the prison where he could say Mass and give the sacraments to the Catholics there. Since they all had keys to their own doors too,

---

[20] Korec, *La Notte dei Barberi*, 207.
[21] Gerard, *Autobiography of a Hunted Priest*, 78.

it was indeed a community in which access to one another was—given the guards' willingness to accept bribes—all but assured.

Even when Gerard was transferred from the Clink to the Tower, where security measures were stricter, he was not entirely alone. He found himself in the cell formerly occupied by another Jesuit, Henry Walpole, who had been hanged two years earlier, in 1595. His unseen but felt presence provided a moving form of companionship for his fellow Jesuit, a presence made almost palpable by the signs Walpole had left behind. As he walked around his new quarters the morning after his arrival, Gerard felt consoled to find "the name of the blessed Father Henry Walpole cut with a chisel on the wall."[22]

On either side of a small blocked-up window, in a space used by Walpole as an oratory, Gerard also found the names he had scratched onto the stone—the orders of angels, with, at the top, "the name of Mary, Mother of God, and then above it the name of Jesus." At the very top was "the name of God written in Latin, Greek and Hebrew characters." Looking at these names, Gerard reflects that "it was a great comfort to me to find myself in a place sanctified by this great and holy martyr, and in the room where he had been tortured so many times."[23] Although unseen and unheard in the physical sense, Walpole's spiritual presence as a fellow Jesuit clearly served as a source of communal support for Gerard, who now faced torture and the prospect of execution himself.

Also able to communicate with one another even while kept separate were the prisoners in Portugal's St. Julien prison, which held many of the Jesuits brought back from the missions at the time of the suppression. Anselm Eckhart describes how they established contact. One of the prisoners devised a system of knocks, with a single knock for each letter of the alphabet. Using a straw blackened with lamp soot, he wrote an explanation of it on the first page of a devotional book that was allowed to circulate. He then glued the edges of this page to the next with his saliva, so that the jailer would not notice the writing as he took the book from cell to cell. But the other prisoners were unaware of this gluing stratagem and did not discover it

---

[22] Ibid., 105.

[23] Ibid., 78, 104–5. In commenting on the fourteen times Walpole was tortured, Gerard notes on p. 105 that the sessions took place in Walpole's cell rather than in the "ordinary public chamber" normally used, because the authorities did not want the frequency of the tortures known.

until three months later, when the two pages accidentally came apart and the code of knocks was understood. From then on, Eckhart says, "the fathers made use of it to encourage one another in their mutual sufferings, to ask prayers for the sick and the dead, and to stay in touch with whatever was of interest."[24] The code, in other words, permitted them to maintain contact among themselves, even though they could neither see nor speak with one another.

Two centuries later in China, the isolation of Dominic Tang was even greater and his time of incarceration far longer—twenty-two years. During those years, he writes in his memoirs, "I never received any letter from my relatives or friends . . . [and] until a few months before my release, I never received any visitors from the outside." The outside world, in fact, assumed he was dead. Nevertheless, isolated though he was, Tang felt in supportive touch with the universal Church: "I knew that the Catholics of the whole Church and the Jesuits supported me; my priests and Catholics were praying for me and I had not been rejected by the people [of his diocese of Shanghai]." These considerations in the midst of his loneliness, he says, gave him "great spiritual strength."[25]

The experience of the unseen but felt support of the Church and his fellow Jesuits also assisted Alfred Delp in Nazi Germany. In his "Letter to the Brethren" at the conclusion of the *Prison Meditations,* he specifically acknowledges his debt in this regard. "Here I am at the parting of the ways. . . . The death sentence has been passed and the atmosphere is so charged with enmity and hatred that no appeal has any hope of succeeding," he begins, and then describes his gratitude to those who had been supportive of him during his imprisonment and trial: "I thank the Order and my brethren for all their loyalty and help, especially during these last weeks. . . . May God shield you all. I ask for your prayers. And I will do my best to catch up, on the other side, with all that I have left undone here on earth." By his reference to "catching up on the other side," Delp implies that even death cannot break the bond of solidarity he has felt with his brother Jesuits and the Society of Jesus itself.[26]

The Jesuit bond could be so intense that at times a Jesuit would

---

[24] Carayon, *Documents Inédits* (*Les Prisons du Marquis de Pombal*) (9):115–18.

[25] Tang, *How Inscrutable His Ways!,* 119–20.

[26] Delp, *Prison Meditations,* 166.

take steps to share in the captivity of others, even when he himself
was not in immediate danger of arrest. After ministering in England
for eighteen years, until 1678, Anthony Turner learned that several
Jesuits had been imprisoned in connection with the Titus Oates plot
against the King's life. The plot was a fabricated effort to discredit
Jesuits and Catholics in general toward the end of the long period of
persecution that had begun with Queen Elizabeth. According to the
account of Turner's arrest in the *Records of the English Province,*
after unsuccessfully attempting to raise funds that would have enabled him to escape to the Continent, "without having been either
accused or proclaimed by name, or sought after by the pursuivants,
he voluntarily gave himself up to a Justice of the Peace, acknowledg-
ing himself to be both a priest and a Jesuit." He thereby—in answer
to his prayer that he "become a sharer with them in their captivity"—
joined the four Jesuits who had already been arrested. All were
hanged the following year.[27]

In an action that went beyond choosing to share in the bondage of
fellow Jesuit prisoners, Juan Julio Wicht refused an offer of freedom
while being held hostage with many others in the Japanese ambassador's residence in Lima, Peru. The leader of the guerrillas, Nestor
Cerpa Cartolini, personally offered him his freedom shortly before
Christmas, 1996. "If there's an armed attack, nobody gets out of here
alive. So, Father," Cerpa Cartolini said to him, "why don't you go?
You are free to, at any moment." Wicht immediately replied, "I'm
staying until there is not a single hostage left."

When the number of hostages was reduced by more than two-
thirds, Wicht again made it clear that he chose to remain with those
who were to be kept. When he heard his name read out as one of
those to be freed, he said, "I am a priest. Can I stay? . . . I would like
to share [in] the trouble of my companions." He deliberately spoke
these words in a loud voice so that the remaining captives could hear,
whereupon "a general applause broke out." It was evident that his
decision was meant to hearten them. Commenting on the applause,
he observed in a subsequent interview: "I had been very much in
doubt about what God wanted of me, and what importance this offer
of mine might have for my companions. I saw now that it made an
impression on everyone." He had bound himself with the others both

---

[27] Foley, *Records of the English Province* (5):862–63.

spiritually and physically, and they felt the support of his communitarian stance.

This communitarian stance, moreover, extended to the captors themselves. Just before the seven-month siege ended in April, 1997, Cerpa Cartolini wished Wicht a happy birthday—he was turning 65. (The relationship between the two, if tense, was always respectful.) Wicht replied: "I am here for my companions who are being held captive, but I am also here for you. You are my brothers. . . . If I can help in any way, I am at your service." He then "went down the line [of the guerrillas] and shook the hand of each of them, looking them in the eye." Just four days later, all the captors died in the commando operation that ended the siege.[28]

Over three centuries before, in 1642, Isaac Jogues's capture was the result of a parallel act of loyalty and solidarity. After an attack by a band of Iroquois, the Hurons in Jogues's party who had eluded capture fled into the woods. Jogues could have done the same, but he was unwilling to leave behind René Goupil and the other Hurons. "[I] surrendered myself to the man who was guarding the prisoners, that I might be made their companion in their perils." The Iroquois warrior guarding the prisoners was amazed "and approached, not without fear, to place me among them." Likewise, as if he were following Jogues's example, one of the Hurons who had escaped—a convert named Eustache Ahatsistari—seeing that Jogues was not with him, turned back "and of his own accord became a prisoner," having said to himself: "I will not forsake my dear Father in the hands of enemies."[29]

In later periods, the spirit of community has also found expression in the identification that Jesuits have felt with non-Jesuit fellow prisoners. When Thomas Phillips was at the Massenet prison in Shanghai, he noticed a Chinese inmate who was holding a small knotted rag in his hand. With barely perceptible signs, the man kept calling his attention to it. Puzzled at first, Phillips gradually came to realize that the man was a Catholic and the knotted rag was a rosary. Holding it in this manner was the man's way of letting him know that the others knew he was a priest and that they were all praying for him.

[28] "Getting Out Alive. An Interview with Juan Julio Wicht," *America*, September 13, 1997, 13–16.

[29] Thwaites, *Jesuit Relations* (39):179–81.

Thus, as the prisoners passed by him, "they signaled: small, apparently insignificant gestures, unnoticed by the watchful guards, to indicate that they were praying for him and for each other. Tiny gestures of blessing. Fleeting smiles and words of acknowledgement."[30]

Eugene Fahy, who also spent time in the Massenet prison, experienced similar support from the Chinese prisoners. "Marching in pairs. . .we could hold whispered conversations at times, during which I received many marks of sympathy—a pleasant revelation in this jail of thoroughly brainwashed men."[31] The hurriedly whispered conversations and the "marks of sympathy" were unquestionably an important factor in his ability to maintain his mental equilibrium.

During his own time in a Chinese Communist prison, John Havas, likewise, received signs of encouragement that conveyed a sense of community. The signs were expressed in a different manner, however—through the use of Latin, a language that the guards could not understand, but which some of the Catholics could, at least with regard to liturgical phrases. By speaking in Latin, he even discovered the presence of another priest in a cell on the same corridor. Because the guards already considered Havas slightly mad, they paid little attention to communications of this kind with the other Catholic prisoners. Havas describes this secret mode of communication as follows:

> I started to sing. As long as they thought me crazy, I decided to use this privilege. "Estne hic sacerdos?" (Is there a priest here or not?) From a distant corner came the answer: "Ita!" (Yes!) Later, I tried to contact him again, but there was no answer anymore. They had taken him to another place. Later, I tried to contact [other] Catholics! "Dominus vobiscum." "Et cum spiritu tuo. ["The Lord be with you." "And with your spirit."]

The combined voices of the nearby Catholics repeating Mass responses such as "et cum Spirito tuo" sounded to him like "a great echo from many places," and then, he writes, "I knew where my sheep were." Once the mutual recognition had taken place, Havas, like Phillips, was able to confer absolution in silence from the window of his cell door as the Chinese prisoners who were Catholic filed past on their way to their forced daily labor: "The Catholics recog-

[30] Becker, *I Met a Traveller*, 133.
[31] Fahy, "Buried above Ground," 143.

nized me as a priest. The next time they passed my grave [cell], each made a cross over his heart. Later on," he continues, "they made their acts of contrition by striking their breast and I gave them absolution in silence. It was an exciting experience," Havas concludes, "even though my service for them was limited."[32]

Latin also served Francis Xavier Ts'ai as a means of communicating with two other Jesuits, Gabriel Cheng and Vincent Chu, who, like him, were kept in separate semi-submerged "prison of water cells." They not only conversed in Latin but also sang sacred songs in Latin as a form of mutual encouragement. Earlier, this experience of community had been intensified when he was confined in the same cell with these Jesuits for a month. "Just being together made us very happy," he said in our interview. "It was almost like the novitiate. We could say the rosary together and even give spiritual conferences to one another." Vincent Chu had studied English in the United States and "taught us some English and even recited passages from Shakespeare for us, like 'To be or not to be.' "[33]

The rare chance to be with fellow Jesuits and other priests provided several periods of relative contentment during George Wong's decades of incarceration in China. After being sentenced in 1967 to fifteen years, he was sent back to the prison of his first confinement. "It was the happiest day of my life," he said in another interview at about the same time, "because they put me in a cell with old friends—thirteen priests, most of them Jesuits."[34]

The Jesuit experience has also included an awareness of the bonds of community among lay prisoners and even atheists. At times Jesuits, albeit peripherally, have shared in the togetherness of nonbelievers. At Dachau, Jacques Sommet found a sense of community not only with other French Catholics, but also with a group of young Russian Communists. When he could do so unnoticed, he slipped away from his work detail and hid with several of these young men behind some haystacks. Although he did not speak Russian, he was able to communicate by using the elementary and coarse form of German that was the common language of the camp. The Russians were simple farm workers who came from the forests and the tundra and were strongly

---

[32] Havas, "Four-Nine-Nine-Six," 101.
[33] Interview with Francis Xavier Ts'ai, May 20, 1995.
[34] Interview with George B. Wong, May 29, 1995.

attached to their homeland and families. On their arms were tattooed inscriptions—sometimes "the last words spoken to them by their mothers when they left their land. Their land, their mothers, that is what remained in their subconscious." One of them once stole a potato, which he roasted and gave to Sommet. He was deeply touched: "It was the only potato I ate during a year at the camp, with the exception of Christmas Day." To give up such a valuable food item was no small sacrifice on the part of the young Russian.

Sommet became aware of the strength of their bonding one Saturday night, a night when the men in his barracks were allowed to have an extra hour of sleep. Around 11 p.m., he was awakened by a vague noise, the sound of someone speaking very quietly. It was one of the Russians, whispering to his companion a story from his life at home. "Then another took up the thread, and so on for the rest of the night. Each told a story of his village or his locality."[35] If they did not take part in the Eucharistic network of Catholics for whom the bond with the body of Christ, the young Russians found their own network of mutual support by endlessly recounting stories from their homeland—a homeland that took the place of the God they did not know and which served to bind them together into a tightly knit community within the camp. Sommet describes the incident as "a surprising experience . . . that I did not find in any other group." Even though he was an outsider, he could to some extent share the experience and be moved by it. And the gift of the potato—rare in a camp plagued by hunger—showed that in their way, they accepted him as one of them.

In a similar but more personal manner, Patricio Cariola writes movingly of hearing the voice of an elderly Chilean in a nearby cell during his 1975 imprisonment. "Are you a priest?" asked the old man. Cariola approached the bars of his own cell and said that he was. The man, Emmanuel, replied, "How wonderful; you are here with us." By the same token, Cariola found in Emmanuel, as well as in other broken people in the Santiago jail, Jesus himself, "the Lord who waits for us in prison."[36]

Experiences like these have led many Jesuits subsequently to view their time of incarceration with gratitude. Later in his reflection, Ca-

---

[35] Sommet, *L'honneur de la liberté*, 100–1.
[36] Cariola, "Dos Meses," 5.

riola expands on this concept in terms reminiscent of the prison writings of others already mentioned in this book. "The bars, the prosecutor, the interrogations, the solitude of being out of touch with others, the guards, the stepping out of the police wagons in handcuffs in the midst of reporters—these are a double grace: the humiliation and the material identification with Christ and many of his saints."[37]

Around the same time, young peace activists and draft resisters in the United States shared a similar kind of bonding at the Danbury federal prison where Daniel Berrigan was serving his sentence in the early 1970s. The bonding arose in part from a deep distrust of the prison social workers, doctors, and most of the guards. Berrigan had a special antipathy for the prison psychiatrist, whom he described as "prowling the yards . . . one drug pusher among many." His group of friends, he says, was not in need of the psychiatrist's overdispensed tranquilizers. Instead, "our little band of survivors had other, different resources: a relentless confidence in the power of our beleaguered community of the incarcerated. We could care for our own, even in such a place"—a community all the stronger precisely because it was beleaguered.[38]

The American peace activist John Dear, in a 1993 letter from his North Carolina jail, describes one of the ways in which he and the two laymen arrested with him kept their sense of community strong. The three—Dear, Philip Berrigan (Daniel's brother), and Bruce Friedrich—were in the same cell. After speaking of his personal early morning prayer, Dear goes on: "I take some time for 'check-in,' to see how each of us is doing, what's on our minds, what our concerns are, what mail we receive, and so forth." This "check-in" at the beginning of the day, he observes, "helps to build community among us." The communal sharing continued as they sat together in their confined space for several hours of scripture study, which, at the time the letter was written, centered on the gospel of Mark, "a few verses each day: We reflect on the message and the life of Jesus, and how it applies to . . . our own lives and our lives in prison. We have had some very rich conversations along the lines of faith, fear, nonviolence, resistance to evil, discipleship . . . and the reign of God." The

---

[37] Ibid.

[38] Daniel Berrigan, *To Dwell in Peace. An Autobiography* (San Francisco: Harper and Row, 1987), 261–62.

Bible study sessions, he explains, are modeled on similar types of discussion in the base communities of Latin America.[39]

Dear, Cariola, and many others were comforted by receiving direct support from their superiors during their imprisonment. Cariola tells of being moved to tears on hearing that his superior general, Pedro Arrupe, sent words of encouragement through his assistant for Latin America. Because of this sign of encouragement and support, he says in "Dos Meses," "I felt the love of the Society." He goes on, "I wrote to Father Arrupe to tell him that now I had seen clearly that paired with obedience is solidarity. You give yourself to the Society, but at the same time, the Society gives itself to you. . . . In fact, the Society gives us much more than we give to it. This awareness gave me much happiness. It was the experience of feeling yourself loved to a degree far greater than anything you could respond to."[40]

Along similar lines, John Dear received visits from James Devereux, a former provincial of the Maryland Province, who also drove hundreds of miles to be present for his trial in Elizabeth City. The Jesuit who was provincial at the time, Edward Glynn, visited as well, coming from the provincial office in Baltimore, Maryland. Of this visit, Dear writes in his journal: "I asked him if he still supported me and my public stand for peace. 'We're very proud of you' he replied. 'Of course, we all support you.' Then, putting his hands up as if to frame a picture, and looking at me through the glass window [of the visiting room], he said, 'You're right where we want you.' We both burst out laughing."[41] He also found support from fellow inmates. "The other prisoners all express interest in our plight. One of the new cell mates pressed me for all the details. Like many others, he said 'I support you. . . . I don't think I could do what you've done, but I agree with you."[42]

Francis Hagerty, likewise, had the support of his New England provincial for his act of civil disobedience. And Joseph Mulligan received numerous demonstrations of support from both superiors and fellow Jesuits after his arrest in Chicago for his activities against the war in Vietnam.

But not all those involved in acts of civil disobedience have felt

[39] Dear, letter to author, January 14, 1994.
[40] Cariola, "Dos Meses," 16.
[41] Dear, *Peace Behind Bars,* 172.
[42] Ibid., 25.

equally supported by other Jesuits. In *Lights On In The House Of The Dead,* Daniel Berrigan refers to his "grievings about the silence and abandonment of the Jesuits" in the aftermath of his arrest and incarceration that followed the first major act of civil disobedience by a priest in protest against the Vietnam War—the burning of draft files in the parking lot outside the Selective Service office in Catonsville, Maryland, in the late 1960s.[43] But during our 1996 interview, he spoke of a kinship among Jesuits that goes deeper than ideologies; he said that despite differences of outlook, he never felt at any time that his bond with the Society had been broken. He, too, had many supporters, both Jesuits and lay friends, who wrote and visited him.

For others, however, isolated from everyone—like John Havas and Dominic Tang in their prisons in China or Walter Ciszek in Siberia—communal support from those on the outside could come only through the realm of faith in the God who is always close to the imprisoned. There were no visits and no letters to serve as tangible reminders of friendship and support.

---

[43] Berrigan, *Lights On In The House Of the Dead,* 156.

SIXTEEN
Conclusion

THE JESUITS whose stories are touched upon in the preceding pages represent only a fraction of those who have undergone some form of incarceration since the time of Ignatius. Their experiences were vastly different, and even their understanding of what arrest and imprisonment might mean varied from person to person. Those sent on the English Mission in the sixteenth and seventeenth centuries knew that they would incur grave danger by returning to their native land to minister to its beleaguered Catholic population. They went there deliberately, nonetheless, even elated by the prospect that some might become martyrs.

A segment of John Gerard's *Autobiography of a Hunted Priest* exemplifies how these men viewed the dangers they might face. On his way to England, Gerard, along with another Jesuit, Edward Oldcorne—who would die a martyr eighteen years later—and two secular priests, stopped at a school for English Catholic boys that the Society had established at Eu. (It was later transferred to St. Omers.) The Jesuits there "all agreed that it would be very unwise to cross to England while things stood as they did. . . . The Spanish Fleet had exasperated the people against the Catholics; everywhere a hunt was being organized for Catholics. . . . In every village and along all the roads and lanes very close watches were kept to catch them." Reluctantly, the group decided to remain at Eu until they received advice from the head of the English Mission, Father Persons, who was in Rome. Persons wrote back that the situation in England had indeed deteriorated, "but the work we had in hand was God's undertaking; we were free either to go ahead with the enterprise or stay back until things in England had quietened down." Gerard and his companions needed no further encouragement. "This was the answer we desired. There was a short discussion, and then we found a ship at once to take us across and drop us in the north of England which seemed the quieter part."[1]

---

[1] Gerard, *Autobiography of a Hunted Priest*, 7–8.

Elsewhere, as in the Philippines during World War II, Jesuits taken prisoner by the Japanese were simply caught up in an international conflict, one they had seen coming. Consequently, imprisonment was just a matter-of-fact reality that had been expected. Then-scholastic Richard McSorley, in his recollections of his years of detention in the Philippines under the Japanese, writes of his wonderment at being regarded as a hero upon his return to his home in Philadelphia in 1945: "I didn't choose to be a prisoner of war; I was so by force. . . . What kind of a hero is that?"[2] For others, however, arrest and imprisonment constituted a shock, leaving them totally unprepared for what was to follow. The Jesuits arrested during the time of the Paris Commune in the 1870s, for instance, were taken totally unawares and had little understanding of why they were being held or what awaited them in the space of a month—violent death. "What is happening. What do they want of us? What are we accused of?" asks Pierre Olivaint at the time of his arrest by the Communards. Perplexed, he concludes, "I do not understand anything about all this."[3]

Once confined, however, many displayed a fortitude that testifies to their belief in the God who first guided them into the Society of Jesus and then promised to stay with them. As seen earlier, some experienced actual happiness at the conditions of their captivity. Ralph Sherwin, who was executed with Edmund Campion, wrote from prison of feeling so consoled that he could hardly refrain from smiling when he heard the rattling of his chains.[4] And for Rupert Mayer, as for Walter Ciszek, there was the happiness of knowing that incarceration meant fulfilling God's will for him. "God has given me to understand in these weeks . . . that He is satisfied with me. That makes me very happy. Nothing can trouble me now."[5]

Prayer, often in a specifically Ignatian mode, is the continuous thread that binds together the stories of those—some still living at the time of this writing—who have set down on paper detailed accounts of their incarceration. They speak of prayer in solitude or with others; prayer under torture or during interrogations; prayer during a dry mass or in the struggle to establish a daily order to secure a

---

[2] McSorley, *My Path to Peace and Justice*, 32.
[3] Ponlevoy, *Actes de la Captivité*, 6th ed., 37.
[4] Edwards, *Elizabethan Jesuits*, 29.
[5] Koerbling, *Father Rupert Mayer*, 128.

desperately needed interior calm. Prayer in its various forms helps to explain the tranquillity of Alois Grimm, a Jesuit imprisoned under Hitler. Two months before he was beheaded at the Brandenburg Prison, he wrote these words to his sister: "What I presently suffer is only a station on the way of the cross that God has traced for me in union with Christ."[6]

But as pointed out in the introduction, others have been crushed both in body and in spirit by the conditions to which they were subjected. Gabriel Malagrida, who became delusional while locked in his underground Portuguese dungeon at the order of the Marquis de Pombal, was only one of many who perished without leaving behind the story of their sufferings. Their own way of the cross, therefore, has a painful quality of isolation that unites them much more closely to the Jesus who prayed alone in Gethsemane.

Ciszek himself, for all his basic optimism and trust in God, knew periods of desolation as he watched at close range the dehumanizing effects of imprisonment. One summer evening, after an exhausting day of forced labor, he paused to admire a mother bird bringing food to the little ones in her nest. Suddenly he saw the mother bird plummet to the ground. A fellow prisoner had killed it with a stone. Ciszek describes his reaction: "I began to shake all over, completely beside myself with rage. I shouted and raved at him almost irrationally. That night," he continues, "I fell into a mood of depression that lasted more than two days."[7]

After his release and return to the United States, Ciszek visited the novitiate of the Maryland Province in Wernersville, Pennsylvania. A Jesuit who was present at one of his talks there told me of hearing Ciszek say that after one especially grueling interrogation, he had been tempted to commit suicide by throwing himself off a staircase as he was being led back to his cell. The incident is not mentioned in either of his books; perhaps it was considered out of keeping with their common theme of survival through trust in God.

Ciszek, along with Campion, Delp, and numerous others, made a conscious decision regarding their apostolic options. Had they so chosen, they could have honorably lived out their lives in safety, without ever facing the dangers and sufferings that overtook them.

---

[6] Lapomarda, *Jesuits and the Third Reich*, 75.
[7] Ciszek, *With God in Russia*, 243.

Rather than exposing himself to the pursuivants of Elizabethan England who eventually found him, Campion might have remained on the Continent using his Oxford education and brilliant mind to write in defense of the Catholic faith. Similarly, after his ordination in Rome, Ciszek served as a parish priest in Poland, which was not a dangerous assignment at the time. But as World War II approached, the American Embassy in Poland pressured him to return immediately to the United States. He not only ignored the embassy's advice, but took the further and far more dangerous step of crossing the border incognito into Russia, thus fulfilling a long-held dream of taking the Gospel into that Communist country. Nor was Alfred Delp obliged to join the Kreisau Circle, the anti-Nazi group wrongly accused of conspiring against Hitler's life. And knowing the dangers, Mayer did not have to continue preaching against Hitler's party; but he would not allow himself to be intimidated, despite Nazi orders to discontinue his preaching activities.

These and many of their fellow Jesuits throughout the centuries entered willingly and even happily into situations that—as they were well aware—placed them in direct conflict with governments that saw them as threats to be eliminated. It is almost a form of testimony to the very effectiveness of their work in such hostile climates that they were eventually arrested, incarcerated, tortured, and frequently executed.

Some could minister behind bars and some could not. Dominic Tang had little opportunity to reach out to his fellow prisoners, but one could hardly call his two decades of incarceration any the less apostolic. Rather, his experience demonstrated what might be called the role of obligatory passivity as a spiritual force. The enforced passivity to which he was subjected was part of his calling to be, as his friend the nun had foreseen, incarcerated for his faith. In joining the Jesuit order as a young man, he had responded to the call to be a contemplative in action. For the twenty-two years of his captivity, however, it was necessarily action of an interior kind.

The freedom felt by many Jesuits to enter into situations that they knew could lead to incarceration and death was a freedom based to some extent on the three vows of poverty, chastity, and obedience. In the interview with Patricio Cariola, for example, he said that it was only after his arrest and imprisonment in Chile that he came to understand fully the liberating effect of the vow of chastity. "When a person marries and has a family," he observed, "it's hard to take the risk of being picked up by the police." He added that members of religious orders in Santiago could become more fully involved in the kinds of situations that led to his own arrest, precisely because they had no dependent family members who would be directly affected by their enforced absence.[8]

A related circumstance for Cariola applied to the vow of poverty. "After the coup, professional people like doctors, who might be asked to treat people who'd been recently tortured, risked their careers." He spoke of a physician he knew who had been obliged to leave Chile for this reason. "His whole career was threatened and with it the source of his livelihood." In contrast, he said that the Jesuit vow of poverty has often freed them from a crippling worry over the possible loss of their careers and sources of income.

Obedience, too, in Cariola's view, is a freeing vow because with it goes an implicit commitment of fraternal support. "When I saw Jesuits waiting in the street as I was being taken in handcuffs from the court and led to the police van, I realized that there was a whole outfit praying for me and providing moral support." Nor had he acted without the permission of his superiors. Before becoming involved in the act that led to his arrest—seeking medical help for the wounded leftist, Nelson Gutierrez—he had asked for and received permission from his provincial and also from the auxiliary bishop of Santiago. The latter even lent him the car with which to pick up Gutierrez.

"I had a good church behind me," Cariola reflected in the interview. When the cardinal, who was away at the time of the arrest, returned from Rome, he visited him in jail the next day. Cariola then summarized what for him was the meaning of obedience: "You give up many things in taking the vow of obedience, but you get back much more by having the support of a team. Once I was behind bars, it was a great consolation to realize this." For John Dear as well, there was the consolation of receiving a letter from Peter-Hans Kolvenbach—the successor to Pedro Arrupe as superior general of the Society—commending him for having requested the permission of the provincial of the Maryland Province before engaging in his act of civil disobedience. "Be sure that I am aware of your situation [in the

---

[8] Interview with Patricio Cariola, July 2, 1994.

jail in North Carolina] and of the blessing of obedience you had for the events leading up to it."[9]

Writing of his incarceration experience, Joseph Mulligan also commented on the role of the vows. In somewhat the same vein as Cariola, he writes, "[T]he choice of celibacy as a life style can help prepare one for the risks of prophetic mission." As for freedom through the vow of poverty, he notes that "prophetic action requires a spirit of detachment, for it will result in persecution and deprivation." Finally, in his comments on obedience, he speaks in terms that call to mind not only Jesuits imprisoned for civil disobedience in this country, but also those earlier Jesuits like John Gerard and Edmund Campion who were confined for "disobedience" to state authorities of their time. For obedience, he says, includes the "possibility of disobedience to lesser lords, systems, and institutions."[10]

During our interview, I asked Mulligan whether he had requested permission before taking part in the Chicago 15 action. He answered that he had discussed the possibility of arrest with one of his superiors who had (as with John Dear twenty years later) been "quietly supportive." After his arrest, he received encouragement from other Jesuits who attended his trial, who testified in his behalf, and who organized a day of support at the time of sentencing. One is reminded that Cariola similarly felt uplifted at seeing fellow Jesuits waiting on the sidewalk as he was led out of the Santiago courthouse.

Others have also written of their experience of the vows in regard to incarceration. With an implicit reference to the vow of chastity—and its ramifications in terms of the renunciation of family life—Jacques Sommet at Dachau expresses relief that "I did not find myself in the situation of the man to whom they say: 'Tomorrow, your wife, your child are going to pay for it if . . . [you do not tell us what we want to know]' "[11] Since he had no wife or children, Sommet knew he was free from this kind of threat from his keepers.

For Peter van Gestel, obedience to religious authority was an important component in the attempt to form a community at Dachau. Once they had a superior, Léo de Coninck, and a spiritual father, Otto Pies, "the full communication with our rules and constitutions

---

[9] Dear, *Peace Behind Bars,* 185.
[10] Mulligan, "Reflections on the War in Vietnam," 20 ff.
[11] Sommet, *L'honneur de la liberté,* 64.

was restored, together with the full merit of a daily life of obedience."
Far from being burdensome, this very "daily life of obedience"
helped the sixty priests, brothers, novices, and scholastics, young and
old alike, to deal with the chaos of their surroundings and the utterly
destructive kind of obedience exacted by the SS guards. So meaningful were the vows to them, in fact, that "there were the regular Tridua
[three days of prayer] for the renovation of vows."[12]

The seriousness with which the vow of obedience was viewed—
and the pain it could sometimes cause—is illustrated in the story of
Edmund Campion, who was captured by priest hunters at the home
of the Yates family at Lyford, half a dozen miles from Oxford. In
July, 1591, he was traveling with the superior of the English Mission,
Robert Persons, and Brother Ralph Emerson. Realizing how close to
the Yates home they were, and remembering that Yates, who had
been incarcerated for his faith, had written to him asking him to
visit the family, Campion asked Persons's permission to stop there.
Persons, however, had to return to London. He knew, too, that stop-
ping could be dangerous since the Yates home was a well-known
gathering place for Catholics. Thus, he granted permission only with
great reluctance and with the strict injunction that Campion was to
spend no more than one day there. To ensure obedience to this command, he ordered Emerson to go with him as acting superior. Campion willingly agreed to this proviso, happy to be placed under
obedience to a brother.

At Lyford, Campion spent the night hearing confessions and giving
spiritual talks. After celebrating Mass in the morning, he rode off
with Emerson, obedient to Person's command. But when new visitors arrived and heard they had just missed an opportunity to be in
the presence of one so renowned in Catholic circles, a chaplain and
several others were sent after him. They pleaded with him to return,
but Campion declined, saying that he could do nothing without the
permission of Brother Emerson. At first Emerson vigorously denied
him permission to return, but the others argued until he relented.
(One can imagine the pressure Emerson felt, under attack on the
matter by the much better educated proponents of Campion's return.) Campion therefore returned to Lyford, while Emerson himself
continued on toward Lancashire. After Campion's capture, Emerson

---

[12] van Gestel, "Jesuits in the Bonds of Dachau," 115–16.

managed to escape to France where he rejoined Persons; but we are told that his "act of concession [by not insisting that Campion obey Parson's injunction] was to Ralph a source of deep repentance for the remainder of his life."[13] In concluding the story, Henry Foley observes in the *Records of the English Province*—somewhat sententiously—that it furnishes "a most useful lesson in the danger of departing in the least point of obedience from the orders of Superiors."[14]

The strong sense of obedience to authority—even to the rules established by prison authorities—turned out to be an indirect source of support for Dominic Tang in China, because it enabled him to adhere to the structure of a daily routine with a clear conscience. "In the prison, I always asked God to grant me the grace to progress in the virtues, e.g. humility and obedience. I considered the prison authorities my superiors. I obeyed them"—although he is careful to add, "only [in regard to] the regulations which did not conflict with the principles of my faith." The regulations he willingly followed included keeping his cell clean, and his obedience in this regard "won the praise of the cadres, who even opened the door so that other prisoners might learn."[15]

For some, however, the struggle to follow the vow of obedience behind bars could produce great stress. One example concerns the obligation to read the prayers of the breviary on a daily basis. Despite his overall sense of peace at being imprisoned, Rupert Mayer wrote to his provincial saying that he was troubled that he was not able to say his breviary as he felt he should. "I have to look closely at my work the whole day long [assembling paper bags], and then in the evening there's the breviary to go through and I have to . . . hurry and rush in order to finish. That puts an end to any calmness or peace of mind." He asks the provincial, "How shall I do it then? Shall I take the whole breviary, or which parts? . . . Please give me an answer." His biographer, Anton Koerbling, describes this incident as an example of "heroic obedience," and in a sense it is. Today, however, it might also be seen as a reflection of an overly rigid adherence to the structure of daily religious observances that for some—as with

---

[13] Foley, *Records of the English Province* (3):26–29.
[14] Ibid.
[15] Tang, *How Inscrutable His Ways!*, 116, 122.

Louis de Jabrun, whose excessively conscientious application to his work in a Nazi concentration camp led to his death—could partially undermine the deeper meaning of the vow of obedience as freeing.[16]

The Jesuits described in these pages have witnessed to their faith in a variety of ways during their periods of imprisonment. In addition, they represent a wide range of outlooks in regard to the mode of their witness. If they were all assembled today for a discussion among themselves, there might well be sharp disagreements along political lines. Would Pierre Olivaint and the other martyrs of the Paris Commune of the 1870s, for instance, have approved of the civil disobedience actions of Daniel Berrigan and others in the peace movement in the United States a hundred years later? Perhaps not, though by the same token they probably would have approved of Francis Hagerty's act of civil disobedience in blocking the abortion clinic in Massachusetts, because it was a form of nonviolent protest that underscored the Church's official teaching with respect to abortion. The actions of Berrigan and his successors, on the other hand, represented challenges to the military establishment, one with which Jesuits have frequently had close and sympathetic ties. (The same has been true in other countries too; for example, before he joined the Society, Olivaint's fellow martyr, Alexis Clerc, had been a captain in the French navy.)

But both Berrigan and Hagerty acted out of the conviction that defying the law could be a valid part of a Jesuit's vocation, just as the Elizabethan Jesuits believed it was their duty to break the laws of Queen Elizabeth in ministering to Catholics in England. "I'd do it again," said Hagerty in our interview. "God called me to it." In a way, the resoluteness of his statement parallels one made by Berrigan: "Jesuits are supposed to be in trouble—it's imbedded by now in the tradition." Being in trouble has always been accepted for reasons of conscience. For instance, arrested in connection with the Gunpowder Plot, Henry Garnet was taken to the Gatehouse prison in London. When he arrived, he called out, "Is there any of you here that be in for the Catholic faith?" Many shouted back, "Yes, yes, we are Catholics and prisoners for our conscience." Garnet replied, "Then I

---

[16] Koerbling, *Father Rupert Mayer*, 41.

am your fellow;" that is, he too saw himself as a prisoner of conscience glad to join those who were spiritual comrades.[17]

No matter how the trouble may come—through deliberately breaking the law, through enthusiastically accepting the kinds of risks that could lead to imprisonment, or through simply being caught up unwittingly in national and international upheavals—the experiences of incarcerated Jesuits form a distinctive part of the Society's history. If that part is painful in terms of hardships endured, it nevertheless attests to the Ignatian desire to find God not only in all things but also in all places, including jails, prisons, and other sites of confinement such as the Iroquois village where Jogues was held.

This part of Jesuit history is not yet over. In December, 1994 and January, 1995, two Chinese Jesuits were taken into custody and imprisoned. More recently, two Mexican Jesuits, Jerónimo Hernández López and Gonzálo Rosas Morales, were arrested in the spring of 1997 in the state of Chiapas. Police dragged them from their vehicle and beat them with their fists. They were held for three days and released only after the intervention of the provincial superior of the Province of Mexico, Mario López Barrio, and Bishop Raúl Vera López, auxiliary bishop of the Diocese of San Cristóbal de las Casas. The underlying reason for the arrest of the two Jesuits stemmed from their support of campesinos evicted from homes they had built on property belonging to a wealthy family in possession of over 3,000 acres of land near Palenque.[18] Hernández López and Rosas Morales are part of the long line of Jesuits extending back over 400 years who have chosen to promote gospel values through confronting unjust regimes that ignore the teachings of Jesus, especially, in this case, those that stem from God's special care for the poor.

More recently, in the United States Stephen Kelly was arrested at the end of 1999 in connection with an antiwar action at the Warfield Air National Guard Base in Middle River, Maryland. As part of a Ploughshares group of four, he took part in hammering and pouring blood on two A-10 Warthog aircraft mounted with a type of weapon that fires depleted uranium. In a letter from prison dated April 15, 2000, he told the author that this and earlier antiwar activities were based on Isaiah 2:4: "They shall beat their swords into ploughshares,

---

[17] Caraman, *Henry Garnet and the Gunpowder Plot*, 347.
[18] *National Jesuit News*, April/May, 1997, p. 1

and their spears into pruning hooks." Having already spent several years behind bars for similar actions, he spoke in his letter of his "prison vigil" as being "in itself my apostolate." The implication would seem to be that incarceration resulting from antiwar protests may indeed be for him an ongoing apostolate.[19]

Whether as Jesuits of the twentieth century in the United States or Mexico, or as Jesuits of centuries past in other parts of the world, throughout their stories of incarceration run the biblical themes of captivity and liberation. By their training and through their own intense prayer lives, they were intimately familiar with these themes as set forth in scripture. The psalms in particular, the heart of the breviary, were often committed to memory and served as reminders that the God of freedom could not forget servants ready to sacrifice their own liberty in service to the Kingdom. Verses from several were relevant to their situation. One, for example, is Psalm 68:34: "The Lord . . . does not despise his own that are in bonds." How comforting these words must have been to Jesuits literally in bonds—whether in the Tower of London in Elizabethan England or the labor camps of Albania in the 1950s—knowing that they were indeed "his own," securely cradled in God's hand no matter what lay before them. Similarly, in Psalm 79, they would have kept in mind verse 11: "Let the groans of the prisoners come before you, according to your great power, preserving those doomed to die." The groans of the prisoners were very real, since many Jesuits were subjected to physical torture and living conditions so debased that they amounted to a form of torture in themselves.

God did not always physically preserve Jesuits "doomed to die," but even those facing death by execution were aware that God was with them, and that in losing their lives they were following in the footsteps not only of St. Paul, "the prisoner of Jesus Christ" (Ephesians 3:1), but also of Jesus, a captive himself. To follow Jesus in his sufferings and—for not a few—in his death was implicitly to share in Christ's redemptive work. This work, they knew, was based on love. For example, when the Hungarian Jesuit John Havas was being expelled from China after two years in a Chinese prison, he could say to the guard who was escorting him to the border that he was leaving

---

[19] In his letter of April 15, 2000, Stephen Kelly was writing from the Roxbury Correction Institute in Hagerstown, Maryland.

against his own wishes. As noted in the chapter on ministry, he made it clear to the guard that he would prefer to die in his Chinese prison than to enjoy freedom in Hong Kong, "because I love you"—that is, the people of China in whose loving service, in or out of prison, he had spent much of his life. Physical liberty meant less to him than the interior freedom he had known in his cell, a freedom based on a knowledge of God's love for him and for all humanity. The same sustaining knowledge was a force in the lives of all the incarcerated Jesuits described in these pages.

GLOSSARY

This list contains the names, dates, and brief biographies of most—but not all—of the Jesuits described in *With Christ in Prison,* along with short explanations of certain relevant terms.

Arbona, Bartolomeo. 1862–1936. Despite religious persecution during the Spanish civil war, celebrated Mass in homes and secretly distributed communion in parks. Arrested in 1936 and jailed for three days before being executed at age 74.

Arrupe, Pedro. 1907–1991. Spanish missionary to Japan; arrested there and jailed for several weeks at beginning of World War II. Later served as Superior General of Society of Jesus (1965–1983).

Battles, Constantine March. 1877–1936. Brother assigned to Ramon Lull Academy in Sarria at time of Spanish Civil War. Executed after five weeks in jail at age 60.

Beaucé, Eugène. 1878–1962. French missionary imprisoned in China with Eugene Fahy (q.v.) and others by Communist authorities in early 1950s. Expelled from country after about a year.

Berrigan, Daniel. b. 1921. Arrested in 1968 after burning draft files in parking lot of Selective Service office near Baltimore, Maryland, as protest against the Vietnam War. Spent two years in Danbury Federal Prison in Connecticut.

Beschet, Paul. b. 1921. While still a scholastic, joined a group of young French Catholics who voluntarily traveled to Germany in 1943 to support Frenchmen conscripted by Nazis as forced laborers. Arrested and sent first to a concentration camp and then to a forced labor factory in Zwickau until liberation.

Bichsel, William J. b. 1928. Arrested several times in connection with civil disobedience protests at Trident submarine base on Puget Sound in Washington State in the early 1980s. In 1997, incarcerated again for protests at the School of the Americas at Fort Benning, Georgia.

Bouchet, Venantius. 1655–1732. French missionary who began working at Madurai Mission in India in 1689. Jailed during anti-Christian persecution.

Brébeuf, Jean de. 1503–1649.French missionary working among Hurons in "New France," with Isaac Jogues (q.v.) and other Jesuits. Captured and tortured to death by Iroquois.

Briant, Alexander. 1553–1581. Sent from Rome to England during persecution of Catholics. During two years in prison, applied to Society and was accepted. Tortured and hanged.

Brito, John de. 1647–1693. Portuguese missionary. Lived as an Indian ascetic in order to approach all castes. Worked mostly in Madurai Province. Held in jail one week before being beheaded.

Campion, Edmund. 1540–1581. Reared as Protestant but reconciled to Church while attending English College in Douai. One of first Jesuits to be assigned to English Mission in 1580. Arrested within a year and tortured prior to execution.

Cariola, Patricio. b. 1928. Incarcerated in Santiago for two months in 1975 for assisting a leftist guerrilla to obtain medical help after being wounded by Chilean security forces.

Carney, James Guadalupe. 1924–1983. Missouri Province Jesuit who worked with campesinos in Honduras. Expelled in 1979. Returned to Latin America in 1980 to work in Nicaragua; secretly crossed border into Honduras with group of guerrillas and disappeared.

Cavanaugh, Paul W. 1901–1975. Chaplain in U.S. Army during World War II. Captured by Germans in 1944 and spent five months in prison camp in Hammelburg.

Chu, Francis Xavier. 1913–1983. Arrested in 1953 in Shanghai by Communist authorities. Incarcerated in prisons and labor camps for thirty years. Died in prison hospital of a heart attack.

Ciszek, Walter. 1904–1984. American son of Polish immigrant parents. After ordination in Rome in 1938, assigned to Poland. Entered

Russia disguised as workman. Following arrest, spent fifteen years in prisons and labor camps. Released in 1955. Allowed to return to United States in 1963.

Clifford, John W. 1917–1984. California Province Jesuit working in China; arrested in early 1950s and imprisoned for a year before being expelled.

Clink. Name of famous London prison that came to be used as a term for penal facilities in general. (According to the *Oxford English Dictionary,* the word may be derived from the word "clinch," meaning to fasten securely.)

Clorivière, Pierre Joseph de. 1735–1820. Imprisoned for five years for alleged complicity in plot against Napoleon. After restoration of the Society, became superior of French Jesuits and novice master.

Collins, Dominic. 1567–1607. As a young man, lived as a soldier until joining the Society in his thirties. Taken prisoner by the English in Ireland and imprisoned. Offered freedom on condition of renouncing faith, but refused and was hanged.

Colombière, Claude de la. 1641–1682. Spiritual director of Margaret Mary Alacoque. Sent to England in 1676 as court preacher to Duchess of York. Falsely accused of complicity in Titus Oates plot (q.v.). Jailed five weeks before being sent back to France.

Commune of 1871. Name given to revolutionary group that occupied Paris in spring of 1871, after municipal government had moved to Versailles out of fear of German occupation of Paris during Franco-Prussian War. Persecution of religious by Commune leaders, with five Jesuits imprisoned and executed:

> **Bengy, Anatole de.** 1824–1871. Member of St. Genevieve School community. Caring for soldiers wounded during Franco-Prussian War at time of arrest with eleven other Jesuits on April 11, 1871.

> **Caubert, Jean.** 1811–1871. Former lawyer who joined the Society as late vocation. Member of rue de Sèvres community. Arrested there with Pierre Olivaint on April 18, 1871.

> **Clerc, Alexis.** 1819–1871. Former naval commander who, like Caubert, joined the Society as late vocation. Taught math at St.

Genevieve School and tended wounded soldiers. Arrested with Léon Ducoudray on April 4, 1871.

Ducoudray, Léon. 1827–1871. Rector of St. Genevieve School community. Arrested with Clerc and de Bengy on April 4, 1871.

Olivaint, Pierre. 1816–1871. Member of St. Genevieve School community who also tended those wounded in Franco-Prussian War. Arrested with Caubert on April 4, 1871, and slain with him and de Bengy by mob on May 16.

Contemplation to Attain the Love of God. A key meditation toward the end of the *Spiritual Exercises* of St. Ignatius. Begins with two points: Love should reveal itself in deeds rather than words, and love consists in a mutual sharing. Ends with prayer of self-offering: "Take, Lord, and receive all my liberty, my memory, my understanding, and my entire will, all that I have and possess."

Corby, Ralph. 1598–1644. Secular priest who entered the Society at age of 28; assigned to English Mission six years later. Ministered in Durham area. Arrested in 1644 by Calvinist soldiers while celebrating Mass in a home. Held for two months in prison and then executed at Tyburn.

Cordier, Jean-Nicolas. 1710–1794. Arrested in 1793 during French Revolution for refusing to adhere to laws and measures attacking the Church. Incarcerated on prison ship at Rochefort along with Joseph Imbert (q.v.) and hundreds of other priests.

Dajani, Daniel. 1906–1946. Albanian who was president of St. Xavier College and rector of Pontifical Seminary in Shkodra. Arrested with Gjon Fausti (q.v.) on December 31, 1945, by Communist authorities. Executed on March 4, 1946.

Dear, John S. b. 1959. As Maryland Province novice, took vow of nonviolence and became active in antiwar activities. Arrested on December 7, 1993 (anniversary of Pearl Harbor) after entering Seymour Johnson Air Force Base in Goldsboro, North Carolina. Sentenced to twelve months, of which seven and a half were served in local jails, then house arrest at Jesuit community in Washington, D.C.

De Coninck, Léo. 1889–1956. Belgian arrested for encouraging clergy to resist Nazis. At Dachau 1942–45. Became superior of Jesuits there and bolstered morale by conferences and retreats.

Delp, Alfred. 1907–1945. An editor of Jesuit periodical *Stimmen der Zeit*. Member of Kreisau Circle, an anti-Nazi group planning for Christian social order after war. Arrested in 1944 following attempt on Hitler's life and executed following pseudo-trial.

Doan, Joseph Nguyen-Công. b. 1941.Superior of Jesuits in Vietnam. Imprisoned for nine years in the 1980s by Vietnamese Communists.

Dominus ac Redemptor. The brief promulgated by Pope Clement XIV in 1773 suppressing the Society of Jesus, a move urged by the Bourbons, the Duc de Choiseul, the Marquis de Pombal (q.v.), and various political factions inimical to the Jesuits. Society restored in 1814 by Pius VII.

Douai. City in northern France and site of a college established by English Catholics after accession of Queen Elizabeth in 1580 to ensure possibility of Catholic education for English youth. Also, a center for publication of Catholic literature.

Dunda, Gerardas. 1914–1996. Lithuanian pastor arrested by Soviet authorities in 1947. Spent more than seven years in prison and labor camps in Siberia.

Eckhart, Anselm. 1721–1809. German working at a Portuguese mission in South America. At time of suppression of Society in Portugal, arrested in 1755 and sent back to Portugal where he spent eighteen years in prison.

Emerson, Ralph. d. 1604. Jesuit brother who assisted Edmund Campion (q.v.) during latter's brief ministry in Elizabethan England. Incarcerated for twenty years.

Esteban, Tomás. 1879–1933. Missionary in China. Arrested by Communists in 1931. Held for ransom and died in their custody after two years.

Evans, Michael A. b. 1954. While working in Northern Sudan with the American Refugee Committee in 1989, arrested by Sudanese secret police. Held incommunicado under house arrest and then expelled.

Fahy, Eugene E. 1911–1997. Arrested by Chinese Communists on August 28, 1951, while associated with Aurora University. Imprisoned for nearly a year in Shanghai. Expelled from China in June 1952.

Fausti, Gjon. 1889–1946. Was vice-provincial for Albanian Jesuits when arrested by Communist authorities on December 31, 1945, with Daniel Dajani (q.v.), president of St. Xavier College in Shkodra. Jailed and executed after six-day trial.

Fekete, Michael. 1907–1973. Hungarian brother assigned to mission in China. Arrested by Communists in 1951, along with Eugene Fahy (q.v.) and other Jesuits, but was released and expelled.

Fernandes, Ambrose. 1551–1620. Portuguese brother arrested in Japan during persecution of Christians and incarcerated with Carlo Spinola (q.v.). Died after two years in prison.

Frater, Robert. 1915–1987. A retreat director in East Germany; arrested by Communist authorities in 1958 with three other Jesuits. Imprisoned for approximately a year.

Gardin, Giacomo (Ják). b. 1905. Italian Jesuit teaching at St. Xavier College in Shkodra when arrested by Albanian Communist authorities. Imprisoned from 1945 until 1955.

Garnet, Henry. 1555–1606. Sent to English Mission with Robert Southwell (q.v.) in 1586. Succeeded William Weston (q.v.) as superior of mission. Arrested in 1606 in connection with Gunpowder Plot (q.v.); imprisoned and executed the same year.

Garnet, Thomas. 1575–1608. Nephew of Henry Garnet (q.v.). Like his uncle, arrested in connection with Gunpowder Plot (q.v.). Banished in 1606; returned to England later and was arrested and executed.

Gerard, John. 1564–1637. Sent to English Mission in 1588. Arrested after eighteen years of ministry. Escaped from Tower of London in 1597 and crossed to Continent. Died in Rome at age 73.

Goupil, René. 1607–1642. North American martyr. Attached self to Society as donné (lay assistant) and sent to New France. Assigned to Huron Mission with Isaac Jogues (q.v.). Pronounced vows as brother shortly before death at hands of Iroquois.

Grimm, Alois. 1886–1944. Arrested by Nazis because of influential work with youth. Incaracerated in Brandenburg Prison and beheaded.

Gunpowder Plot. Conspiracy by group of Catholic laymen angered by James I's failure to show more tolerance to Catholics. Intended to blow up Parliament and the king on November 5, 1605. Government tried to implicate Jesuits, but could prove nothing.

Hagerty, Francis O. "Skip." 1916–1997. Spent four and a half months in jail in Boston area for helping to block abortion clinic in Brookline as part of Operation Rescue action.

Hausmann, Carl W. 1898–1945. American missioned to Philippines. Chaplain in U.S. Army during World War II. Interned by Japanese for three years. Died of hunger in prison-transport ship.

Havas, John A. 1908–1994. Hungarian missioned to China. Arrested by Communists and incarcerated for twenty-two months, from September 1952 until May 1954. Expelled from country on release.

Hernández López, Jerónimo. b. 1955. Arrested with fellow-Mexican Jesuit Gonzálo Rosas Morales (q.v.) in March of 1996 in Chiapas and briefly jailed; both had been defending the rights of the indigenous people.

Holtby, Richard. 1552–1646. Sent to English Mission in 1579. Ministered there for fifty years without ever being arrested. After execution of Henry Garnet (q.v) in 1606, became superior of mission until 1609.

Houle, John A. 1914–1997. Missioned to China and worked in Christ the King Parish in Shanghai. Arrested and imprisoned from 1953 to 1957.

Ignatius of Loyola. 1491–1556. Founder of the Jesuit order (Society of Jesus), who was briefly incarcerated in Spain by the Inquisition.

Imbert, Joseph. ca. 1720–1794. Imprisoned with Jean-Nicolas Cordier (q.v.) and other priests and held on prison ship at Rochefort during the French Revolution. Died of typhoid.

Jabrun, Louis de. 1883–1943. French. Arrested by Nazis and sent to Buchenwald. Died at hands of a kapo in a concentration camp hospital.

Jalics, Franz. b. 1927. Hungarian. Worked with poor in Argentina in the 1970s; arrested by right-wing military group in 1976. Held captive for five months.

Jogues, Isaac. 1607–1646. North American martyr. Worked with Hurons in New France for six years. Captured by Iroquois with René Goupil (q.v.); escaped to France, but killed on return.

Kavanagh, Joseph J. 1915–1999. While a scholastic in Philippines, taken captive by Japanese early in World War II. Interned at Los Baños with other Jesuits.

Kelly, Stephen M. b. 1949. Arrested and imprisoned for antiwar activities–first, in August, 1995 in California (damaging missile shells); then in February, 1997 in Maine (damaging equipment on guided missile launcher); and in December 1999 at Warfield Air National Guard Base in Middle River, Maryland (damaging weapons using depleted uranium).

Kisai, James. 1533–1597. Novice brother who was martyred with Paul Miki in Nagasaki during a persecution of Christians.

Koláček, Aloysius. 1887–1970. Arrested by Nazis in March, 1941 while superior of St. Ignatius Church in Prague. Imprisoned at Dachau; secretly said Mass for other prisoners.

Korec, Ján. b. 1924. Czech. While studying theology, arrested by Communists. Released and worked as laborer. Secretly ordained a bishop at age 27 in order to be able to ordain priests. Served eight years in prison.

Lalemant, Gabriel. 1610–1649. North American martyr. Captured by Iroquois and tortured to death with Jean de Brébeuf (q.v.).

Laynez, Francis. 1656–1715. Portuguese, sent to Madurai Mission. Imprisoned during anti-Christian persecution and sentenced to death in 1693, but later released. Became bishop of San Thomé.

Lenz, John (Johan Maria). b. 1902. Austrian parish priest arrested by Nazis for criticizing Hitler's National Socialist party. Six years at Dachau. (Left the Society after the war to become a secular priest.)

Lillie, John. b. ca. 1560. Layman who, while imprisoned in Tower of London with John Gerard (q.v.), helped him to escape. Later escaped himself and became a Jesuit brother in Rome.

Luli, Anton. b. 1910. Albanian assigned to Xavier College in Shkodra. Arrested after Communist takeover in 1944. Seventeen years of forced labor.

Lusher, Edward. 1587–1665. To English Mission in 1633. After arrest of Henry Morse (q.v.), took over latter's ministry to plague victims. Died of disease during second outbreak.

Malagrida, Gabriel. 1689–1761. Arrested in Portugal at instigation of Marquis de Pombal (q.v.) in connection with alleged attempt on king's life. Executed after two and a half years in prison.

Martin, Clarence A. b. 1918. Interned as scholastic by Japanese in Philippines during World War II. Held at Los Baños.

Matulionis, Jonas Kastytis. b. 1931. Lithuanian secretly ordained in 1980. While serving as parish priest, arrested by Communists in 1984 and sent to labor camp.

Maya, Sebastian de. 1598–1638. Portuguese assigned to Madurai Mission who was arrested and incarcerated with Roberto de Nobili (q.v.) during anti-Christian persecution.

Mayer, Rupert. 1876–1945. Arrested several times in the 1930s for speaking out against National Socialist Party. At outbreak of World War II, sent to Sachsenhausen concentration camp and later held in Benedictine monastery until end of war.

McSorley, Richard T. b. 1914. Interned by Japanese while a scholastic in Philippines. Became peace activist after war.

Menzel, Josef. b. 1916. In retreat work in former East Germany when arrested by state police in July 1958 with three other Jesuits also engaged in pastoral work there. Sentenced to a year and a half in prison.

Middleton, Robert. 1570–1601. Secular priest who became Jesuit while in Gatehouse prison in London before being hanged.

Miki, Paul. 1564–1597. Japanese scholastic arrested during anti-Christian persecution. Executed after five months in prison, along with another scholastic (John Soan de Goto), a novice brother (James Kisai), six Franciscans, and their fifteen tertiaries.

More, Henry. 1586–1661. Sent to English Mission in 1621 and arrested eleven years later. Imprisoned for a year. Later wrote first account of the mission published in 1660. Not to be confused with Henry Morse (q.v.).

Morse, Henry. 1595–1645. Secular priest ministering in England. After arrest, became Jesuit in prison with Jesuit prisoner (John Robinson) as novice master. On release, worked among plague victims. Arrested again and executed.

Moussé, Jean. b. 1921. Unable to enter Society because of war conditions in France; arrested by Nazis and sent to Buchenwald. Became Jesuit soon after war.

Moyano Walker, Juan Luís. b. 1946. Scholastic working with poor in barrio of Buenos Aires when arrested by right-wing military in 1974. Tortured and held for three months.

Müldner, Josef. 1911–1984. Parish priest in the Zwickau area of East Germany. Arrested in 1958 by Communist authorities and sentenced to a year and three months in prison.

Mulligan, Joseph E. b. 1943. While scholastic, arrested as peace protester during Vietnam War as one of Chicago 15. Served two years in federal prison in Minnesota.

Murphy, Edward "Ned" J. b. 1937. Frequently arrested and jailed in connection with Vietnam antiwar protests and other civil disobedience issues.

Nagascima, Michael. 1582–1628. Provided hospitality to Jesuit priests and other missionaries during persecution in Japan. Received into Society as brother in 1627. Arrested and, after four months in prison, died under torture.

Nobili, Roberto de. 1577–1656. Missioned to India after ordination. Adapted self to native customs, living as a sannyasi (holy ascetic) and thereby gained acceptance. Jailed twice because of anti-Christian pressure.

Ogilvie, John. 1579–1615. Worked among Catholics in Scotland for eleven months before arrest. Imprisoned for five months and tortured before being hanged.

Owen, Nicholas. d. 1606. Entered as brother and worked with Edmund Campion (q.v.) and Henry Garnet (q.v.) on English Mission. Built hiding places for priests in Catholic homes. Arrested after discovery of Gunpowder Plot (q.v.) and died under torture.

Pacheco, Francis. 1565–1626. Portuguese serving on Japanese Mission. Expelled in 1614 when Christianity was outlawed, but returned in disguise. Imprisoned and burned at stake.

Paez, Pedro. 1564–1622. Spaniard sent to reestablish Jesuit mission in Ethiopia. Underwent various forms of captivity for seven years, including a period as galley slave.

Pantalija, Gjon. 1887–1947. Italian brother working in Albania. Arrested by Communist authorities in 1946 and imprisoned. Died as a result of torture.

Pérez Aguirre, Luís. b. 1941. Social activist and founder of Uruguayan branch of Servicio Paz y Justicia (SERPAJ), a human rights organization. Arrested and tortured in the 1980s during military dictatorship.

Persons, Robert. 1546–1612. Accompanied Edmund Campion (q.v.) and Brother Ralph Emerson (q.v.) to England to begin mission there in 1580. Returned to Continent in 1546 and served as focus of opposition to anti-Catholic policy in England.

Phillips, Thomas. 1904–1968. California Jesuit who was rector of Christ the King Parish in Shanghai. Arrested by Chinese Communists in early 1950s with John Clifford (q.v.); incarcerated for three years.

Pies, Otto. 1901–1960. Prior to arrest by Nazis, had been novice master for Eastern Province of Germany. Imprisoned at Dachau in 1941. Served Jesuits there as spiritual father.

Pombal, Marquis [Marqûes] de (Sebastião José de Carvalho). 1699–1782. Powerful political figure in Portugal and enemy of the Society of Jesus. As prime minister, helped bring about the suppression of the order and the expulsion of Jesuits from Portugal and its missions in 1759.

Pounde, Thomas. 1539–1615. Layman who helped Campion (q.v.) and Persons (q.v.) after their arrival to begin English Mission. Incarcerated for thirty years. Received into Society while in prison.

Prescott, Cuthbert. 1592–1647. Entered Society as brother and sent to English Mission to assist Catholic youth to enroll in Catholic schools abroad. Died in prison at age 55.

Pro, Miguel. 1891–1927. During prohibition of Catholic worship in Mexico, secretly said Mass for groups and distributed communion. Arrested after attempt on life of General Alvaro Obregon; confined in jail for a week before execution.

Ricci, Lorenzo. 1703–1775. Eighteenth superior general of Society of Jesus. Imprisoned after suppression for two and a half years in Rome's Castel Sant'Angelo, where he died.

Robinson, John. 1598–1675. Imprisoned twice on English Mission. During first incarceration, served as novice master to fellow prisoner Henry Morse (q.v.). Sentenced to death in 1653, but sentence never carried out.

Rosas Morales, Gonzálo. b. 1955. While working with indigenous people in Mexico, arrested on March 14, 1997, with Jerónimo Hernández López (q.v.) and briefly detained.

Rösch, Augustin. 1893–1961. Provincial of Upper German Province and superior of Alfred Delp (q.v.) and Rupert Mayer (q.v.). Imprisoned after the 1944 attempt on Hitler's life.

Rueter, Wilhelm. 1911–1987. One of four Jesuits in pastoral work in Communist East Germany. Arrested by state security police in 1958. Sentenced to one year and five months in prison.

St. Omer's College. School for English youth established in northern France in 1593 by Robert Persons (q.v.) during persecution of Catholics under Elizabeth I.

Salès, Jacques. 1556–1593. Arrested by French Calvinists while ministering in Aubenas. Held briefly with Brother Guillaume Saultemouche (q.v.) and killed in town square.

Saultemouche, Guillaume. 1557–1593. Brother working with Jacques Salès (q.v.) in Aubenas when arrested by French Calvinists. Refused offer of freedom and was killed with Salès.

Šeškevičius, Antanas. b. 1914. Lithuanian imprisoned by Russian KGB because of youth work. Sent to Soviet concentration camp and later to forced-labor factory.

Shen, Louis. b. 1936. Joined Society between periods of incarceration in China. After release, studied theology in California and ordained there in 1993.

Soan de Goto, John. 1578–1597. Scholastic martyred with Paul Miki (q.v.) and James Kisai (q.v.) in Nagasaki during persecution of Christians.

Sommet, Jacques. b. 1912. While a scholastic in France, arrested by Nazis in 1944 because of resistance work. Imprisoned for a year at Dachau.

Southwell, Robert. 1561–1595. Assigned to English Mission with Henry Garnet (q.v.) as superior. Ministered for six years before arrest; imprisoned for three years, tortured, and finally executed.

Spinola, Carlo. 1564–1622. Italian missionary in Japan. Arrested with Brother Ambrose Fernandes (q.v) during anti-Christian persecution. After four years in prison, burned at stake.

Suppression of the Society of Jesus. 1773–1814. Caused by enmity toward Jesuits on part of powerful political groups and individuals like Pombal (q.v.). Began in Portugal in 1759, then France and Spain. Under pressure, Pope Clement XIV finally ordered suppression of the whole Society in 1773 with his brief, *Dominus ac Redemptor* (q.v.).

Tamkevičius, Sigitas. b. 1938. Lithuanian pastor arrested by Russian KGB and tried in 1983. Sentenced to six years in labor camps.

Tang, Dominic. 1908–1995. Archbishop of Canton, arrested in 1958 for refusing to approve government-controlled Catholic Patriotic Association. Imprisoned for twenty-two years. Died in Connecticut.

Third Degree of Humility. A key meditation in the Second Week of *Spiritual Exercises* of St. Ignatius that focuses on desire to share in poverty, humiliation, and insults endured by Christ.

Thornton, James Enda. 1910–1993. Californian serving in Shanghai at time of Communist take-over. Imprisoned in 1950–51.

Titus Oates Plot. Alleged plot fabricated by Titus Oates, who claimed Jesuits and others planned to assassinate Charles II in 1678. Provoked large-scale persecution of English Catholics.

Ts'ai, Francis Xavier. 1907–1997. Arrested in 1953 while pastor of St. Ignatius Parish in Shanghai. Not tried until 1960. In prisons and labor camps for thirty-five years, 1953–88. Died in New York.

Turner, Anthony. 1628–1679. Gave himself up to be with fellow Jesuits arrested during persecution in wake of Titus Oates plot (q.v.). Condemned with four other Jesuits and executed.

Van Gestel, Peter. 1897–1972. At time of arrest by Nazis in September 1941, was rector of Jesuit theologate at Maastricht in Holland. Sent to Dachau in 1941.

Walpole, Henry. 1558–1595. Arrested on arrival at English Mission. Imprisoned and frequently tortured before being hanged.

Weston, William. 1550–1615. Missioned to England in 1584. Spent eighteen years in various prisons. Exiled in 1603 after accession of James I.

White, Andrew. 1579–1656. Sent to North American Mission with Lord Baltimore's expedition to Maryland. Captured by Puritans and sent back to England as prisoner.

Wicht, Juan Julio. b. 1932. One of many taken hostage in December, 1996 by rebel Peruvian group in residence of Japanese ambassador in Lima, Peru. Held captive in embassy for four months.

Wong, George B. b. 1918. Arrested by Communists in Shanghai in 1955. In Chinese prisons and labor camps for more than twenty-four years.

BIBLIOGRAPHY

Anonymous. "Philippine Jesuits under the Japanese." *Woodstock Letters* 74(3) (October 1945).

———. "Varia: Germany." (re Aloysius Koláček). *Woodstock Letters* 74(4) (December 1945).

———. "Witness to the Faith" (re Augustin Rösch). *Yearbook of the Society of Jesus 1962–63.* Rome: General Curia of the Society of Jesus, 85. (Published yearly)

———. *Jesuits in China 1949–1990: Ignatian Year.* Hong Kong: China P. Macau Hong Kong P. DCA, 1990.

Anderson, George M., S.J. "A Jesuit prisoner in Vietnam. An interview with Joseph Doan." *America* (September 16, 1995):12–18.

———. "A Prisoner for Peace: An Interview with Stephen Kelly." *America* (October 17, 1998):14–18.

Bailey, David C. *!Viva Cristo Rey! The Cristero Revolution and the Church–State Conflict in Mexico.* Austin: University of Texas Press, 1974.

Bangert, William V., S.J. *A History of the Society of Jesus.* St. Louis: Institute of Jesuit Sources, 1972.

Bannon, Edwin. *Refractory Men, Fanatical Women: Fidelity to Conscience during the French Revolution.* Harrisburg, Pa.: Morehouse Publishing Co., 1992.

Bartoli, Daniello, S.J. *Dell'Istoria della Compagnia di Gesù.* Ancona: Giuseppi Ameli, 1843.

Bashati, Myfit Q. "An Eye-witness Account of the Last Days of Fr. Daniel Dajani, S.J." *Albanian Catholic Bulletin* (University of San Francisco, Xavier Hall), 15 (1994).

Bazelaire, Max de, S.J. *Le Père de Clorivière.* Paris: Société de l'Apostolat de la Prière, 1966.

Beaucé, Eugène. "Quelques Expériences Communistes en Chine." Unpublished manuscript, Manila, 1952.

Becker, Kurt. *I Met a Traveller: The Triumph of Father Phillips.* New York: Farrar, Straus and Cudahy, 1958.

Belli, Gino (Pseudonym). Interview, October 20, 1993.

Berrigan, Daniel. *No Bars to Manhood*. New York: Doubleday, 1970.

——. *Lights On In The House Of The Dead*. New York: Doubleday, 1974.

——. *To Dwell in Peace. An Autobiography*. San Francisco: Harper and Row, 1987.

——. Interview, January 4, 1994.

Beschet, Paul. *Mission en Thuringe au Temps du Nazism*. Paris: Éditions Ouvrières, 1989.

Bichsel, William J., S.J. Telephone interview with author, January 24, 1995.

Blanc, Jules. *Les Martyrs d'Aubenas*. Valence: Chez l'Auteur, 1906.

Blomme, Yves. *Les Prêtres Déportés sur les Pontons de Rochefort*. Saint-Jean-d'Angély: Éditions Bourdessoules, 1994.

Boero, Giuseppe, S.J. *Istoria della Vita e del Martirio dei Santi Giapponesi Paolo Michi, Giovanni Soan de Goto e Giacomo Chisai*. Rome: Civiltà Cattolica, 1862.

——. *Relazione della Gloriosa Morte de duecento e cinque beati martiri nel Giappone*. Rome: Civiltà Cattolica, 1867.

Braie, Pierre, and Emile Temimé. *The Revolution and the Civil War in Spain*. Cambridge: MIT Press, 1970.

——. *Henry Morse: Priest of the Plague*. New York: Farrar, Straus and Cudahy, 1957.

——. *The Lost Empire. The Story of the Jesuits in Ethiopia 1555–1634*. London: Sidgwick and Jackson, 1985.

Carayon, Auguste. *Documents Inédits sur la Compagnie de Jésus*. 16 vols. Poitiers: Henri Oudin, Imprimeur; 1870. (These *Documents* include his *Les Prisons du Marquis de Pombal*, published as a separate volume in 1865. Paris: L'Ecureux Librairie.)

Cariola, Patricio, S.J. "Dos Meses." In *Noticias Jesuitas Chile* (Santiago) (July/August 1976).

——. Interview with author, July 2, 1994.

Carmelite sister of Macao [Sr. Teresa of Jesus]. *If the Grain of Wheat Dies*. [Life of Francis Xavier Chu]. Privately printed, through Provincial for the China Apostolate, Xavier House, 167 Argyle St., Kowloon, Hong Kong, n.d.

Carney, James Guadalupe. *To Be a Revolutionary*. San Francisco: Harper and Row, 1985.

Carnota, John Smith Athelstane. *Memoirs of the Marquis of Pombal*. London: Longman, Brown, and Green, 1843.

Catholic Records Society. *Unpublished Documents Relating to the English Martyrs*, vol. 1, 1584–1603. Collected and edited by John Hungerford Pollen, S.J. London: J. Whitehead and Son, 1908.

Cavanaugh, Paul W., S.J. Circular letter to Missouri Province military chaplains, July 23, 1945.

Challoner, Richard, D. D. *Memoirs of Missionary Priests*. New York: P. J. Kenedy and Sons, 1924.

Cheke, Marcus. *Dictator of Portugal: A Life of the Marquis of Pombal 1699–1782*. London: Sidgwick and Jackson, 1938.

Chenu, Bruno, Claude Prud'homme, France Queré, and Jean-Claude Thomas. *The Book of Christian Martyrs*. New York: Crossroads, 1990.

Chronicle of the Catholic Church in Lithuania. Translated by Casimir Pugevicius. Lithuanian Catholic Religious Aid, Brooklyn, N.Y. Nos. 58 (October 1, 1983); 61 (April 9, 1984); 63 (November 15, 1984); 68 (March 19, 1987); 70 (December 14, 1986); 72 (January 8, 1988); 77 (September 28, 1988); and 78 (January 30, 1989).

Ciszek, Walter J., S.J. *With God in Russia*. New York: Doubleday/Image, 1966.

———. *He Leadeth Me*. New York: Doubleday/Image, 1973.

Clair, Charles. *Pierre Olivaint*. Paris: Librairie Victor Palme, 1890.

Clifford, John W. *In the Presence of My Enemies*. New York: W.W. Norton and Co., 1963.

Collins. Thomas. *Martyr In Scotland. The Life and Times of John Ogilvie*. London: Burns and Oates, 1955.

The Constitutions of the Society of Jesus. Translated by George E. Ganss, S.J. St. Louis: Institute of Jesuit Sources, 1970.

Cooper, Michael, S.J. *Rodrigues the Interpreter*. New York: Weatherhill, 1974.

Crétineau-Joly, Jacques. *Histoire religieuse politique et littéraire de la Compagnie de Jésus*. 6 vols. Paris: 1844–56.

Dear, John S., S.J. Letter to author, January 14, 1994.

———. *Peace Behind Bars*. Kansas City, Mo.: Sheed and Ward, 1995.

Debs, Eugene Victor. *Walls and Bars*. Chicago: Charles H. Kerr and Co., 1973.

De Coninck, Léo, S.J. "The Priests of Dachau." *The Month* CLXXXII (950), March–April 1946.

Decorme, Gerard, S.J. *La Obra de los Jesuítas Mexicanos durante la Epoca Colonial 1572–1767.* 2 vols. Mexico City: Antigua Libreria Robredo de José Porrua y Hijos, 1941.

Delp, Alfred, S.J. *The Prison Meditations of Alfred Delp.* New York: Herder and Herder, 1963.

Devlin, Christopher. *The Life of Robert Southwell.* London: Sidgwick and Jackson, 1967.

Dietsch, Jean-Claude, S.J. *One Jesuit's Spiritual Journey: Autobiographical Conversations with Pedro Arrupe, S.J.* Translated by Ruth Bradley. St. Louis: Institute of Jesuit Sources, 1986.

Diocese of Dublin. "Cause for the Beatification and Canonization of the Servants of God Dermot O'Hurley, Archbishop and Companions, who died in Ireland in defense of the Catholic faith 1579–1654." Rome, 1988.

Doan, Joseph Nguyen-Công. Interview, April 11, 1995.

Dragon, Antonio, S.J. *Blessed Miguel Pro, S.J.* Translated by Sr. Mary Agnes Chevalier, F.M.I. Anand, India: Gujarat Sahitya Prakash, 1959.

Duffy, John E., S.J. "He Kept Silence in Seven Languages: A Short Sketch of Carl W. Hausmann, S.J." *Woodstock Letters* 75(4) (December 1946).

Dunda, Gerardas, S.J. Unpublished memoir, n.d.

Dunne, George H., S.J. *Generation of Giants: The Story of the Jesuits in China in the Last Decades of the Ming Dynasty.* South Bend, Ind.: Notre Dame Press, 1962.

Echaniz, Ignatius, S.J. *A Symphony of Love. Stories of Jesuit Brothers.* Anand, India: Gujarat Sahitya Prakash, 1985.

Eckhart, Anselmo, S.J. *Memórias de um Jesuíta Prisioneiro de Pombal.* Braga: Livraria A.I., 1987.

Edwards, Francis, S.J. *The Jesuits in England: From 1580 to the Present Day.* London: Burns and Oates, 1985.

The Elizabethan Jesuits: Historia Missionis Anglicanae Societatis Jesu (1660) of Henry More. Translated by Francis Edwards, S.J. London: Phillimore, 1981.

Endo, Shusaku. *Silence.* New York: Taplinger Publishing Co., 1980.

Evans, Michael A., S.J. Letter to author, December 7, 1995.

Fahy, Eugene E., S.J. "Buried above Ground." *Life* (September 8, 1952).

————. "The Red Take-Over of a Mission and My Ten Months in Communist Jails." Unpublished manuscript, n.d.

Filosomi, Luigi, S.J. *St. Claude de la Colombière: His Life and Personality*. Rome: Secretariatus ad Promovendam Ignatianam Spirtualitatem, 1992.

Fleming, Peter Joseph, S.J. "Chosen For China: The California Province Jesuits in China 1928–1957: A Case Study in Mission and Culture." Ph.D. Diss., Graduate Theological Union, Berkeley, Calif., 1987. Facsimile printed by UMI Dissertation Services, Ann Arbor, Mich., 1994.

Foley, Henry, S.J. *Jesuits in Conflict: or, Historic Facts Illustrative of the Labours and Sufferings of the English Mission and Province of the Society of Jesus*. London: Burns and Oates, 1873.

————. *Records of the English Province of the Society of Jesus*. 7 vols. London: Burns and Oates, 1875–1883.

Frankl, Viktor E. *Man's Search for Meaning*. New York: Simon and Schuster/Pocket Books, 1963.

Gardin, Giacomo, S.J. *Banishing God in Albania. The Prison Memoirs of Giacomo Gardin, S.J.* San Francisco: Ignatius Press, 1988.

————. "Father Gjon Karma's Slow Road to Martyrdom." *Albanian Catholic Bulletin* 11(1990):57.

Gerard, John. *The Autobiography of a Hunted Priest*. Translated by Philip Caraman. New York: Pellegrini and Cudahy, 1952.

Gil, Pablo, S.J. *Misionero y Mártir. Vida del Padre Tomás Esteban, S.J.* Pamplona: Ediciones los Misioneros, 1956.

Gillow, Joseph. *A Literary and Biographical Dictionary of the English Catholics, from the Breach in Rome in 1534 to the Present Time*. 5 vols. London: Burns and Oates, 1885.

Gobien, Charles le, S.J., ed. *Lettres Édifiantes et Curieuses Écrites des Missions Étrangères par quelques missionaires de la Compagnie de Jésus*. 27 vols. Paris: Chez Nicolas le Clerc, 1707.

Guilday, Peter. *The Life and Times of John Carroll, Archbishop of Baltimore*. New York: Encyclopedia Press, 1977.

Guillon, Abbé Aimé. *Les Martyrs de la Foi pendant la Révolution Française*. 4 vols. Paris: Chez Germain Mathiot, Libraire, 1821.

Guitton, Georges, S.J. *Perfect Friend: The Life of Blessed Claude de la Colombière, S.J.* Translated by William J. Young, S.J. St. Louis: B. Herder Book Co., 1955.

Hagerty, Francis O., S.J. Telephone interview with author, January 17, 1994.

Havas, John A., S.J. "Four, Nine, Nine, Six." Unpublished manuscript, n.d.

Herbert, Lady (Baroness Mary Elizabeth). *A Martyr from the Quarterdeck: Alexis Clerc, S.J.* London: Burnes and Oates, 1890.

Hoffman, Bedrich. *And Who Will Kill You? The Chronicles of the Life and Sufferings of Priests in the Concentration Camps.* Pl. Puznan Poland: Pallotinum, 1994.

Hogan, Edward, S.J. *Distinguished Irishmen of the 16th Century.* London: Burns and Oates, 1894.

Houle, John A., S.J. "Thoughts in Prison." *The Catholic Mind* 56 (May–June 1958):266.

Houpert, J.C., S.J. *The Madurai Mission Manual.* Trichinopoli: St. Joseph Industrial School Press, 1916.

Ignatius of Loyola. *St. Ignatius' Own Story.* Translated by William J. Young, S.J. Chicago: Loyola University Press, 1956. (Reprinted in 1980.)

Jalics, Franz. *Ejercicios de Contemplación.* Buenos Aires: San Pablo Press, 1995.

Kelley, Francis Clement. *Blood Drenched Altars.* Milwaukee: Bruce Publishing Co., 1935.

Kelly, Stephen. Letter to author, April 15, 2000.

King, Marie Gentert, ed. *Foxe's Book of Martyrs.* Westwood, N.J.: Fleming H. Revell Co., Spire Books, 1968.

Koerbling, Anton, S.J. *Father Rupert Mayer.* Cork: Mercier Press, 1950.

Korec, Ján. *La Notte dei Barberi.* Rome: Edizioni Piemme, 1993.

Lamet, Miguel Pedro. *Arrupe: Una Explosión en la Iglesia.* Madrid: Ediciones Temas de Hoy, 1989.

Lapomarda, Vincent A. *The Jesuits and the Third Reich.* Lewiston, N.Y.: Edwin Mellen Press, 1989.

Lenz, John M. *Christ in Dachau.* Translated by Countess Barbara Waldstein. Modling Bei Wien: Missiondruckerie St. Gabriel, 1960.

Lopes, António, S.J. *Roteiro Histórico dos Jesuítas em Lisboa.* Braga: Livraria A.I., 1985.

Luli, Anton, S.J. "Dearest: The Painful Ordeal of an Albanian Jesuit." *National Jesuit News* (December/January 1994).

Martin, Clarence A., S.J. Interview, January 7, 1994.

McCoog, Thomas M., S.J., ed. "English and Welsh Jesuits: Catalogues 1555–1640," in *Monumenta Angliae I and II* in *Monumenta Missionium Societatis Jesu*, vols. 55–56, in *Monumenta Historica Societatis Jesu*, vols. 142–143. Rome: Institutum Historicum Societatis Jesu, 1992.

McSorley, Richard T., S.J. *My Path to Peace and Justice*. Marion, S. Dak.: Fortkamp Publishing/Rose Hill Books, 1996.

Menzel, Josef, S.J. "Personal Recollections." Unpublished manuscript, n.d.

Morrisey, Thomas, S.J. "Among the Irish Martyrs: Dominic Collins, S.J. In His Time." *Studies* (Dublin) 81(323) (Autumn 1992).

Moussé, Jean. "La Planète Buchenwald." *Études* (Paris) 362/3 (March 1985).

———. *Libre à Buchenwald*. Paris: Bayard Éditions/Centurion, 1995.

———. Letters to author, November 7 and 25, 1995.

Moyano Walker, Juan Luís. Letters to author, April 18 and June 6, 1995.

Mulligan, Joseph E. "Reflections on Resistance against the War in Vietnam." *St. Luke's Journal of Theology* (Sewanee, Tenn.) 28 (September 1985).

———. Interview with author, July 12, 1994.

Murphy, Edward J., S.J. Interview with author, November 27, 1994.

Neill, Stephen, F.B.A. *A History of Christianity in India 1707–1858*. Cambridge: Cambridge University Press, 1985.

Ogilvie, John. *An Authentic Account of the Imprisonment and Martyrdom in the High Street at Glasgow, in the year 1675 of Father John Ogilvie of the Society of Jesus*. Translated by Charles J. Karslake, S.J. London: Burns and Oates, 1877.

O'Grady, Desmond. *The Turned Card: Christianity before and after the Wall*. Chicago: Loyola University Press, 1997.

Pacheco, E. "Carcere e Vita Religiosa." In *Dizionario degli Instituti di Perfezione*. vol. II. Edited by Guerino Pellicia and Giancarlo Rocca. Rome: Edizioni Paoline, 1975.

Pastor, Ludwig Freiherr von. *History of the Popes*, vol. 38. (40 vols.) Translated by E. F. Peeler. St. Louis: B. Herder Book Co., 1952.

Pies, Otto. *The Victory of Father Karl*. Translated by Salvator Attanasio. New York: Farrar, Straus, and Cudahy, 1957.

Ponlevoy, Armand de, S.J. *Actes de la Captivité et de la Mort des RR.*

PP. P. Olivaint, L. Ducoudray, J. Caubert, A. Clerc, A. de Bengy. 5ᵗʰ ed. Paris: G. Téqui, Librairie-Éditeur, 1872.

Rajamanickam, S. "De Nobili in the Madurai Jail: A Letter of Sebastian de Maya." *Indian Church History Review* XVIII(2) (December 1984).

Reynolds, E. E. *Campion and Persons. The Jesuit Missions of 1580–81.* London: Sheed and Ward, 1980.

Roche, Alfred. "P. Otto Pies." *Mitteilungen* 19 (1960–62).

Roland, Manon Jeanne de la Platière. *Memoires de Madame Roland Ecrits durant Sa Captivité.* Edited by M. P. Faugère. Paris: Librairie de La Hachette et Cie, 1804.

Royer, Fanchon. *Padre Pro.* New York: P. J. Kenedy and Sons, 1954.

Rudé, George F. *The Crowd and the French Revolution.* Oxford: Clarendon Press, 1959.

Šeškevičius., Antanas. Interview with Edward Schmidt, S.J., 1994.

Shen, Louis. "Growing Up in the Church: China and the USA." *America* (January 23, 1993).

Shestani, Msgr. Zef. "Brother Gjon Pantalija, S.J., the Man and the Martyr." In Gjon Sinishta, *The Fulfilled Promise. A Documentary Account of Religious Persecution in Albania.* Santa Clara, Calif.: H and F Composing Service, 1976.

Silvestri, Giorgi. "Fr. Gjon Fausti, S.J. Strength in Serenity: The Account of an Eyewitness of His Mission." In Gjon Sinishta, *The Fulfilled Promise. A Documentary Account of Religious Persecution in Albania.* Santa Clara, Calif.: H and F Composing Service, 1976.

Sinishta, Gjon. *The Fulfilled Promise. A Documentary Account of Religious Persecution in Albania.* Santa Clara, Calif.: H and F Composing Service, 1976.

——— ed., "The Diary of Father Ják [Giacomo] Gardin, S.J. In Gjon Sinishta, *The Fulfilled Promise. A Documentary Account of Religious Persecution in Albania.* Santa Clara, Calif.: H and F Composing Service, 1976.

Sommet, Jacques. *L'honneur de la liberté.* Paris: Éditions du Centurion, 1987.

Sommet, Jacques, and Albert Longchamps. *L'Acte de Mémoire: 50 ans après la déportation.* Paris: Les Éditions Ouvrières, 1995.

Spinola, P. Fabio Ambrosio. *Vita del P. Carlo Spinola.* Bologna: L'Herede del Benacci, 1628.

Tang, Dominic, S.J. *How Inscrutable His Ways! Memoirs, 1951–81.* Hong Kong: Aidan Publicities and Printing, 1987.

Thornton, James Enda, S.J. "The New Proletarian Man." Unpublished manuscript, n.d.

Thwaites, Reuben Gold, ed. *Jesuit Relations and Allied Documents.* 73 vols. Cleveland: Burrows Brothers Co., 1896–1901.

Todorov, Tzvetan. *Facing the Extreme. Moral Life in the Concentration Camps.* Translated by Arthur Danner and Abigail Pollack. New York: Henry Holt and Co., 1996.

Torrens, James, S.J. "Getting Out Alive: An Interview with Juan Julio Wicht." *America* (September 13, 1997):13–16.

Ts'ai, Francis Xavier. Interview, May 20, 1995.

Tylenda, Joseph N., S.J. *Jesuit Saints and Martyrs.* Chicago: Loyola University Press, 1983.

Ullrich, Josef, S.J., ed. "Regarding the Trial of Four Jesuits in the Year 1958 in the Former German Democratic Republic." Archives, North German Province of the Society of Jesus, n.d.

Van Gestel, Peter, S.J. "Jesuits in the Bonds of Dachau." *Woodstock Letters* 76(2) (June 1947).

Weschler, Lawrence. "A Reporter at Large" (Uruguay). *The New Yorker* (April 3, 10, 1989).

———. *A Miracle, A Universe: Settling Accounts with Torturers.* New York: Penguin Books, 1990.

Weston, William. *An Autobiography from the Jesuit Underground.* Translated by Philip Caraman. New York: Farrar, Straus and Cudahy, 1955.

Wong, George B., S.J. (pen name: Bernard Brown). "Candle in the Wind: A Prisoner's Testimony." *The Tablet* (London) (December 24/31, 1994).

———. Interviews with author, May 5 and 29, 1995.

INDEX

For the major themes of this book (e.g., prayer, Mass, ministry), see the chapter headings in the table of contents (page v). "Baptism" and "confession" are mentioned repeatedly throughout the book and are not indexed here except for specially memorable circumstances. For books of the Old and New Testaments, see the entries under "Bible."

For summaries of the principal persons, places, and topics, see the glossary (page 261). For the principal countries, see the geographical chart (page vii). The bibliography (page 272) contains the sources for this book, including previously unpublished data (interviews and letters).

See "Prisons" (in this index) for the jails, prisons, labor camps, religious houses, ships, and other facilities in which Jesuits have been incarcerated. See "*Spiritual Exercises*" for entries related to this work by Ignatius of Loyola. "Saint" is added to a name only if it is commonly used without any other identification (e.g., Augustine, Paul).